10 New Pattern Mock Tests for NTA JEE Main 2023

5 Online & 5 in Book
(90 Question Pattern)

DISHA Publications Inc.

45, 2nd Floor, Maharishi Dayanand Marg,
Corner Market, Malviya Nagar, new Delhi -110017
Tel: 49842349/ 49842350

Typeset By

DISHA DTP Team

Contents

Mock Tests

Solutions

Link for 5 Online Mock Test NTA JEE Main

Scan QR Code OR Visit

https://bit.ly/3xvf7YN

1 Mock Test

INSTRUCTIONS

1. This test will be a 3 hours Test.
2. This test consists of Physics, Chemistry and Mathematics questions with equal weightage of 100 marks.
3. Each question is of 4 marks.
4. There are three sections in the question paper consisting of Physics (Q.no.1 to 30), Chemistry (Q.no.31 to 60) and Mathematics (Q. no.61 to 90). Each section is divided into two parts, Part I consists of 20 multiple choice questions & Part II consists of 10 Numerical value type Questions, attempt any 5 questions out of 10.
5. There will be only one correct choice in the given four choices in Part I. For each question 4 marks will be awarded for correct choice, 1 mark will be deducted for incorrect choice for Part I Questions and zero mark will be awarded for not attempted question. For Part II Questions 4 marks will be awarded for correct answer and zero for unattempted and incorrect answer.
6. Any textual, printed or written material, mobile phones, calculator etc. is not allowed for the students appearing for the test.
7. All calculations / written work should be done in the rough sheet provided.

PHYSICS

PART-I (Multiple Choice Questions)

1. Two stars each of mass M and radius R are approaching each other for a head-on collision. They start approaching each other when their separation is $r >> R$. If their speeds at this separation are negligible, the speed v with which they collide would be

(a) $v=\sqrt{GM\left(\frac{1}{R}-\frac{1}{r}\right)}$

(b) $v=\sqrt{GM\left(\frac{1}{2R}-\frac{1}{r}\right)}$

(c) $v=\sqrt{GM\left(\frac{1}{R}+\frac{1}{r}\right)}$

(d) $v=\sqrt{GM\left(\frac{1}{2R}+\frac{1}{r}\right)}$

2. A block of mass M is kept on a platform which is accelerated upward with a constant acceleration 'a' during the time interval T. The work done by normal reaction between the block and platform is

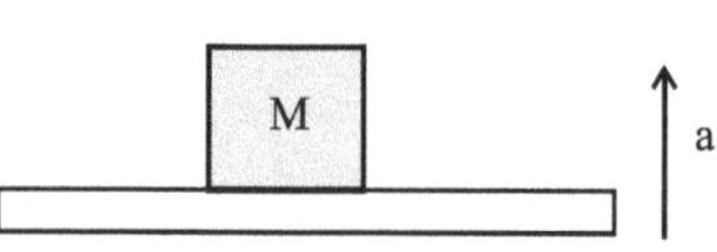

(a) $-\frac{MgaT^2}{2}$

(b) $\frac{1}{2}M(g+a)aT^2$

(c) $\frac{1}{2}Ma^2T$

(d) Zero

3. A large number of water drops each of radius r combine to have a drop of radius R. If the surface tension is T and the mechanical equivalent of heat is J, then the rise in temperature will be

(a) $\frac{2T}{rJ}$

(b) $\frac{3T}{RJ}$

(c) $\frac{3T}{J}\left(\frac{1}{r}-\frac{1}{R}\right)$

(d) $\frac{2T}{J}\left(\frac{1}{r}-\frac{1}{R}\right)$

4. Three charges are placed at the vertices of an equilateral triangle of side 'a' as shown in the following figure. The force experienced by the charge placed at the vertex A in a direction normal to BC is

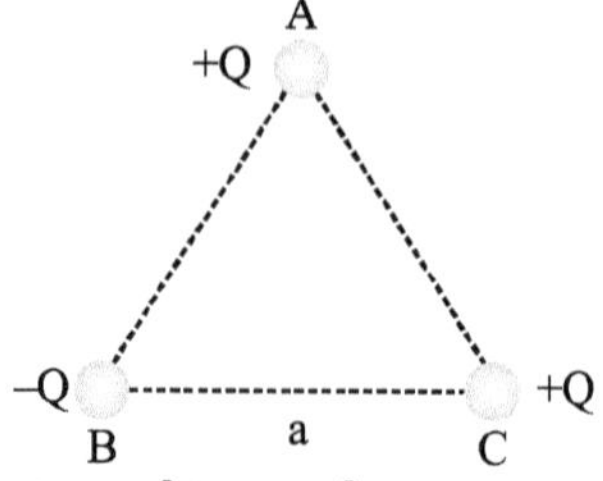

(a) $Q^2/(4\pi\varepsilon_0 a^2)$

(b) $-Q^2/(4\pi\varepsilon_0 a^2)$

(c) Zero

(d) $Q^2/(2\pi\varepsilon_0 a^2)$

5. Axis of a solid cylinder of infinite length and radius R lies along y-axis, it carries a uniformly distributed current i along +y direction. Magnetic field at a point $\left(\frac{R}{2}, y, \frac{R}{2}\right)$ is

(a) $\frac{\mu_0 i}{4\pi R}(\hat{i}-\hat{k})$

(b) $\frac{\mu_0 i}{2\pi R}(\hat{j}-\hat{k})$

(c) $\frac{\mu_0 i}{4\pi R}\hat{j}$

(d) $\frac{\mu_0 i}{4\pi R}(\hat{i}+\hat{k})$

6. Two identical short bar magnets, each having magnetic moment of 10 Am^2, are arranged such that their axial lines are perpendicular to each other and their centres be along the same straight line in a horizontal plane. If the distance

between their centres is 0.2 m, the resultant magnetic induction at a point midway between them is ($\mu_0 = 4\pi \times 10^{-7}\,\text{Hm}^{-1}$)

(a) $\sqrt{2} \times 10^{-7}$ tesla

(b) $\sqrt{5} \times 10^{-7}$ tesla

(c) $\sqrt{2} \times 10^{-3}$ tesla

(d) $\sqrt{5} \times 10^{-3}$ tesla

7. Two boys are standing at the ends A and B of a ground where $AB = a$. The boy at B starts running in a direction perpendicular to AB with velocity v_1. The boy at A starts running simultaneously with velocity v and catches the other boy in a time t, where t is

(a) $a/\sqrt{v^2 + v_1^2}$

(b) $a/(v + v_1)$

(c) $a/(v - v_1)$

(d) $\sqrt{a^2/(v^2 - v_1^2)}$

8. A block is placed on a rough horizontal plane. A time dependent horizontal force $F = kt$ acts on the block. Here, k is a positive constant. The acceleration-time graph of the block is

(a)

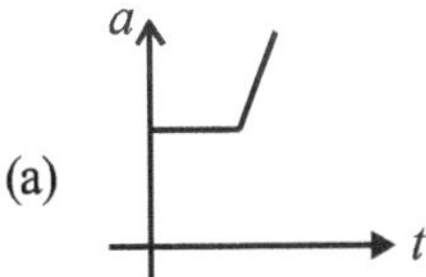

(b)

(c)

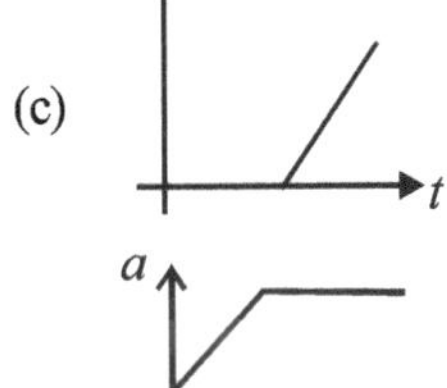

(d)

9. A new system of units is proposed in which unit of mass is α kg, unit of length is β m and unit of time is γ s. What wil be value of 5 J in this new system?

(a) $5\alpha\beta^2\gamma^{-2}$

(b) $5\alpha^{-1}\beta^{-2}\gamma^2$

(c) $5\alpha^{-2}\beta^{-1}\gamma^{-2}$

(d) $5\alpha^{-1}\beta^2\gamma^2$

10. Television signals on earth cannot be received at distances greater than 100 km from the transmission station. The reason behind this is that

(a) the receiver antenna is unable to detect the signal at a disance greater than 100 km

(b) the TV programme consists of both audio and video signals

(c) the TV signals are less powerful than radio signals
(d) the surface of earth is curved like a sphere

11. A sinusoidal voltage of amplitude 25 volt and frequency 50Hz is applied to a half wave rectifier using P-n junction diode. No filter is used and the load resistor is 1000Ω. The forward resistance R_f of ideal diode is 10Ω. The percentage rectifier efficiency is

(a) 40% (b) 20%
(c) 30% (d) 15%

12. When photon of energy 4.25 eV strike the surface of a metal A, the ejected photoelectrons have maximum kinetic energy T_A eV and de-Brolie wavelength λ_A. The maximum kinetic energy of photoelectrons liberated from another metal B by photon of energy 4.70 eV is $T_B = (T_A - 1.50)$ eV. If the de-Broglie wavelength of these photoelectrons is $\lambda_B = 2\lambda_A$, then

(a) the work function of A is 3.40 eV
(b) the work function of B is 6.75 eV
(c) $T_A = 2.00\, eV$
(d) $T_B = 2.75\, eV$

13. Given is the graph between $\frac{PV}{T}$ and P for 1 g of oxygen gas at two different temperatures T_1 and T_2, as shown in figure. Given, density of oxygen = 1.427 kg m^{-3}. The value of PV/T at the point A and the relation between T_1 and T_2 are respectively

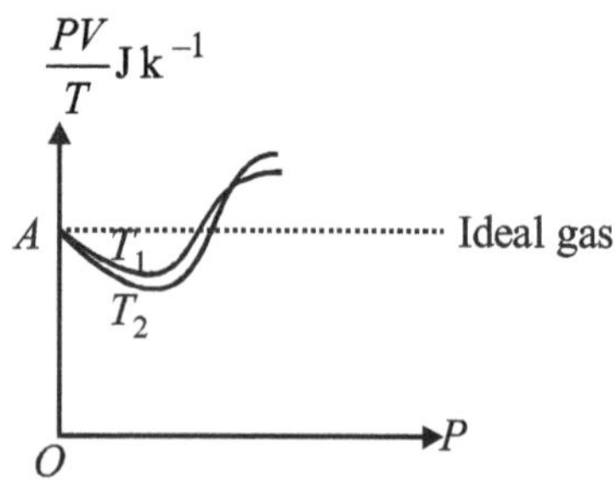

(a) 0.259 J K^{-1} and $T_1 < T_2$
(b) 8.314 J mol^{-1}K^{-1} and $T_1 > T_2$
(c) 0.259 J K^{-1} and $T_1 > T_2$
(d) 4.28 g J K^{-1} and $T_1 < T_2$

14. An observer moves towards a stationary source of sound with a speed 1/5th of the speed of sound. The wavelength and frequency of the sound emitted are λ and f respectively. The apparent frequency and wavelength recorded by the observer are respectively.

(a) 0.8f, 0.8λ (b) 1.2f, 1.2λ
(c) 1.2f, λ (d) f, 1.2λ

15. The figure shows a system of two concentric spheres of radii r_1 and r_2 are kept at temperatures T_1 and T_2, respectively. The radial rate of flow of heat in a substance between the two concentric spheres is proportional to

(a) $In\left(\frac{r_2}{r_1}\right)$

(b) $\frac{(r_2 - r_1)}{(r_1 r_2)}$

(c) $(r_2 - r_1)$

(d) $\frac{r_1 r_2}{(r_2 - r_1)}$

16. A gas is compressed isothermally to half its initial volume. The same gas is compressed separately through an adiabatic process until its volume is again reduced to half. Then :

(a) Compressing the gas isothermally will require more work to be done.

(b) Compressing the gas through adiabatic process will require more work to be done.

(c) Compressing the gas isothermally or adiabatically will require the same amount of work.

(d) Which of the case (whether compression through isothermal or through adiabatic process) requires more work will depend upon the atomicity of the gas.

17. A ray PQ incident on the refracting face BA is refracted in the prism BAC as shown in the figure and emerges from the other

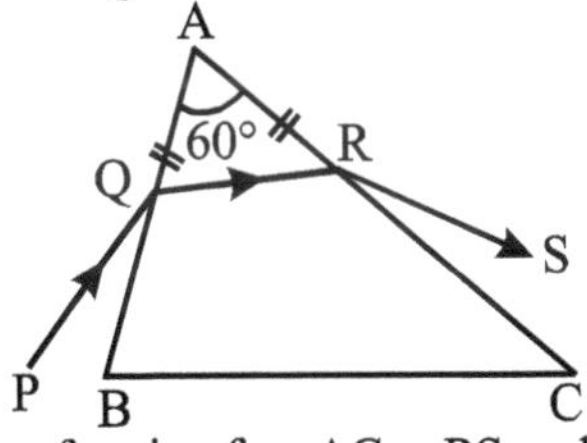

refracting face AC as RS such that AQ = AR. If the angle of prism A = 60° and the refractive index of the material of prism is $\sqrt{3}$, then the angle of deviation of the ray is

(a) 60°
(b) 45°
(c) 30°
(d) None of these

18. Which of the following has/have zero average value in a plane electromagnetic wave ?

(a) Both magnetic and electric field
(b) Electric field only
(c) Magnetic energy
(d) Electric energy

19. Two inductors L_1 (inductance 1 mH, internal resistance 3Ω) and L_2 (inductance 2 mH, internal resistance 4Ω), and a resistor R (resistance 12Ω) are all connected in parallel across a 5V battery. The circuit is switched on a time t = 0. The ratio of the maximum to the minimum current (I_{max}/I_{min}) drawn from the battery is

(a) 8 (b) 10
(c) 12 (d) 14

20. In a diffraction pattern due to a single slit of width 'a', the first minimum is observed at an angle 30° when light of wavelength 5000 Å is incident on the slit. The first secondary maximum is observed at an angle of :

(a) $\sin^{-1}\left(\frac{1}{4}\right)$ (b) $\sin^{-1}\left(\frac{2}{3}\right)$

(c) $\sin^{-1}\left(\frac{1}{2}\right)$ (d) $\sin^{-1}\left(\frac{3}{4}\right)$

PART-II (Numerical Answer Questions)

21. Figure shows use of potentiometer for comparison of two resistances. The balance point with standard resistance R = 10Ω is at 58.3 cm, while that with unknown resistance X is 68.5 cm. Find X (in Ω).

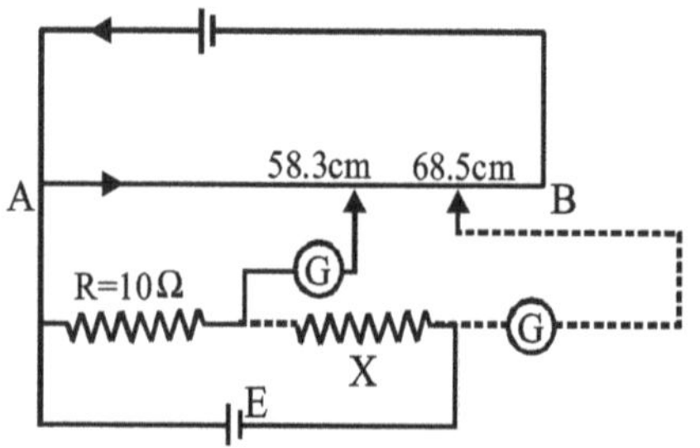

22. An automobile moves on a road with a speed of 54 km h^{-1}. The radius of its wheels is 0.45 m and the moment of inertia of the wheel about its axis of rotation is 3 kg m^2. If the vehicle is brought to rest in 15s, the magnitude of average torque (in kgm^2s^{-2}) transmitted by its brakes to the wheel is :

23. A coil of effective area 4 m^2 is placed at right angles to the magnetic induction B. The e.m.f. of 0.32 V is induced in the coil, when the field is reduced to 20% of its initial value in 0.5 sec. Find B (in wb/m^2).

24. A disc of radius $R = 10$ cm oscillates as a physical pendulum about an axis perpendicular to the plane of the disc at a distance r from its centre. If $r = \frac{R}{4}$, the approximate period of oscillation (in second) is (Take $g = 10$ m s^{-2})

25. Taking the wavelength of first Balmer line in hydrogen spectrum (n = 3 to n = 2) as 660 nm, the wavelength (in nm) of the 2nd Balmer line (n = 4 to n = 2) will be;

26. The radius of a sphere is measured to be (7.50 + 0.85) cm. Suppose the percentage error in its volume is x. The value of x, to the nearest x, is ________.

27. An asteroid is moving directly towards the centre of the earth. When at a distance of 10 R (R is the radius of the earth) from the earths centre, it has a speed of 12 km/s. Neglecting the effect of earths atmosphere, what will be the speed of the asteroid when it hits the surface of the earth (escape velocity from the earth is 11.2 km/ s)? Give your answer to the nearest integer in kilometer/s _____.

28. Magnetic fields at two points on the axis of a circular coil at a distance of 0.05 m and 0.2 m from the centre are in the ratio 8 : 1. The radius of coil is _____.

29. An α particle and a proton are accelerated from rest by a potential difference of 200 V. After this, de Broglie wavelengths are λ_α and λ_P respectively. The ratio $\frac{\lambda_p}{\lambda_\alpha}$ is :

30. A particle executes S.H.M. with amplitude 'a' and time period 'T'. The displacement of the particle when its speed is half of maximum speed is $\frac{\sqrt{x}\,a}{2}$. The value of x is ______.

CHEMISTRY

PART-I (Multiple Choice Questions)

31. Which of the following has the highest $p\pi - p\pi$ bonding tendency?
(a) N (b) P
(c) As (d) Sb

32. Among the following, the compound that is both paramagnetic and coloured, is
(a) $KMnO_4$
(b) CuF_2
(c) $K_2Cr_2O_7$
(d) All are coloured

33. The bond angle between two hybrid orbitals is 105°. The percentage of *s*-character of hybrid orbital is between
(a) 50 - 55% (b) 9 - 12%
(c) 21 - 23% (d) 11 - 12%

34. Identify Z in the following sequence of reactions –

$$CH_3-COONH_4 \xrightarrow{\Delta} X \xrightarrow{P_2O_5} Y \xrightarrow{H_2O/H^{\oplus}} Z$$

(a) $CH_3-CH_2-CO-NH_2$
(b) CH_3-CN
(c) $(CH_3CO)_2O$
(d) CH_3-COOH

35. Correct order of first IP among following elements Be, B, C, N, O is
(a) $B < Be < C < O < N$
(b) $B < Be < C < N < O$
(c) $Be < B < C < N < O$
(d) $Be < B < C < O < N$

36. Select the rate law that corresponds to data shown for the following reaction

$A + B \longrightarrow$ products.

Exp.	[A]	[B]	Initial rate
1	0.012	0.035	0.1
2	0.024	0.070	0.8
3	0.024	0.035	0.1
4	0.012	0.070	0.8

(a) rate $= k\,[B]^3$
(b) rate $= k\,[B]^4$
(c) rate $= k\,[A]\,[B]^3$
(d) rate $= k\,[A]^2\,[B]^2$

37. The pH of 0.1 M solution of the following species increases in the order :
(a) $NaCl < NH_4Cl < NaCN < HCl$
(b) $HCl < NH_4Cl < NaCl < NaCN$
(c) $NaCN < NH_4Cl < NaCl < HCl$
(d) $HCl < NaCl < NaCN < NH_4Cl$

38. Aldehydes and ketones are distinguished by which of the following test ?

(a) Lucas test
(b) Tollen's test
(c) $KMnO_4$ solution (Baeyer's test)
(d) None of these

39. Which is not a true statement?
(a) α-Carbon of α-amino acid is asymmetric
(b) All proteins are found in L-form
(c) Human body can synthesize all proteins they need
(d) At pH = 7 both amino and carboxylic groups exist in ionised form

40. Which of the following products are obtained when Na_2CO_3 is added to a solution of copper sulphate ?
(a) Basic copper carbonate $[CuCO_3.Cu(OH)_2]$, sodium sulphate and CO_2.
(b) Copper hydroxide, sodium sulphate and CO_2.
(c) Copper carbonate, sodium sulphate and CO_2.
(d) Copper carbonate and sodium sulphate.

41. Which of the following statement is incorrect with respect to metallic or electronic conductivity?
(a) Metallic conductivity depends on the structure of metal and its charactristics.
(b) Metallic conductivity depends on the number of electrons in the valence shell of atom of metal.
(c) The electrical conductivity of metal increases with increase in temperature.
(d) There is no change in the structure of metal during electrical conduction.

42. Given below are two statements.
Statement I : Frenkel defects are vacancy as well as interstitial defects.
Statement II : Frenkel defect leads to colour in ionic solids due to presence of F-centres.
Choose the **most appropriate** answer for the statements from the options given below :
(a) Statement I is false but Statement II is true
(b) Both Statement I and Statement II are true
(c) Statement I is true but Statement II is false
(d) Both Statement I and Statement II are false

43. When phenol is treated with excess bromine water. It gives
(a) *m*-Bromophenol
(b) *o*-and *p*-Bromophenols
(c) 2,4-Dibromophenol
(d) 2,4, 6-Tribromophenol.

44. Given below, catalyst and corresponding process/reaction are matched. The one with mismatch is
(a) $[RhCl(PPh_3)_2]$: Hydrogenation
(b) $TiCl_4 + Al(C_2H_5)_3$: Polymerization
(c) V_2O_5 : Haber-Bosch process
(d) Nickel : Hydrogenation

45. Match list-I with list-II

List-I (Molecule)	List-II (Bond order)
(A) Ne_2	(I) 1
(B) N_2	(II) 2
(C) F_2	(III) 0
(D) O_2	(IV) 3

Choose the correct answer from the options given below

(a) (A)-(IV); (B)-(III); (C)-(II); (D)-(I)
(b) (A)-(II); (B)-(I); (C)-(IV); (D)-(III)
(c) (A)-(I); (B)-(II); (C)-(III); (D)-(IV)
(d) (A)-(III); (B)-(IV); (C)-(I); (D)-(II)

46. One mole of NaCl (*s*) on melting absorbed 30.5 kJ one of heat and its entropy is increased by 28.8 $JK^{-1}mol^{-1}$. The melting point of NaCl is

(a) 1059 K (b) 30.5 K
(c) 28.8 K (d) 28800 K

47. Which alkene on ozonolysis gives CH_3CH_2CHO and CH_3COCH_3 ($CH_3\overset{\overset{O}{\|}}{C}CH_3$)?

(a) $CH_3CH_2CH=C(CH_3)_2$
(b) $CH_3CH_2CH=CHCH_2CH_3$
(c) $CH_3CH_2CH=CHCH_3$
(d) $CH_3-\underset{\underset{CH_3}{|}}{C}=CHCH_3$

48. On reduction of $KMnO_4$ by oxalic acid in acidic medium, the oxidation number of Mn changes. What is the magnitude of this change?

(a) From 7 to 2
(b) From 6 to 2
(c) From 5 to 2
(d) From 7 to 4

49. The half-life for radioactive decay of C–14 is 5730 years. An archaeological artifact containing wood had only 80% of the C–14 found in a living tree. The age of the sample is

(a) 1485 years
(b) 1845 years
(c) 530 years
(d) 4767 years.

50. Which one of the following complexes is an outer orbital complex?

(a) $[Co(NH_3)_6]^{3+}$
(b) $[Mn(CN)_6]^{4-}$
(c) $[Fe(CN)_6]^{4-}$
(d) $[Ni(NH_3)_6]^{2+}$

(Atomic nos. : Mn = 25; Fe = 26; Co=27, Ni=28)

PART-II (Numerical Answer Questions)

51. If pressure of a gas is reduced by 25%, then what should be the temperature required to make its volume twice at NTP?

52. An aromatic compound of formula C_7H_7Cl has in all ..... isomers :

53. Calculate the volume strength of 1.5 N H_2O_2 solution.

54. A metal crystallizes into a lattice containing a sequence of layers of atoms of ABABAB.......What percentage by volume of this lattice has empty space?

55. In an experiment, 4 g of M_2O_x oxide was reduced to 2.8 g of the metal. Calculate the number of O atoms in the oxide.
(Given : Atomic mass of the metal = 56 g mol^{-1})

56. The total number of negative charge in the tetrapeptide, Gly-Glu-Asp-Tyr, at pH 12.5 will be ________.

57. For a chemical reaction $A \rightarrow B$, it was found the concentration of B increased by 0.2 mol L^{-1} in 30 mn. The average rate of the reaction is ________ $\times 10^{-1}$ mol L^{-1} h^{-1}.

58. If the concentration of glucose $(C_6H_{12}O_6)$ in blood is 0.72 g L^{-1}, the molarity of glucose in blood is ________ $\times 10^{-3}$ M.
Given : Atomic mass of C = 12, H = 1, O = 16 u]

59. The pH of ammonium phosphate solution, if pk_a of phosphoric acid and pk_b of ammonium hydroxide are 5.23 and 4.75 respectively, is ________.

60. The dihedral angle in staggered form of Newman projection of 1, 1, 1-Trichloro ethane is .... degree.

MATHEMATICS

PART-I (Multiple Choice Questions)

61. If the coefficient of 4th term in the expansion of $\left(x+\frac{\alpha}{2x}\right)^n$ is 20, then the respective values of α and n are
(a) 2, 7
(b) 5, 8
(c) 3, 6
(d) 2, 6

62. If the roots of the quadratic equation $x^2+px+q=0$ are tan 30° and tan 15°, respectively, then the value of $2+q-p$ is
(a) 2
(b) 3
(c) 0
(d) 1

63. If a^2, b^2, c^2 are in A.P. then $\frac{1}{b+c}, \frac{1}{c+a}, \frac{1}{a+b}$ are in-
(a) A.P.
(b) G.P.
(c) H.P.
(d) None of these

64. Let C be the circle with centre (0, 0) and radius 3 units. The equation of the locus of the mid points of the chords of the circle C that subtend an angle of $\frac{2\pi}{3}$ at its center is
(a) $x^2+y^2=\frac{3}{2}$
(b) $x^2+y^2=1$
(c) $x^2+y^2=\frac{27}{4}$
(d) $x^2+y^2=\frac{9}{4}$

65. If $y=\tan^{-1}\left(\frac{\log_e(e/x^2)}{\log_e(ex^2)}\right)+\tan^{-1}\left(\frac{3+2\log_e x}{1-6\log_e x}\right)$, then $\frac{d^2y}{dx^2}$ is
(a) 2
(b) 1
(c) 0
(d) −1

66. If { } denotes the fractional part of x, the range of the function

$f(x)=\sqrt{\{x\}^2-2\{x\}}$ is

(a) ϕ (b) $[0, 1/2]$

(c) $\{0, 1/2\}$ (d) $\{0\}$

67. The length of the perpendicular from the origin to a line is 7 and line makes an angle of 150° with the positive direction of y-axis, then the equation of the line is

(a) $\sqrt{3}\,x+y=7$

(b) $\sqrt{3}\,x-y=14$

(c) $\sqrt{3}\,x+y+14=0$

(d) $\sqrt{3}\,x+y-14=0$

68. $\int\frac{dx}{\cos x+\sqrt{3}\sin x}$ equals

(a) $\log\tan\left(\frac{x}{2}+\frac{\pi}{12}\right)+C$

(b) $\log\tan\left(\frac{x}{2}-\frac{\pi}{12}\right)+C$

(c) $\frac{1}{2}\log\tan\left(\frac{x}{2}+\frac{\pi}{12}\right)+C$

(d) $\frac{1}{2}\log\tan\left(\frac{x}{2}-\frac{\pi}{12}\right)+C$

69. If $\frac{\tan 3\theta-1}{\tan 3\theta+1}=\sqrt{3}$, then the general value of θ is

(a) $\frac{n\pi}{3}-\frac{\pi}{12}$ (b) $n\pi+\frac{7\pi}{12}$

(c) $\frac{n\pi}{3}+\frac{7\pi}{36}$ (d) $n\pi+\frac{\pi}{12}$

70. Three normals are drawn to the parabola $y^2 = x$ through point $(a, 0)$. Then

(a) $a=1/2$

(b) $a=1/4$

(c) $a>1/2$

(d) None of these

71. If four vertices of a regular octagon are chosen at random, then the probability that the quadrilateral formed by them is a rectangle is

(a) $\frac{1}{8}$ (b) $\frac{2}{21}$

(c) $\frac{1}{32}$ (d) $\frac{1}{35}$

72. The function

$f(x)=x^3-3x^2-24x+5$ is an increasing function in the interval given below

(a) $(-\infty,-2)\cup(4,\infty)$

(b) $(-2,\infty)$

(c) $(-2,4)$

(d) $(-\infty,4)$

73. If $y = y(x)$ and it follows the relation $x\cos y + y\cos x = \pi$ then $y''(0) =$

(a) 1 (b) -1

(c) π (d) $-\pi$

74. ABC is triangular park with $AB=AC=100$ m. A clock tower is situated at the mid-point of *BC*. The angles of elevation of the top of the tower at *A* and *B* are $\cot^{-1} 3.2$ and $\operatorname{cosec}^{-1} 2.6$ respectively. The height of the tower is

(a) 50 m
(b) 25 m
(c) 40 m
(d) None of these

75. If the vectors $\overrightarrow{AB} = -3\hat{i} + 4\hat{k}$ and $\overrightarrow{AC} = 5\hat{i} - 2\hat{j} + 4\hat{k}$ are the sides of a triangle ABC, then the length of the median through A is

(a) $\sqrt{14}$ (b) $\sqrt{18}$
(c) $\sqrt{29}$ (d) 4

76. The negation of the compound proposition $p \vee (\sim p \vee q)$ is

(a) $(p \wedge \sim q) \wedge \sim p$
(b) $(p \wedge \sim q) \vee \sim p$
(c) $(p \vee \sim q) \vee \sim p$
(d) None of these

77. Let $f(x) = \begin{cases} x^p \sin\frac{1}{x}, & x \neq 0 \\ 0 & , x = 0 \end{cases}$ then $f(x)$ is continuous but not differentiable at $x = 0$ if

(a) $0 < p \le 1$
(b) $1 \le p < \infty$
(c) $-\infty < p < 0$
(d) $p = 0$

78. The length and foot of the perpendicular from the point (7, 14, 5) to the plane $2x + 4y - z = 2$, are

(a) $\sqrt{21}, (1, 2, 8)$
(b) $3\sqrt{21}, (3, 2, 8)$
(c) $21\sqrt{3}, (1, 2, 8)$
(d) $3\sqrt{21}, (1, 2, 8)$

79. If $\Delta(x) = \begin{vmatrix} e^x & \sin x \\ \cos x & \ln(1 + x^2) \end{vmatrix}$, then the value of $\lim_{x \to 0} \frac{\Delta(x)}{x}$ is

(a) 0 (b) 2
(c) –1 (d) –2

80. The number of positive integral solutions of the equation

$\tan^{-1} x + \cot^{-1} y = \tan^{-1} 3$, is

(a) two
(b) one
(c) infinite
(d) None of these

PART-II (Numerical Answer Questions)

81. A box contains two white balls, three black balls and four red balls. The number of ways such that three balls can be drawn from the box if at least one black ball is to be included in the draw is ______.

82. Find the median from the following distribution.

Class	5–10	10–15	15–20	20–25	25–30	30–35	35–40	40–45
frequency	5	6	15	10	5	4	2	2

83. If α, β are the roots of the equation $2x^2 + 3x + 5 = 0$, then the absolute value of the determinant $\begin{vmatrix} 0 & \beta & \beta \\ \alpha & 0 & \alpha \\ \beta & \alpha & 0 \end{vmatrix}$ is ______.

84. $\int_{-3}^{2} \{|x+1| + |x+2| + |x-1|\} dx$ is ______.

85. The area bounded by the curve $y = 2x - x^2$ and the line $y = -x$ is ______.

86. Let $\tan\alpha$, $\tan\beta$ and $\tan\gamma$; $\alpha, \beta, \gamma \neq \frac{(2n-1)\pi}{2}$, $n \in N$ be the slopes of three line segments OA, OB and OC, respectively, where O is origin. If circumcentre of ΔABC coincides with origin and its orthocentre lies on y-axis, then the value of $\left(\frac{\cos 3\alpha + \cos 3\beta + \cos 3\gamma}{\cos\alpha \cos\beta \cos\gamma}\right)^2$ is equal to ______.

87. An electric instrument consists of two units. Each unit must function independently for the instrument to operate. The probability that the first unit functions is 0.9 and that of the second unit is 0.8. The instrument is switched on and it fails to operate. If the probability that only the first unit failed and second unit is functioning is p, then 98 p is equal to ______.

88. The number of integral values of 'k' for which the equation $3\sin x + 4\cos x = k + 1$ has a solution, $k \in R$ is ______.

89. If for the complex numbers z satisfying $|z - 2 - 2i| \leq 1$, the maximum value of $|3iz + 6|$ is attained at $a + ib$, then $a + b$ is equal to ______.

90. If $(x) = \int \frac{5x^8 + 7\,7x^6}{(x^2 + 1 + 2x^7)^2} dx$, $(x \geq 0)$, $f(0) = 0$ and, then the value of K is ______.

RESPONSE SHEET

PHYSICS		CHEMISTRY		MATHEMATICS	
1.	ⓐⓑⓒⓓ	31.	ⓐⓑⓒⓓ	61.	ⓐⓑⓒⓓ
2.	ⓐⓑⓒⓓ	32.	ⓐⓑⓒⓓ	62.	ⓐⓑⓒⓓ
3.	ⓐⓑⓒⓓ	33.	ⓐⓑⓒⓓ	63.	ⓐⓑⓒⓓ
4.	ⓐⓑⓒⓓ	34.	ⓐⓑⓒⓓ	64.	ⓐⓑⓒⓓ
5.	ⓐⓑⓒⓓ	35.	ⓐⓑⓒⓓ	65.	ⓐⓑⓒⓓ
6.	ⓐⓑⓒⓓ	36.	ⓐⓑⓒⓓ	66.	ⓐⓑⓒⓓ
7.	ⓐⓑⓒⓓ	37.	ⓐⓑⓒⓓ	67.	ⓐⓑⓒⓓ
8.	ⓐⓑⓒⓓ	38.	ⓐⓑⓒⓓ	68.	ⓐⓑⓒⓓ
9.	ⓐⓑⓒⓓ	39.	ⓐⓑⓒⓓ	69.	ⓐⓑⓒⓓ
10.	ⓐⓑⓒⓓ	40.	ⓐⓑⓒⓓ	70.	ⓐⓑⓒⓓ
11.	ⓐⓑⓒⓓ	41.	ⓐⓑⓒⓓ	71.	ⓐⓑⓒⓓ
12.	ⓐⓑⓒⓓ	42.	ⓐⓑⓒⓓ	72.	ⓐⓑⓒⓓ
13.	ⓐⓑⓒⓓ	43.	ⓐⓑⓒⓓ	73.	ⓐⓑⓒⓓ
14.	ⓐⓑⓒⓓ	44.	ⓐⓑⓒⓓ	74.	ⓐⓑⓒⓓ
15.	ⓐⓑⓒⓓ	45.	ⓐⓑⓒⓓ	75.	ⓐⓑⓒⓓ
16.	ⓐⓑⓒⓓ	46.	ⓐⓑⓒⓓ	76.	ⓐⓑⓒⓓ
17.	ⓐⓑⓒⓓ	47.	ⓐⓑⓒⓓ	77.	ⓐⓑⓒⓓ
18.	ⓐⓑⓒⓓ	48.	ⓐⓑⓒⓓ	78.	ⓐⓑⓒⓓ
19.	ⓐⓑⓒⓓ	49.	ⓐⓑⓒⓓ	79.	ⓐⓑⓒⓓ
20.	ⓐⓑⓒⓓ	50.	ⓐⓑⓒⓓ	80.	ⓐⓑⓒⓓ
21.		51.		81.	
22.		52.		82.	
23.		53.		83.	
24.		54.		84.	
25.		55.		85.	
26.		56.		86.	
27.		57.		87.	
28.		58.		88.	
29.		59.		89.	
30.		60.		90.	

2 Mock Test

INSTRUCTIONS

1. This test will be a 3 hours Test.
2. This test consists of Physics, Chemistry and Mathematics questions with equal weightage of 100 marks.
3. Each question is of 4 marks.
4. There are three sections in the question paper consisting of Physics (Q.no.1 to 30), Chemistry (Q.no.31 to 60) and Mathematics (Q. no.61 to 90). Each section is divided into two parts, Part I consists of 20 multiple choice questions & Part II consists of 10 Numerical value type Questions, attempt any 5 questions out of 10.
5. There will be only one correct choice in the given four choices in Part I. For each question 4 marks will be awarded for correct choice, 1 mark will be deducted for incorrect choice for Part I Questions and zero mark will be awarded for not attempted question. For Part II Questions 4 marks will be awarded for correct answer and zero for unattempted and incorrect answer.
6. Any textual, printed or written material, mobile phones, calculator etc. is not allowed for the students appearing for the test.
7. All calculations / written work should be done in the rough sheet provided.

PHYSICS

PART-I (Multiple Choice Questions)

1. A bus is moving with a velocity of 10m/s on a straight road. A scooterist wishes to overtake the bus in 100 seconds. If the bus is at a distance of 1 km from the scooterist, at what velocity should the scooterist chase the bus?

(a) 50 m/sec (b) 40 m/sec
(c) 30 m/sec (d) 20 m/sec

2. The length of an elastic string is x when the tension is 5N. Its length is y when the tension is 7N. What will be its length, when the tension is 9N?

(a) $2y+x$ (b) $2y-x$
(c) $7x-5y$ (d) $7x+5y$

3. A rod of length L is placed on x – axis between x = 0 and x = L. The linear density i.e., mass per unit length denoted by ρ, of this rod, varies as, ρ = a + bx. What should be the dimensions of b?

(a) $M^2L^1T^0$
(b) $M^1L^{-2}T^0$
(c) $M^{-1}L^3T^1$
(d) $M^{-1}L^2T^3$

4. A wheel is rolling on a plane road. The linear velocity of centre of mass is v. Then velocities of the points A and B on circumference of wheel relative to road will be

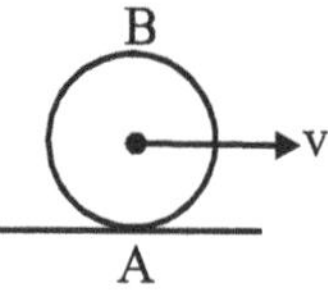

(a) $v_A = v, v_B = 0$
(b) $v_A = v_B = 0$
(c) $v_A = 0, v_B = v$
(d) $v_A = 0, v_B = 2v$

5. A metallic wire of density d is lying horizontal on the surface of water. The maximum length of wire so that it may not sink will be

(a) $\sqrt{\frac{2Tg}{\pi d}}$ (b) $\sqrt{\frac{2\pi T}{dg}}$

(c) $\sqrt{\frac{2T}{\pi dg}}$ (d) any length

6. Two points of a rod move with velocities 3v and v perpendicular to the rod and in the same direction, separated by a distance r. Then the angular velocity of the rod is

(a) 3v/r (b) 4v/r
(c) 5v/r (d) 2v/r

7. For hydrogen gas $C_p - C_v = a$ and for oxygen gas $C_p - C_v = b$. So, the relation between a and b is given by

(a) a = 16 b (b) 16a = b
(c) a = 4b (d) a = b

8. A bucket full of hot water is kept in a room and it cools from 75°C to 70°C in T_1 minutes, from 70°C to 65°C in T_2 minutes and from 65°C to 60°C in T_3 minutes. Then

(a) $T_1 = T_2 = T_3$
(b) $T_1 < T_2 < T_3$
(c) $T_1 > T_2 > T_3$
(d) $T_1 < T_3 < T_2$

9. The equivalent capacity of the network, (with all capacitors having the same capacitance C)

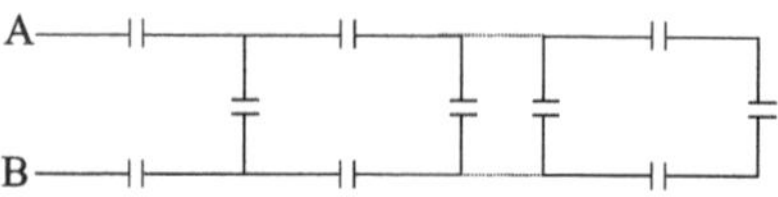

(a) ∞
(b) zero
(c) $C[(\sqrt{3} - 1) / 2]$
(d) $C[(\sqrt{3} + 1) / 2]$

10. The current I vs voltage V graphs for a given metallic wire at two different temperatures T_1 and T_2 are shown in the figure. It is concluded that

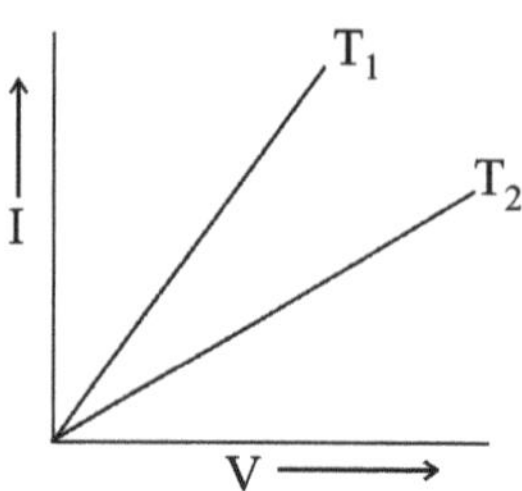

(a) $T_1 > T_2$ (b) $T_1 < T_2$
(c) $T_1 = T_2$ (d) $T_1 = 2T_2$

11. In the circuit shown the effective resistance between B and C is

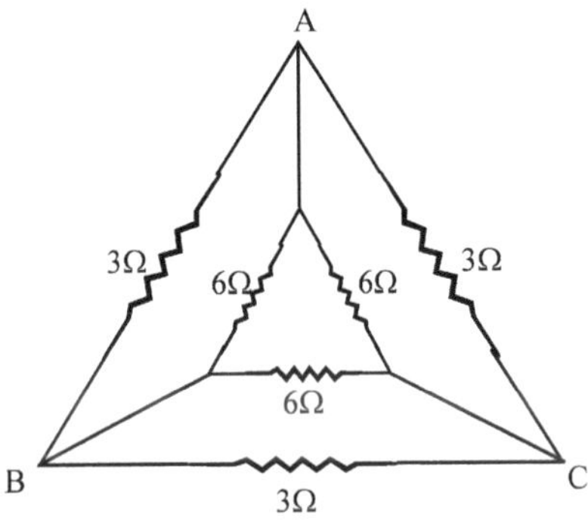

(a) 3 Ω (b) 4 Ω
(c) 4/3 Ω (d) 3/4 Ω

12. In the given circuit, the current drawn from the source is

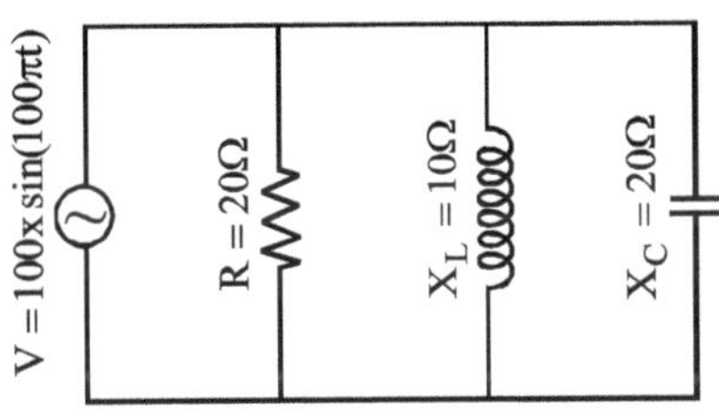

(a) 20 A (b) 10 A
(c) 5 A (d) $5\sqrt{2}$ A

13. A flat plate P of mass 'M' executes SHM in a horizontal plane by sliding over a frictionless surface with a frequency V. A block 'B' of mass 'm' rests on the plate as shown in figure. Coefficient of friction between the surface of B and P is μ. What is the maximum amplitude of oscillation that the plate block system can have if the block B is not to slip on the plate :

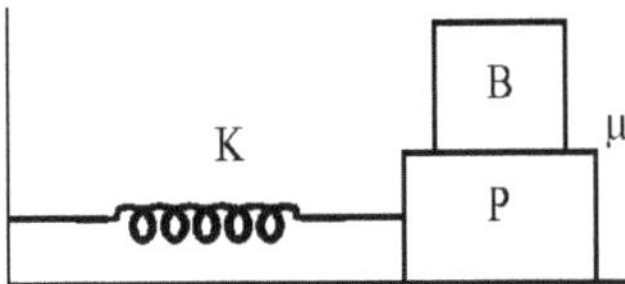

(a) $\frac{\mu g}{4\pi^2 V^2}$ (b) $\frac{\mu g}{4\pi^2 V}$

(c) $\frac{\mu}{4\pi^2 V^2 g}$ (d) $\frac{\mu g}{2\pi^2 V^2}$

14. A glass slab has the left half of refractive index n_1, and the right half of $n_2=3n_1$. The effective refractive index of the whole slab is

(a) $\frac{n_1}{2}$ (b) 2n

(c) $\frac{3n_1}{2}$ (d) $\frac{2n_1}{3}$

15. In the arrangement shown L_1, L_2 are slits and S_1, S_2 two independent sources on the screen, interference fringes

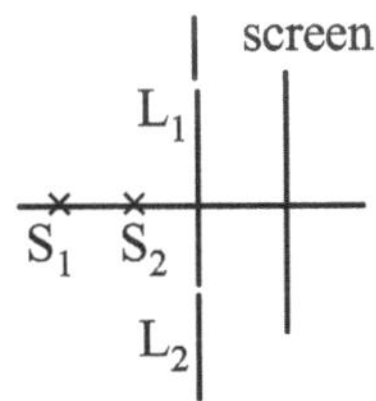

(a) will not be there
(b) will not be there if the intensity of light reaching the screen from S_1 and S_2 are equal.
(c) will be there under all circumstances
(d) we will have only the central fringe

16. What is the ratio of the circumference of the first Bohr orbit for the electron in the hydrogen atom to the de Brogile wavelength of electrons having the same velocity as the electron in the first Bohr orbit of the hydrogen atom?
(a) 1 : 1 (b) 1 : 2
(c) 1 : 4 (d) 2 : 1

17. The radioactivity of a sample is R_1 at a time T_1 and R_2 at a time T_2. If the half life of the specimen is T, the number of atoms that have disintegrated in the time $(T_2–T_1)$ is proportional to
(a) $(R_1T_1 - R_2T_2)$
(b) $(R_1 - R_2)$
(c) $(R_1 - R_2)/T$
(d) $(R_1–R_2) \times T$

18. P–V plots for two gases during adiabatic processes are shown in the figure. Plots 1 and 2 should correspond respectively to

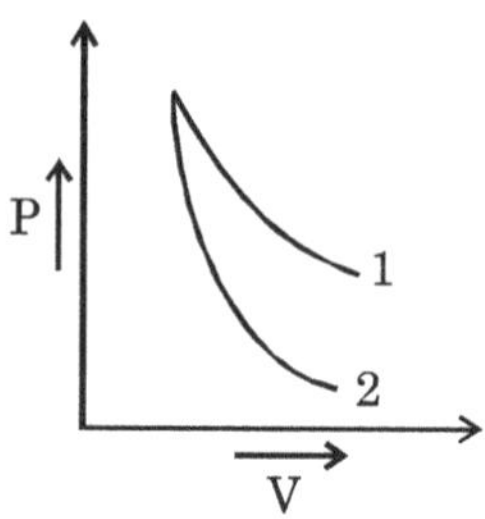

(a) He and Ar (b) He and O_2
(c) O_2 and N_2 (d) O_2 and He

19. Two identical thin rings, each of radius R metres, are coaxially placed at a distance R metres apart. If Q_1 coulomb and Q_2 coulomb are respectively, the charges uniformly spread on the two rings, the work done in moving a charge q from the centre of one ring to that of the other is

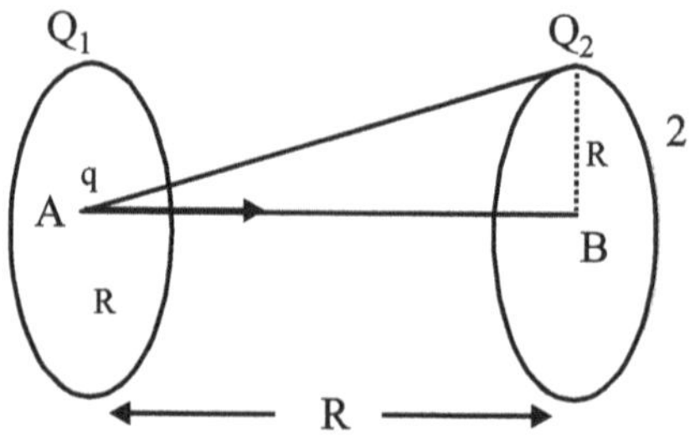

(a) zero
(b) $q(Q_1–Q_2)(\sqrt{2}-1)/\sqrt{2}\, 4\pi\varepsilon_0 R$
(c) $q\sqrt{2}\,(Q_1 + Q_2)/4\pi\varepsilon_0 R$
(d) $q(Q_1+Q_2)(\sqrt{2}+1)/\sqrt{2}\, 4\pi\varepsilon_0 R$

20. The ratio of the coefficient of volume expansion of a glass container to that of a viscous liquid kept inside the container is 1 : 4. What fraction of the inner volume of the container should the liquid occupy so that the volume of the remaining vacant space will be same at all temperatures ?
(a) 2 : 5 (b) 1 : 4
(c) 1 : 64 (d) 1 : 8

PART-II (Numerical Answer Questions)

21. The masses of the blocks A and B are 0.5 kg and 1 kg respectively. These are arranged as shown in the figure and are connected by a massless string. The coefficient of friction between all contact surfaces is 0.4. The force (in N) necessary to move the block B with constant velocity will be ($g = 10 m/s^2$)

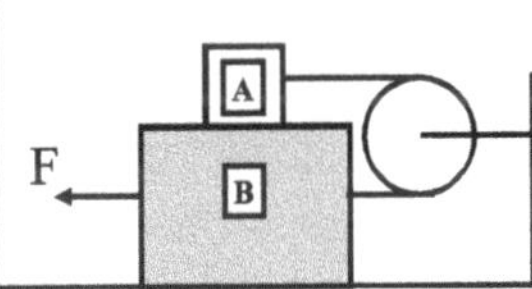

22. A body is thrown vertically upwards from the surface of earth in such a way that it reaches upto a height equal to $10R_e$. The velocity (in km/s) imparted to the body will be

23. A non-conducting partition divides a container into two equal compartments. One is filled with helium gas at 200 K and the other is filled with oxygen gas at 400 K. The number of molecules in each gas is the same. If the partition is removed to allow the gases to mix, the final temperature (in K) will be

24. A transformer is used to light a 140 W, 24 V bulb from a 240 V a.c. mains. The current in the main cable is 0.7 A. The efficiency (in %) of the transformer is

25. Two circular coils X and Y, having equal number of turns, carry equal currents in the same sense and subtend same solid angle at point O. If the smaller coil X is midway between O and Y, then if we represent the magnetic induction due to bigger coil Y at O as B_Y and due to smaller coil X at O as B_X then the ratio $\frac{B_Y}{B_X}$ is

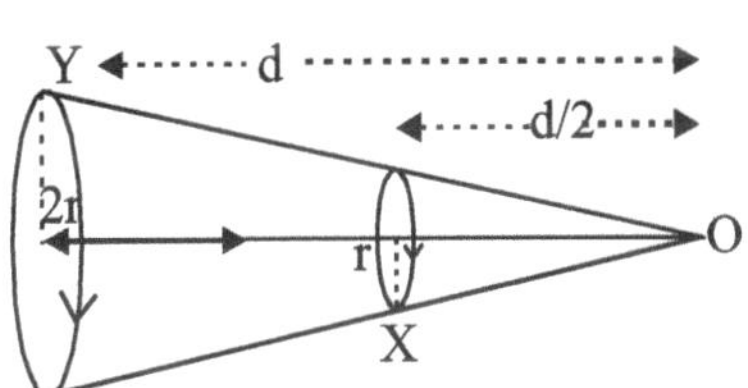

26. The speed verses time graph for a particle is shown in the figure. The distance travelled (in m) by the particle during the time interval $t = 0$ to $t = 5$ s will be ________.

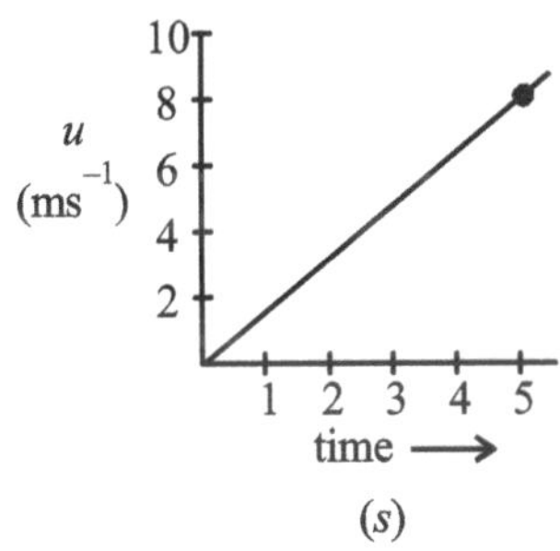

27. The nuclear activity of a radioactive element becomes $\left(\frac{1}{8}\right)^{th}$ of its initial

value in 30 years. The half-life of radioactive element is ________ years.

28. A body of mass 2 kg moving with a speed of 4 m/s makes an elastic collision with another body at rest and continues to move in the original direction but with one fourth of its initial speed. The speed of the two body centre of mass is $\frac{x}{10}$ m/s. Then the value of x is________.

29. If the maximum value of accelerating potential provided by a radio frequency oscillator is 12 kV. The number of revolution made by a proton in a cyclotron to achieve one sixth of the speed of light is ________

[$m_p = 1.67 \times 10^{-27}$ kg, $e = 1.6 \times 10^{-19}$ C, Speed of light $= 3 \times 10^8$ m/s]

30. In the reported figure, heat energy absorbed by a system in going through a cyclic process is ______ πJ.

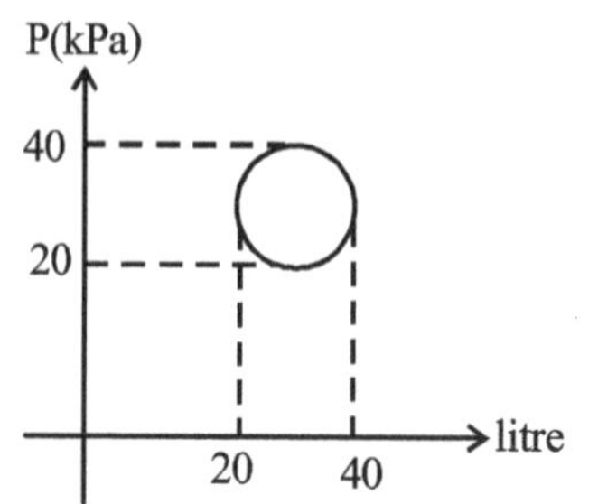

CHEMISTRY

PART-I (Multiple Choice Questions)

31. Which of the following structures does not contain any chiral C atom but represent the chirality in the structure.

(a) 2 – Ethyl – 3 – hexene
(b) 2, 3-Pentadiene
(c) 1,3 – Butadiene
(d) Pent – 3 – en – 1 – yne

32. The root mean square speed of gas molecules at 25K & 1.5×10^5 Nm^{-2} is 100.5 ms^{-1}. If the temperature is raised to 100K & pressure to 6.0×10^5 Nm^{-2}, the root mean square speed becomes.

(a) 100.5 ms^{-1} (b) 201.0 ms^{-1}
(c) 402 ms^{-1} (d) 1608 ms^{-1}

33. Reduction with aluminium isopropoxide in excess of isopropyl alcohol is called Meerwein Ponndorff-Verley reduction (MPV). What will be the final product when cyclohex-2-enone is selectively reduced in MPV reaction ?

(a) Cyclohexanol
(b) Cyclohex-2-enol
(c) Cyclohexanone
(d) Benzene

34. N_2 and O_2 are converted to mono cations N_2^+ and O_2^+ respectively, which of the following is wrong?

(a) In N_2^+, the N – N bond weakens
(b) In O_2^+, the O – O bond order increases

(c) In O_2^+, paramagnetism decreases

(d) N_2^+ becomes diamagnetic

35. The reaction in which hydrogen peroxide acts as a reducing agent is

(a) $PbS + 4H_2O_2 \rightarrow PbSO_4 + 4H_2O$

(b) $2KI + H_2O_2 \rightarrow 2KOH + I_2$

(c) $2FeSO_4 + H_2SO_4 + H_2O_2 \rightarrow Fe_2(SO_4)_3 + 2H_2O$

(d) $Ag_2O + H_2O_2 \longrightarrow 2Ag + H_2O + O_2$

36. Reaction of $CH_2—CH_2$ (bridged by O) with RMgX leads to formation of

(a) RCHOHR

(b) $RCHOHCH_3$

(c) RCH_2CH_2OH

(d) 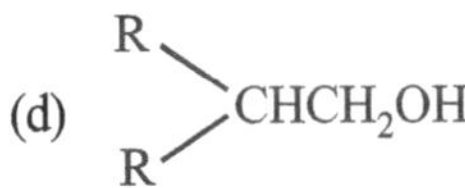

37. The correct match between Item - I (starting material) and Item - II (reagent) for the preparation of benzaldehyde is :

	Item - I		Item - II
(I)	Benzene	(P)	HCl and $SnCl_2$, H_3O^+
(II)	Benzonitrile	(Q)	H_2, Pd-$BaSO_4$, quinoline
(III)	Benzoyl Chloride	(R)	CO, HCl and $AlCl_3$

(a) (I) - (Q), (II) - (R) and (III) - (P)

(b) (I) - (P), (II) - (Q) and (III) - (R)

(c) (I) - (R), (II) - (P) and (III) - (Q)

(d) (I) - (R), (II) - (Q) and (III) - (P)

38. Given below are two statements, one is labelled as **Assertion (A)** and other is labelled as **Reason (R).**

Assertion (A) : Sucrose is a disaccharide and a non-reducing sugar.

Reason (R) : Sucrose involves glycosidic linkage between C_1 of β-glucose and C_2 of β-fructose.

Choose the **most appropriate** answer from the options given below :

(a) Both (A) and (R) are true but (R) is not the true explanation of (A)

(b) (A) is false but (R) is true.

(c) (A) is true but (R) is false

(d) Both (A) and (R) are true and (R) is the true explanation of (A)

39. When tert-butyl chloride is made to react with sodium methoxide, the major product is

(a) dimethyl ether

(b) di-tert-butyl ether

(c) tert-butylmethyl ether

(d) isobutylene

40. If s_0, s_1, s_2 and s_3 are the solubilities of AgCl in water, 0.01 M $CaCl_2$, 0.01 M NaCl and 0.05 M $AgNO_3$ solutions, respectively, then

(a) $s_0 > s_1 > s_2 > s_3$

(b) $s_0 > s_2 > s_1 > s_3$

(c) $s_0 > s_2 > s_3 > s_1$

(d) $s_0 > s_1 = s_2 > s_3$

41. An organic compound is treated with $NaNO_2$ and dil. HCl at 0°C. The resulting solution is added to an alkaline solution of β-naphthol where by a brilliant red dye is produced. It shows the presence of

(a) $-NO_2$ group

(b) aromatic $-NH_2$ group

(c) $-CONH_2$ group

(d) aliphatic $-NH_2$ group

42. Point out the incorrect statment among the following :

(a) The oxidation state of oxygen is +2 in OF_2.

(b) Acidic character follows the order $H_2O < H_2S < H_2Se < H_2Te$.

(c) The tendency to form multiple bonds increases in moving down the group from sulphur to tellurium (towards C and N)

(d) Sulphur has a strong tendency to catenate while oxygen shows this tendency to a limited extent.

43. Removal of Fe, Cu, W from Sn metal after smelting is by .... because ....

(a) Poling; of more affinity towards oxygen for impurities

(b) Selective oxidation; of more affinity towards oxygen for impurities

(c) Electrolytic refining; impurities undissolved in electrolyte

(d) Liquation; Sn having low melting point compared to impurities.

44. Among KO_2, AlO_2^-, BaO_2 and NO_2^+, unpaired electron is present in

(a) NO_2^+ and BaO_2

(b) KO_2 and AlO_2^-

(c) KO_2 only

(d) BaO_2 only

45. If a 0.1 M solution of glucose (Mol. wt 180) and 0.1 molar solution of urea (Mol. wt. 60) are placed on two sided semipermeable membrane to equal heights, then it will be correct to say that

(a) there will be no net movement across the membrane

(b) glucose will flow across the membrane into urea solution

(c) urea will flow across the membrane into glucose solution

(d) water will flow from urea solution to glucose solution

46. When pink $[Co(H_2O)_6]^{2\oplus}$ is dehydrated the colour changes to blue. The correct explanation for the change is :

(a) The octahedral complex becomes square planar.

(b) A tetrahedral complex is formed.

(c) Distorted octahedral structure is obtained.
(d) Dehydration results in the formation of polymeric species.

47. Amongst the following the compound that is both paramagnetic and coloured is
(a) $K_2Cr_2O_7$
(b) $(NH_4)_2[TiCl_6]$
(c) $CoSO_4$
(d) $K_3[Cu(CN)_4]$

48. A reaction rate constant is given by $K = 1.2 \times 10^{10} e^{-2500/RT}$ · It means
(a) log K vs T will give a straight line
(b) log K vs 1/T gives a straight line with a slope –2500/2.303 R
(c) half life of reaction will be more at higher temperature
(d) log K vs 1/T gives a straight line with a slope 2500/R

49. The correct statement among the following is :
(a) The alkali metals when strongly heated in oxygen form superoxides.
(b) Caesium is used in photoelectric cells.
(c) $NaHCO_3$ is more soluble in water than $KHCO_3$.
(d) The size of hydrated ions of alkali metals increases from top to bottom.

50. The e.m.f. of a Daniell cell,

$$Zn\left|\underset{(0.01M)}{ZnSO_4}\right|\left|\underset{(1.0M)}{CuSO_4}\right|Cu \text{, at 298 K}$$

is E_1. When the concentration of $ZnSO_4$ is 1.0 M and that of $CuSO_4$ is 0.01 M, the e.m.f. changed to E_2. What is the relationship between E_1 and E_2?
(a) $E_1 < E_2$ (b) $E_1 = E_2$
(c) $E_2 = 0 \neq E_1$ (d) $E_1 > E_2$

PART-II (Numerical Answer Questions)

51. The vapour pressure of benzene at a certain temperature is 640 mm of Hg. A non volatile and non electrolyte solid weighing 2.175 g is added to 39.08 g of benzene. If the vapour pressure of the solution is 600mm of Hg, what is the molecular weight of solid substance?

52. What will be the uncertainty in the position of an electron (mass 9.1×10^{-28}g) moving with a velocity of 3.0×10^4 cm s^{-1} accurate up to 0.011%

53. When CO_2 dissolves in water, the following equilibrium is established

$$CO_2 + 2H_2O \rightleftharpoons H_3O^+ + HCO_3^-;$$

for which the equilibrium constant is 3.8×10^{-6} and pH = 6.0. What would be the ratio of concentration of bicarbonate ion to carbon dioxide?

54. The wave number of first line of Balmer series of hydrogen is 15200 cm^{-1}. Wht will be the wave number of first Balmer line of Li^{2+} ion?

55. A cylinder of gas supplied by Bharat Petroleum is assumed to contain 14 kg of butane. If a normal family requires 20,000 kJ of energy per day for cooking, butane gas in the cylinder last for .... Days.
(ΔH_c of C_4H_{10} = –2658 JK per mole)

56. 40 g of glucose (Molar mass = 180) is mixed with 200 mL of water. The freezing point of solution is _____ K.
[Given : K_f = 1.86 K kg mol^{-1} ; Density of water = 1.00 g cm^{-3}; Freezing point of water = 273.15 K]

57. The number of nitrogen atoms in a semicarbazone molecule of acetone is _________.

58. In Carius method for estimation of halogens, 0.2 g of an organic compound gave 0.188 g of AgBr. The percentage of bromine in the compound is ________.
[Atomic mass : Ag = 108, Br = 80]

59. The total number of reagents from those given below, that can convert nitrobenzene into aniline is ______. (Integer answer)

I. Sn – HCl
II. Sn – NH_4OH
III. Fe – HCl
IV. Zn – HCl
V. H_2 – Pd
VI. H_2 – Raney Nickel

60. In the electrolytic refining of blister copper, the total number of main impurities, from the following, removed as anode mud is ________

Pb, Sb, Se, Te, Ru, Ag, Au, Pt

MATHEMATICS

PART-I (Multiple Choice Questions)

61. If a, b, c, d and p are distinct non zero real numbers such that $(a^2 + b^2 + c^2)p^2 - 2(ab + bc + cd)p + (b^2 + c^2 + d^2) \leq 0$ then a,b,c,d are in

(a) A.P.
(b) G.P.
(c) H.P.
(d) satisfy ab = cd

62. Which of the following is correct?

(a) If $a^2 + 4b^2 = 12ab$, then

$$\log(a+2b) = \frac{1}{2}(\log a + \log b)$$

(b) If $\frac{\log x}{b-c} = \frac{\log y}{c-a} = \frac{\log z}{a-b}$,

then $x^a.y^b.z^c = abc$

(c)

$$\frac{1}{\log_{xy} xyz} + \frac{1}{\log_{yz} xyz} + \frac{1}{\log_{zx} xyz} = 2$$

(d) All are correct

63. If $0 < \alpha, \beta, \gamma < \pi/2$ such that $\alpha + \beta + \gamma = \frac{\pi}{2}$ and $\cot \alpha$, $\cot \beta$, $\cot \gamma$ are in arithmetic progression, then the value of $\cot \alpha \cot \gamma$ is

(a) 1
(b) 3
(c) $\cot^2 \beta$
(d) $\cot \alpha + \cot \gamma$

64. If $\omega = \cos\frac{\pi}{n} + i \sin\frac{\pi}{n}$, then value of $1 + \omega + \omega^2 + ... + \omega^{n-1}$ is

(a) $1 + i$
(b) $1 + i \tan(\pi/n)$
(c) $1 + i \cot(\pi/2n)$
(d) None of these

65. The circles $x^2 + y^2 - 2x - 15 = 0$ and $x^2 + y^2 + 4y + 3 = 0$ have
   (a) no common tangent
   (b) one common tangent
   (c) three common tangents
   (d) four common tangents

66. Which of the following is correct?
   (a) If A and B are square matrices of order 3 such that $|A| = -1$, $|B| = 3$, then the determinant of 3 AB is equal to 27.
   (b) If A is an invertible matrix, then det (A^{-1}) is equal to det (A)
   (c) If A and B are matrices of the same order, then $(A+B)^2 = A^2 + 2AB + B^2$ is possible if AB = I
   (d) None of these

67. If the solution of the linear equations $x - 2y + z = 0$; $2x - y + 3z = 0$ and $\lambda x + y - z = 0$ is trivial then the value of λ is given by
   (a) $\lambda = -\frac{4}{5}$ (b) $\lambda \neq -\frac{4}{5}$
   (c) $\lambda = 2$ (d) $\lambda \neq 2$

68. Let $f(x) = |x - 1|$. Then
   (a) $f(x^2) = (f(x))^2$
   (b) $f(x+y) = f(x) + f(y)$
   (c) $f(|x|) = |f(x)|$
   (d) None of these

69. If

$$\sin^{-1}\frac{2a}{1+a^2} + \sin^{-1}\frac{2b}{1+b^2} = 2\tan^{-1} x,$$

then x is equal to
   (a) $\frac{a-b}{1+ab}$ (b) $\frac{b}{1+ab}$
   (c) $\frac{b}{1-ab}$ (d) $\frac{a+b}{1-ab}$

70. If AB = 0, then for the matrices

$$A = \begin{bmatrix} \cos^2\theta & \cos\theta\sin\theta \\ \cos\theta\sin\theta & \sin^2\theta \end{bmatrix}$$

and $B = \begin{bmatrix} \cos^2\phi & \cos\phi\sin\phi \\ \cos\phi\sin\phi & \sin^2\phi \end{bmatrix}$,

$\theta - \phi$ is
   (a) an odd number of $\frac{\pi}{2}$
   (b) an odd multiple of π
   (c) an even multiple of $\frac{\pi}{2}$
   (d) 0

71. The set of points where $f(x) = (x-1)^2 (x + |x-1|)$ is thrice differentiable, is
   (a) R (b) R – {0}
   (c) R – {1} (d) R – {0,1}

72. Let $f(x) = 1/(x-1)$ and $g(x) = 1/(x^2+x-2)$. Then the set of points where (gof)(x) is discontinuous, is
   (a) {1} (b) {–2,1}
   (c) {1/2, 1, 2} (d) {1/2, 1}

73. $\sum_{r=0}^{m} {}^{n+r}C_n$ is equal to :
   (a) ${}^{n+m+1}C_{n+1}$
   (b) ${}^{n+m+2}C_n$
   (c) ${}^{n+m+3}C_{n-1}$
   (d) None of these

74. Let $f(x)=\dfrac{x-\{x+1\}}{x-\{x+2\}}$; where $\{x\}$ is the fractional part of x, then $\lim_{x\to 1/3} f(x)$

(a) has value 0
(b) has value 1
(c) has value $-\infty$
(d) has value ∞

75. The order of the differential equation

$$\left[1+5\left(\frac{dy}{dx}\right)^2\right]^{3/2}=11\left(\frac{d^2y}{dx^2}\right)^5$$ is

(a) 1 (b) 2
(c) 3 (d) 4

76. The value of

$$\int_{-\pi/4}^{\pi/4}(x|x|+\sin^3 x+x\tan^2 x+1)\,dx$$ is

(a) 0 (b) 1
(c) $\pi/4$ (d) $\pi/2$

77. Let $(1-x-2x^2)^6=1+a_1x+a_2x^2+\ldots.+a_{12}x^{12}$. Then

$$\frac{a_2}{2^2}+\frac{a_4}{2^4}+\frac{a_6}{2^6}+\ldots\ldots+\frac{a_{12}}{2^{12}}$$ is equal to

(a) -1 (b) $-1/2$
(c) 0 (d) 1/2

78. The equation of a common tangent to $y^2=4x$ and the curve $x^2+4y^2=8$ can be

(a) $x-2y+2=0$
(b) $x+2y+4=0$
(c) $x-2y=4$
(d) $x+2y=4$

79. The function $f(x)=(x-3)^2$ satisfies all the conditions of mean value theorem in $\{3, 4\}$. A point on $y=(x-3)^2$, where the tangent is parallel to the chord joining (3, 0) and (4,1) is

(a) $\left(\frac{7}{2},\frac{1}{2}\right)$ (b) $\left(\frac{7}{2},\frac{1}{4}\right)$
(c) (1,4) (d) (4, 1)

80. If $x+y-z+xyz=0$, then $\frac{2x}{1-x^2}+\frac{2y}{1-y^2}-\frac{2z}{1-z^2}$ is equal to

(a) $\dfrac{xyz}{[(1-x^2)(1-y^2)(1-z^2)]}$

(b) $\dfrac{-xyz}{[(1-x^2)(1-y^2)(1-z^2)]}$

(c) $\dfrac{8xyz}{[(1-x^2)(1-y^2)(1-z^2)]}$

(d) $\dfrac{-8xyz}{[(1-x^2)(1-y^2)(1-z^2)]}$

PART-II (Numerical Answer Questions)

81. If one root of the equation $x^2+px+12=0$ is 4 while the equation $x^2+px+q=0$ has equal roots, the value of q is ________.

82. The value of $\cos 36^0 \cos 42^0 \cos 78^0$ is

$$\left[\text{Given} : \sin 18 = \frac{\sqrt{5}-1}{4} \text{ and } \cos 36 = \frac{\sqrt{5}+1}{4}\right]$$

83. If x =1/5, the absolute value of $\cos(\cos^{-1}x + 2\sin^{-1}x)$ is ______.

84. If θ_1, θ_2 are the solutions of the equation $2\tan^2\theta - 4\tan\theta + 1 = 0$, then $\tan(\theta_1 + \theta_2)$ is equal to _____.

85. In a ΔABC, if $\begin{vmatrix} 1 & a & b \\ 1 & c & a \\ 1 & b & c \end{vmatrix} = 0$, then

$\sin^2 A + \sin^2 B + \sin^2 C =$ _____.

86. The least positive integer n such that $\frac{(2i)^n}{(1-i)^{n-2}}, i = \sqrt{-1}$

is a positive integer, is ______.

87. If $^1P_1 + 2.\,^2P_2 + 3.\,^3P_3 + ... + 15.\,^{15}P_{15} = \,^qP_r - s, 0 \le s \le 1$, then $^{q+s}C_{r-s}$ is equal to ________.

88. For real numbers α, β, γ and δ, if

$$\int \frac{\left(x^2-1\right) + \tan^{-1}\left(\frac{x^2+1}{x}\right)}{\left(x^4+3x^2+1\right)\tan^{-1}\left(\frac{x^2+1}{x}\right)} dx$$

$$= \alpha \log_e\left(\tan^{-1}\left(\frac{x^2+1}{x}\right)\right) + \beta\tan^{-1}\left(\frac{\gamma\left(x^2-1\right)}{x}\right) + \delta\tan^{-1}\left(\frac{x^2+1}{x}\right) + C$$

Where C is an arbitrary constant, then the value of $10(\alpha + \beta\gamma + \delta)$ is equal to _______ .

89. Let $\vec{a} = \hat{i} + 5\hat{j} + \alpha\hat{k}, \vec{b} = \hat{i} + 3\hat{j} + \beta\hat{k}$ and $\vec{c} = -\hat{i} + 2\hat{j} - 3\hat{k}$ be three vectors such that, $\left|\vec{b} \times \vec{c}\right| = 5\sqrt{3}$ and $\vec{a}$ is perpendicular to $\vec{b}$. Then the greatest amongst the values of $\left|\vec{a}\right|^2$ is _____.

90. The number of integral values of 'k' for which the equation 3sinx + 4cosx = k + 1 has a solution, k ∈ R is ________.

RESPONSE SHEET

PHYSICS		CHEMISTRY		MATHEMATICS	
1.	ⓐⓑⓒⓓ	31.	ⓐⓑⓒⓓ	61.	ⓐⓑⓒⓓ
2.	ⓐⓑⓒⓓ	32.	ⓐⓑⓒⓓ	62.	ⓐⓑⓒⓓ
3.	ⓐⓑⓒⓓ	33.	ⓐⓑⓒⓓ	63.	ⓐⓑⓒⓓ
4.	ⓐⓑⓒⓓ	34.	ⓐⓑⓒⓓ	64.	ⓐⓑⓒⓓ
5.	ⓐⓑⓒⓓ	35.	ⓐⓑⓒⓓ	65.	ⓐⓑⓒⓓ
6.	ⓐⓑⓒⓓ	36.	ⓐⓑⓒⓓ	66.	ⓐⓑⓒⓓ
7.	ⓐⓑⓒⓓ	37.	ⓐⓑⓒⓓ	67.	ⓐⓑⓒⓓ
8.	ⓐⓑⓒⓓ	38.	ⓐⓑⓒⓓ	68.	ⓐⓑⓒⓓ
9.	ⓐⓑⓒⓓ	39.	ⓐⓑⓒⓓ	69.	ⓐⓑⓒⓓ
10.	ⓐⓑⓒⓓ	40.	ⓐⓑⓒⓓ	70.	ⓐⓑⓒⓓ
11.	ⓐⓑⓒⓓ	41.	ⓐⓑⓒⓓ	71.	ⓐⓑⓒⓓ
12.	ⓐⓑⓒⓓ	42.	ⓐⓑⓒⓓ	72.	ⓐⓑⓒⓓ
13.	ⓐⓑⓒⓓ	43.	ⓐⓑⓒⓓ	73.	ⓐⓑⓒⓓ
14.	ⓐⓑⓒⓓ	44.	ⓐⓑⓒⓓ	74.	ⓐⓑⓒⓓ
15.	ⓐⓑⓒⓓ	45.	ⓐⓑⓒⓓ	75.	ⓐⓑⓒⓓ
16.	ⓐⓑⓒⓓ	46.	ⓐⓑⓒⓓ	76.	ⓐⓑⓒⓓ
17.	ⓐⓑⓒⓓ	47.	ⓐⓑⓒⓓ	77.	ⓐⓑⓒⓓ
18.	ⓐⓑⓒⓓ	48.	ⓐⓑⓒⓓ	78.	ⓐⓑⓒⓓ
19.	ⓐⓑⓒⓓ	49.	ⓐⓑⓒⓓ	79.	ⓐⓑⓒⓓ
20.	ⓐⓑⓒⓓ	50.	ⓐⓑⓒⓓ	80.	ⓐⓑⓒⓓ
21.		51.		81.	
22.		52.		82.	
23.		53.		83.	
24.		54.		84.	
25.		55.		85.	
26.		56.		86.	
27.		57.		87.	
28.		58.		88.	
29.		59.		89.	
30.		60.		90.	

3 Mock Test

INSTRUCTIONS

1. This test will be a 3 hours Test.
2. This test consists of Physics, Chemistry and Mathematics questions with equal weightage of 100 marks.
3. Each question is of 4 marks.
4. There are three sections in the question paper consisting of Physics (Q.no.1 to 30), Chemistry (Q.no.31 to 60) and Mathematics (Q. no.61 to 90). Each section is divided into two parts, Part I consists of 20 multiple choice questions & Part II consists of 10 Numerical value type Questions; attempt any 5 questions out of 10.
5. There will be only one correct choice in the given four choices in Part I. For each question 4 marks will be awarded for correct choice, 1 mark will be deducted for incorrect choice for Part I Questions and zero mark will be awarded for not attempted question. For Part II Questions 4 marks will be awarded for correct answer and zero for unattempted and incorrect answer.
6. Any textual, printed or written material, mobile phones, calculator etc. is not allowed for the students appearing for the test.
7. All calculations / written work should be done in the rough sheet provided.

PHYSICS

PART-I (Multiple Choice Questions)

1. Astronauts look down on earth surface from a space ship parked at an altitude of 500 km. They can resolve objects of the earth of the size (It can be assumed that the pupils diameter is 5mm and wavelength of light is 500 nm)

(a) 0.5m (b) 5m
(c) 50m (d) 500m

2. The wavelength of sodium light in air is 5890Å. The velocity of light in air is 3×10^{-8} ms^{-1}. The wavelength of light in a glass of refractive index 1.6, would be close to

(a) 5890 Å (b) 3680 Å
(c) 9424 Å (d) 15078 Å

3. A space craft of mass 'M', moving with velocity 'v' suddenly breaks into two pieces. After the explosion mass 'm' becomes stationary. What is the velocity of the other part of the craft ?

(a) $\frac{Mv}{M-m}$ (b) v
(c) $\frac{mv}{M}$ (d) $\frac{M-m}{m}v$

4. Using mass(M), length(L), time(T) and electric current (A) as fundamental quantities the dimensions of permittivity will be
 (a) $MLT^{-1}A^{-1}$
 (b) $MLT^{-2}A^{-2}$
 (c) $M^{-1}L^{-3}T^{+4}A^{2}$
 (d) $M^{2}L^{-2}T^{-2}A^{2}$

5. A black body at a temperature of 227°C radiates heat at the rate of 20 cal m^{-2} s^{-1}. When its temperature rises to 727°C the heat radiated will be
 (a) 40 units (b) 160 units
 (c) 320 units (d) 640 units

6. Two waves of wavelengths 99 cm and 100 cm both travelling with velocity 396 m/s are made to interfere. The number of beats produced by them per second are
 (a) 1 (b) 2
 (c) 4 (d) 8

7. A sphere of mass 'm' and radius 'r' is falling in the column of a viscous fluid. Terminal velocity attained by falling object is proportional to
 (a) r^2 (b) 1/r
 (c) r (d) $-1/r^2$

8. There are two wires of the same length. The diameter of second wire is twice that of the first. On applying the same load to both the wires, the extension produced in them will be in ratio of
 (a) 1 : 4 (b) 1 : 2
 (c) 2 : 1 (d) 4 : 1

9. When a proton, anti-proton annihilate the energy released is
 (a) 1.5×10^{-10} J
 (b) 28.8×10^{-10} J
 (c) 6×10^{-10} J
 (d) 9×10^{-10} J

10. $y = 2\,(\text{cm}) \sin\left[\frac{\pi t}{2} + \phi\right]$
 What is the maximum acceleration of the particle doing the SHM
 (a) $\frac{\pi}{2}$ cm/s^2 (b) $\frac{\pi^2}{2}$ cm/s^2
 (c) $\frac{\pi^2}{4}$ cm/s^2 (d) $\frac{\pi}{4}$ cm/s^2

11. What is the electric potential at the centre of the square?

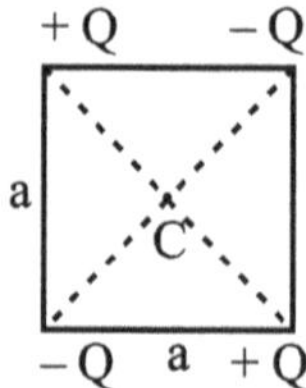

 (a) zero
 (b) $kq/a\sqrt{2}$
 (c) kq/a^2
 (d) None of these

12. A rectangular block of mass m and area of cross-section A floats in a liquid of density ρ. If it is given a small vertical displacemnet from equilibrium it undergoes oscillation with a time period T. Then
 (a) $T \propto \frac{1}{\sqrt{A}}$ (b) $T \propto \frac{1}{\rho}$
 (c) $T \propto \frac{1}{\sqrt{m}}$ (d) $T \propto \sqrt{\rho}$

13. While determining the specific resistance of a wire using a metre

bridge the formula used is (where X, D, L and ρ denote unknown resistance, diameter of the wire, the length of the wire and the specific resistance of the wire)

(a) $\rho = \frac{X\pi D}{4L}$

(b) $\rho = \frac{X\pi D^2}{4L}$

(c) $\rho = \frac{X^2\pi D^2}{4L}$

(d) $\rho = \frac{X\pi D^2}{4L^2}$

14. Consider the following u-v diagram regarding the experiment to determine the focal length of a convex lens.

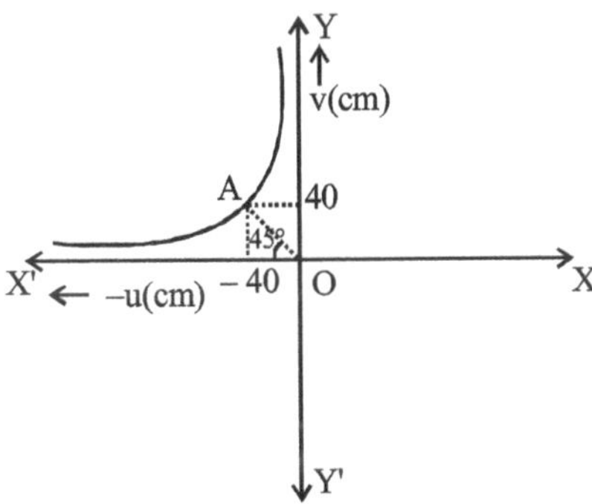

At the point A, the values of u and v are equal. The focal length of the lens is

(a) 40 cm (b) 20 cm
(c) 10 cm (d) 15 cm

15. Two metallic plates A and B, each of area $5 \times 10^{-4} m^2$, are placed parallel to each other at a separation of 1 cm. Plate B carries a positive charge of 33.7×10^{-12}C. A mono-chromatic beam of light, with photons of energy 5 eV each, starts falling on plate A at t = 0 so that 10^{16} photons fall on it per square meter per second. Assume that one photoelectron is emitted for every 10^6 incident photons. Also assume that all the emitted photoelectrons are collected by plate B and the work function of plate A remains constant at the value 2 eV.

No. of photoelectrons emitted up to 10 sec

(a) 5×10^7 (b) 2×10^6
(c) 5×10^6 (d) 2×10^7

16. The circuit shown here has two batteries of 8.0 V and 16.0 V and three resistors 3 Ω, 9 Ω and 9 Ω and a capacitor of 5.0 μF.

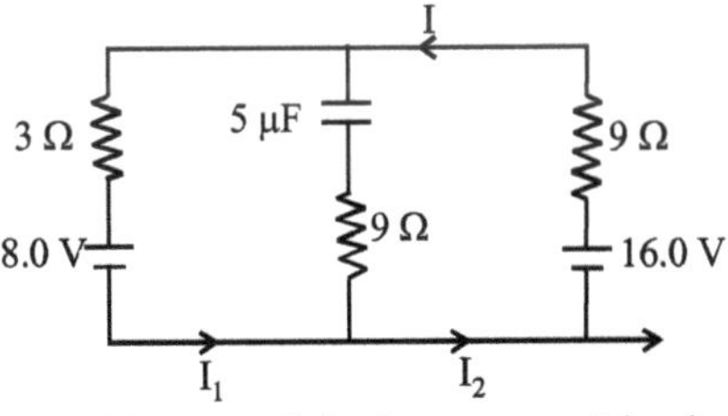

How much is the current I in the circuit in steady state?

(a) 1.6 A (b) 0.67 A
(c) 2.5 A (d) 0.25 A

17. An electromagnetic wave of frequency 1×10^{14} hertz is propagating along z-axis. The amplitude of electric field is 4 V/m. If $\varepsilon_0 = 8.8 \times 10^{-12}$ C²/N-m², then average energy density of electric field will be:

(a) 35.2×10^{-10} J/m³
(b) 35.2×10^{-11} J/m³
(c) 35.2×10^{-12} J/m³
(d) 35.2×10^{-13} J/m³

18. A block is placed on a frictionless horizontal table. The mass of the

block is m and springs are attached on either side with force constants K_1 and K_2. If the block is displaced a little and left to oscillate, then the angular frequency of oscillation will be

(a) $\left(\frac{K_1+K_2}{m}\right)^{\frac{1}{2}}$

(b) $\left[\frac{K_1K_2}{m(K_1+K_2)}\right]^{\frac{1}{2}}$

(c) $\left[\frac{K_1K_2}{(K_1-K_2)m}\right]^{\frac{1}{2}}$

(d) $\left[\frac{K_1^2+K_2^2}{(K_1+K_2)m}\right]^{\frac{1}{2}}$

19. A sphere is placed in front of a convex lens of focal length f. The radius of the sphere is much smaller compared to f. The image of the sphere would look spherical if the object distance is

(a) f (b) $\frac{3f}{2}$

(c) 2f (d) $\frac{f}{2}$

20. Which of the following expressions corresponds to simple harmonic motion along a straight line, where x is the displacement and a, b, c are positive constants?

(a) $a+bx-cx^2$

(b) bx^2

(c) $a-bx+cx^2$

(d) $-bx$

PART-II (Numerical Answer Questions)

21. The source of sound generating a frequency of 3 kHz reaches an observer with a speed of 0.5 times in air. The frequency (in kHz) heard by the observer is

22. The temperature of reservoir of Carnot's engine operating with an efficency of 70% is 1000 kelvin. The temperature (in kelvin) of its sink is

23. The escape velocity for a body of mass 1 kg from the earth surface is 11.2 kms^{-1}. The escape velocity (in kms^{-1}) for a body of mass 100 kg would be

24. At the centre of a circular coil of radius 5 cm carrying current, magnetic field due to earth is 0.5×10^{-5} W/m^2. What should be the current (in A) flowing through the coil so that it annuls the earth's magnetic field

25. A beam of light of intensity 12 $watt/cm^2$ is incident on a totally reflecting plane mirror of area 1.5 cm^2, then the force (in newton) acting on the mirror will be

26. Two persons A and B perform same amount of work in moving a body through a certain distance d with application of forces acting at angle 45° and 60° with the direction of displacement respectively. The ratio of force applied by person A to the force applied by person B is $\frac{1}{\sqrt{x}}$. The value of x is ________.

27. White light is passed through a double slit and interference is observed on a screen 1.5 m away.

The separation between the slits is 0.3 mm. The first violet and red fringes are formed 2.0 mm and 3.5 mm away from the central white fringes. The difference in wavelengths of red and violet light is ________ nm.

28. A steel rod with $Y = 2.0 \times 10^{11}$ Nm^{-2} and $\alpha = 10^{-5}$ $°C^{-1}$ of length 4 m and area of cross-section 10 cm^2 is heated from 0° C to 400°C without being allowed to extend. The tension produced in the rod is $x \times 10^5$ N where the value of x is ________

29. Two radioactive substance X and Y originally have N_1 and N_2 nuclei respectively. Half life of X is half of the half life of Y. After three half lives of Y, number of nuclei of both are equal.

The ratio $\frac{N_1}{N_2}$ will equal to:

30. Wires W_1 and W_2 are made of same material having the breaking stress of 1.25×10^9 N/m^2. W_1 and W_2 have cross-sectional area of 8×10^{-7} m^2 and 4×10^{-7} m^2, respectively. Masses of 20 kg and 10 kg hang from them as shown in the figure. The maximum mass that can be placed in the pan without breaking the wires is ____ kg.
(Use $g = 10$ m/s^2)

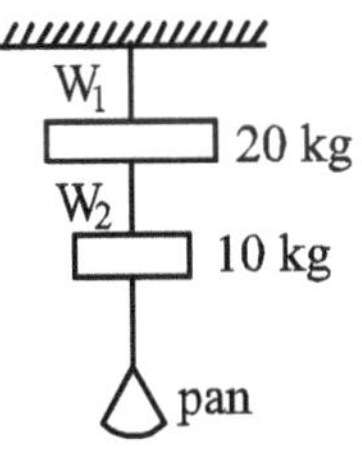

CHEMISTRY

PART-I (Multiple Choice Questions)

31. Ethylene dicholoride and ethylidine chloride are isomeric compounds. The false statement about these isomers is that they :
(a) react with alcoholic potash and give the same product
(b) are position isomers
(c) contain the same percentage of chlorine
(d) are both hydrolysed to the same product

32. An aqueous solution of sodium carbonate has a pH greater than 7 because :
(a) it contains more carbonate ions than H_2O molecules
(b) contains more sodium ions than carbonate ions
(c) Na^+ ions react with water
(d) carbonate ions react with H_2O

33. By what ratio the average velocity of the molecule in gas changes when the temperature is raised from 50 to 200°C ?
(a) $\frac{1.21}{1}$ (b) $\frac{1.46}{1}$
(c) $\frac{2}{1}$ (d) $\frac{4}{1}$

34. How many H-atoms are present in 0.046 g of ethanol ?

(a) 6×10^{20} (b) 1.2×10^{21}
(c) 3×10^{21} (d) 3.6×10^{21}

35. A metal M reacts with N_2 to give a compound 'A' (M_3N). 'A' on heating at high temperature gives back 'M' and 'A' on reacting with H_2O gives a gas 'B'. 'B' turns $CuSO_4$ solution blue on passing through it. M and B can be :
(a) Al & NH_3 (b) Li & NH_3
(c) Na & NH_3 (d) Mg & NH_3

36. When ethanal reacts with CH_3MgBr and C_2H_5OH/dry HCl, the product formed are :
(a) ethyl alcohol and 2-propanol
(b) ethane and hemi acetal
(c) 2-propanol and acetal
(d) propane and methyl acetate

37. If the solutions of NaCl and $NaNO_3$ are mixed in one beaker and the temperature adjusted to 383° K, the contents of the beaker will most likely:
(a) freeze
(b) boil
(c) exhibit precipitation of $NaNO_3$
(d) exhibit a marked color change

38. Given the molecular formula of the hexa-coordinated complexes (i) $CoCl_3.6NH_3$, (ii) $CoCl_3.5NH_3$, (iii) $CoCl_3.4NH_3$
If the number of co-ordinated NH_3 molecules in i, ii and iii respectively are 6, 5, 4, the primary valencies in (i), (ii) and (iii) are :
(a) 6, 5, 4 (b) 3, 2, 1
(c) 0, 1, 2 (d) 3, 3, 3

39. Polyethylene is
(a) Random copolymer
(b) Homopolymer
(c) Alternate copolymer
(d) Crosslinked copolymer

40. Given below are two statements :
Statement I : Penicillin is a bacteriostatic type antibiotic.
Statement II : The general structure of Penicillin is:

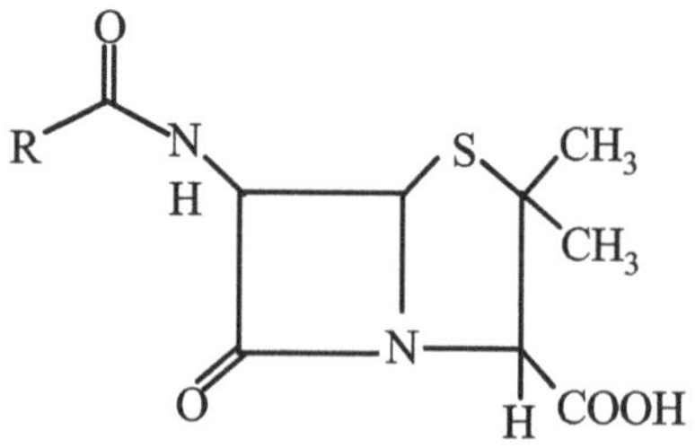

Choose the correct option :
(a) Both statement I and statement II are false.
(b) Statement I is incorrect but statement II is true.
(c) Both statement I and statement II are true.
(d) Statement I is correct but statement II is false.

41. With a change in hybridization of the carbon bearing the charge, the stability of a carbanion decreases in the order :
(a) $sp < sp^2 < sp^3$
(b) $sp < sp^3 < sp^2$
(c) $sp^3 < sp^2 < sp$
(d) $sp^2 < sp < sp^3$

42. In O_2^-, O_2 and O_2^{2-} molecular species, the total number of antibonding electrons respectively are :
(a) 7, 6, 8 (b) 1, 0, 2
(c) 6, 6, 6 (d) 8, 6, 8

43. Which of the given sets of temperature and pressure will cause a gas to exhibit the greatest deviation from ideal gas behaviour?
(a) 100 °C & 4 atm
(b) 100 °C & 2 atm
(c) –100 °C & 4 atm
(d) 0 °C & 2 atm

Space for Rough Work

44. Which of the following pairs has heat of neutralisation equal to 13.7 kcals ?
(a) HCl, NH_4OH
(b) HNO_3, KOH
(c) $NaOH, CH_3COOH$
(d) H_2SO_4, NH_4OH

45. The relative abundance of two isotopes of atomic weight 85 and 87 is 75% and 25% respectively. The average atomic weight of element is
(a) 75.5 (b) 85.5
(c) 40.0 (d) 86.0

46. In Kjeldahl's method, nitrogen present in the organic compound is quantitatively converted into
(a) ammonium nitrite
(b) ammonium sulphate
(c) ammonium phosphate
(d) ammonium nitrate

47. An organic amino compound reacts with aqueous nitrous acid at low temperature to produce an oily nitrosoamine. The compound is:
(a) CH_3NH_2
(b) $CH_3CH_2NH_2$
(c) $CH_3CH_2NH.CH_2CH_3$
(d) $(CH_3CH_2)_3N$

48. Which reaction characteristics are changed by the addition of a catalyst to a reaction at constant temperature ?
(i) Activation energy
(ii) Equilibrium constant
(iii) Reaction enthalpy
(a) (i) only
(b) (iii) only
(c) (i) and (ii) only
(d) all of these

49. Match List-I with List-II

List-I (Elements)	List-II (Properties)
(A) Ba	(i) Organic solvent soluble compounds
(B) Ca	(ii) Outer electronic configuration $6s^2$
(C) Li	(iii) Oxalate insoluble in water
(D) Na	(iv) Formation of very strong monoacidic base

Choose the correct answer from the options given below:
(a) (A)-(ii), (B)-(iii), (C)-(i) and (D)-(iv)
(b) (A)-(iv), (B)-(i), (C)-(ii) and (D)-(iii)
(c) (A)-(iii), (B)-(ii), (C)-(iv) and (D)-(i)
(d) (A)-(i), (B)-(iv), (C)-(ii) and (D)-(iii)

50. A fire of lithium, sodium and potassium can be extinguished by
(a) H_2O
(b) Nitrogen
(c) CO_2
(d) Asbestos blanket

PART-II (Numerical Answer Questions)

51. What is the molarity of H_2SO_4 solution if 25ml is exactly neutralized with 32.63 ml of 0.164 M, NaOH?

52. 3.92 g of ferrous ammonium sulphate react completely with 50 ml $\frac{N}{10}$ $KMnO_4$ solution. What will be the percentage purity of the sample?

53. An '*fcc*' in a unit cell of aluminium contains the equivalent of how many atoms ?

54. If K_{sp} of Ag_2CO_3 is 8, the molar solubility of Ag_2CO_3 in 0.1 M $AgNO_3$ is :

55. When 5 litres of a gas mixure of methane and propane is perfectly combusted at 0 °C and 1 atmosphere, 16 litres of oxygen at the same temperature and pressure is consumed. The amount of heat released from this combustion in kJ

$[\Delta H_{comb.}(CH_4) = 890\ kJ\ mol^{-1}$, $\Delta H_{comb.}(C_3H_8) = 2220 kJ\ mol^{-1}]$ is

56. At 298 K, the enthalpy of fusion of a solid (X) is 2.8 kJ mol^{-1} and the enthalpy of vaporisation of the liquid (X) is 98.2 kJ mol^{-1}. The enthalpy of sublimation of the substance (X) in kJ mol^{-1} is

________ .

57. The empirical formula for a compound with a cubic close packed arrangement of anions and with cations occupying all the octahedral sites in A_xB. The value of x is ________.

58. 3.12 g of oxygen is adsorbed on 1.2 g of platinum metal. The volume of oxygen adsorbed per gram of the adsorbent at 1 atm and 300 K in L is

________ .

$[R = 0.0821\ L\ atm\ K^{-1}\ mol^{-1}]$

59. In the ground state of atomic Fe(Z = 26), the spin-only magnetic moment is________ $\times 10^{-1}$ BM.

[Given : $\sqrt{3} = 1.73, \sqrt{2} = 1.41$]

60. To synthesise 1.0 mole of 2-methylpropan-2-ol from Ethylethanoate ________ equivalents of CH_3MgBr reagent will be required.

MATHEMATICS

PART-I (Multiple Choice Questions)

61. The function $f(x) = \tan^{-1}(\sin x + \cos x)$ is an increasing function in

(a) $\left(0, \frac{\pi}{2}\right)$ (b) $\left(-\frac{\pi}{2}, \frac{\pi}{2}\right)$

(c) $\left(\frac{\pi}{4}, \frac{\pi}{2}\right)$ (d) $\left(-\frac{\pi}{2}, \frac{\pi}{4}\right)$

62. The degree of differential equation satisfying the relation

$$\sqrt{1+x^2} + \sqrt{1+y^2} = \lambda(x\sqrt{1+y^2} - y\sqrt{1+x^2})$$ is

(a) 1 (b) 2

(c) 3 (d) 4

63. $\int_0^2 [x^2]dx$, where [x] is the greatest integer $\leq$ x is

(a) $5+\sqrt{2}+\sqrt{3}$

(b) $-5+\sqrt{2}-\sqrt{3}$

(c) $5-\sqrt{2}-\sqrt{3}$

(d) $-4+\sqrt{3}-\sqrt{2}$

64. α, β be the roots of $x^2 - 3x + a = 0$ and γ, δ be the roots of $x^2 - 12x + b = 0$ and numbers α, β, γ, δ (in order) form an increasing G.P. then
(a) $a = 3, b = 12$
(b) $a = 12, b = 3$
(c) $a = 2, b = 32$
(d) $a = 4, b = 16$

65. Assume R and S are (non-empty) relations in a set A. Which of the following relation given below is false
(a) If R and S are transitive, then $R \cup S$ is transitive.
(b) If R and S are transitive, then $R \cap S$ is transitive.
(c) If R and S are symmetric, then $R \cup S$ is symmetric.
(d) If R and S are reflexive, Then $R \cap S$ is reflexive.

66. $\int \log 2x \, dx$ is
(a) $x \log 2x - \frac{x^2}{2}$
(b) $x \log 2x - \frac{x}{2}$
(c) $x^2 \log 2x - \frac{x}{2}$
(d) $x \log 2x - x + c$

67. For a given integer k, in the interval $\left[2\pi k + \frac{\pi}{2}, 2\pi k - \frac{\pi}{2}\right]$ the graph of sin x is
(a) increasing from –1 to 1
(b) decreasing from –1 to 0
(c) decreasing from 0 to 1
(d) None of these

68. $\frac{dy}{dx} + y = 2e^{2x}$ then y is
(a) $ce^{-x} + \frac{2}{3}e^{2x}$
(b) $(1 + x)e^{-x} + \frac{2}{3}e^{2x} + c$
(c) $ce^{-x} + \frac{2}{3}e^{2x} + c$
(d) $e^{-x} + \frac{2}{3}e^{2x} + c$

69. If $\begin{vmatrix} a+x & a-x & a-x \\ a-x & a+x & a-x \\ a-x & a-x & a+x \end{vmatrix} = 0$ then x is
(a) 0, 2a
(b) a, 2a
(c) 0, 3a
(d) None of these

70. The equation of a circle with origin as centre and passing through the vertices of an equilateral triangle whose median is of length 3a is
(a) $x^2 + y^2 = 9a^2$
(b) $x^2 + y^2 = 16a^2$
(c) $x^2 + y^2 = 4a^2$
(d) $x^2 + y^2 = a^2$

71. If a positive integer n is divisible by 9, then the sum of the digits of n is divisible by 9. So which statement is it contrapositive.
(a) (sum of digits of n is divisible by 9)
$\Rightarrow$ (n is divisible by 9)

(b) (sum of digits of n is not divisible by 9) $\Rightarrow$ (n is not divisible by 9)
(c) (sum of digits of n is divisible by 9) $\Rightarrow$ (n is divisible by 9)
(d) none of these

72. Fifteen coupons are numbered 1, 2 ..... 15,respectively. Seven coupons are selected at random one at a time with replacement. The probability that the largest number appearing on a selected coupon is 9, is

(a) $\left(\frac{9}{16}\right)^6$ (b) $\left(\frac{8}{15}\right)^7$

(c) $\left(\frac{3}{5}\right)^7$

(d) None of these

73. If $a \le 0$ then roots of $x^2 - 2a|x-a| - 3a^2 = 0$ is

(a) $(-1+\sqrt{6})a$
(b) $(\sqrt{6}-1)a$
(c) a
(d) None of these

74. If X and Y are two sets, then $X \cap (X \cup Y)^c$ equals.

(a) X
(b) Y
(c) ϕ
(d) None of these

75. If $y = \log_2\{\log_2(x)\}$, then $\frac{dy}{dx}$ is

(a) $\frac{\log_2 e}{x\,ln\,x}$

(b) $\frac{2.3026}{x\,ln\,x\,ln\,2}$

(c) $\frac{1}{ln(2x)^x}$

(d) None of these

76. $f(x) = \sin|x|.f(x)$ is not differentiable at

(a) $x = 0$ only
(b) all x
(c) multiples of π
(d) multiples of $\frac{\pi}{2}$

77. $\int_0^{\pi/3} \frac{\cos x + \sin x}{\sqrt{1+\sin 2x}} dx$ is

(a) $\frac{4\pi}{3}$ (b) $\frac{2\pi}{3}$

(c) π (d) $\frac{\pi}{3}$

78. The angle between the pair of tangents drawn to the ellipse $3x^2 + 2y^2 = 5$ from the point (1,2) is

(a) $\tan^{-1}\left(\frac{12}{5}\right)$

(b) $\tan^{-1}\left(6\sqrt{5}\right)$

(c) $\tan^{-1}\left(\frac{12}{\sqrt{5}}\right)$

(d) $\tan^{-1}\left(12\sqrt{5}\right)$

79. Let α and β be the roots of the equation $x^2+x+1=0$ the equation whose roots are α^{19}, β^7 is

(a) $x^2-x-1=0$

(b) $x^2-x+1=0$

(c) $x^2+x-1=0$

(d) $x^2+x+1=0$

80. The x satisfying

$\sin^{-1}x+\sin^{-1}(1-x)=\cos^{-1}x$

are

(a) $1, 0$

(b) $1, -1$

(c) $0, \frac{1}{2}$

(d) None of these

PART-II (Numerical Answer Questions)

81. Area between curves $y=x^2, x=y^2$ is ________.

82. The probability of A = Probability of B = Probability of $C = \frac{1}{4}$

$P(A)\cap P(B)\cap P(C)=0,\ P(B\cap C)=0$

and $P(A\cap C)=\frac{1}{8},\ P(A\cap B)=0$

the probability that atleast one of the events A, B, C exists is

83. Coefficient of x^6 in the expansion $\left(x+\frac{1}{x^2}\right)^6$ is ________.

84. $f(x)=\frac{\sin 3x}{\sin x}$, when $x\neq 0$

$=k$, when $x=0$

for the function to be continuous k should be ________.

85. A line passes through (2,2) and is perpendicular to the line $3x+y=3$ its y intercept is ________.

86. Let $A_1, A_2, A_3,.....$ be squares such that for each $n \geq 1$, the length of the side of A_n equals the length of diagonal of A_{n+1}. If the length of A_1 is 12 cm, then the smallest value of n for which area of A_n is less than one, is__________.

87. There are 5 students in class 10, 6 students in class 11 and 8 students in class 12. If the number of ways, in which 10 students can be selected from them so as to include at least 2 students from each class and at most 5 students from the total 11 students of class 10 and 11 is 100 k, then k is equal to ________.

88. If $x\phi(x)=\int_5^x\left(3t^2-2\phi'(t)\right)dt$, $x>-2$, and $\phi(0)=4$, then $\phi(2)$ is ________.

89. The area bounded by the lines $y=||x-1|-2|$ is ______.

90. If $\sqrt{3}\left(\cos^2 x\right)=\left(\sqrt{3}-1\right)\cos x+1$, the number of solutions of the given equation when $x\in\left[0,\frac{\pi}{2}\right]$ ________.

RESPONSE SHEET

PHYSICS		CHEMISTRY		MATHEMATICS	
1.	ⓐⓑⓒⓓ	31.	ⓐⓑⓒⓓ	61.	ⓐⓑⓒⓓ
2.	ⓐⓑⓒⓓ	32.	ⓐⓑⓒⓓ	62.	ⓐⓑⓒⓓ
3.	ⓐⓑⓒⓓ	33.	ⓐⓑⓒⓓ	63.	ⓐⓑⓒⓓ
4.	ⓐⓑⓒⓓ	34.	ⓐⓑⓒⓓ	64.	ⓐⓑⓒⓓ
5.	ⓐⓑⓒⓓ	35.	ⓐⓑⓒⓓ	65.	ⓐⓑⓒⓓ
6.	ⓐⓑⓒⓓ	36.	ⓐⓑⓒⓓ	66.	ⓐⓑⓒⓓ
7.	ⓐⓑⓒⓓ	37.	ⓐⓑⓒⓓ	67.	ⓐⓑⓒⓓ
8.	ⓐⓑⓒⓓ	38.	ⓐⓑⓒⓓ	68.	ⓐⓑⓒⓓ
9.	ⓐⓑⓒⓓ	39.	ⓐⓑⓒⓓ	69.	ⓐⓑⓒⓓ
10.	ⓐⓑⓒⓓ	40.	ⓐⓑⓒⓓ	70.	ⓐⓑⓒⓓ
11.	ⓐⓑⓒⓓ	41.	ⓐⓑⓒⓓ	71.	ⓐⓑⓒⓓ
12.	ⓐⓑⓒⓓ	42.	ⓐⓑⓒⓓ	72.	ⓐⓑⓒⓓ
13.	ⓐⓑⓒⓓ	43.	ⓐⓑⓒⓓ	73.	ⓐⓑⓒⓓ
14.	ⓐⓑⓒⓓ	44.	ⓐⓑⓒⓓ	74.	ⓐⓑⓒⓓ
15.	ⓐⓑⓒⓓ	45.	ⓐⓑⓒⓓ	75.	ⓐⓑⓒⓓ
16.	ⓐⓑⓒⓓ	46.	ⓐⓑⓒⓓ	76.	ⓐⓑⓒⓓ
17.	ⓐⓑⓒⓓ	47.	ⓐⓑⓒⓓ	77.	ⓐⓑⓒⓓ
18.	ⓐⓑⓒⓓ	48.	ⓐⓑⓒⓓ	78.	ⓐⓑⓒⓓ
19.	ⓐⓑⓒⓓ	49.	ⓐⓑⓒⓓ	79.	ⓐⓑⓒⓓ
20.	ⓐⓑⓒⓓ	50.	ⓐⓑⓒⓓ	80.	ⓐⓑⓒⓓ
21.		51.		81.	
22.		52.		82.	
23.		53.		83.	
24.		54.		84.	
25.		55.		85.	
26.		56.		86.	
27.		57.		87.	
28.		58.		88.	
29.		59.		89.	
30.		60.		90.	

4 Mock Test

INSTRUCTIONS

1. This test will be a 3 hours Test.
2. This test consists of Physics, Chemistry and Mathematics questions with equal weightage of 100 marks.
3. Each question is of 4 marks.
4. There are three sections in the question paper consisting of Physics (Q.no.1 to 30), Chemistry (Q.no.31 to 60) and Mathematics (Q. no.61 to 90). Each section is divided into two parts, Part I consists of 20 multiple choice questions & Part II consists of 10 Numerical value type Questions, attempt any 5 questions out of 10.
5. There will be only one correct choice in the given four choices in Part I. For each question 4 marks will be awarded for correct choice, 1 mark will be deducted for incorrect choice for Part I Questions and zero mark will be awarded for not attempted question. For Part II Questions 4 marks will be awarded for correct answer and zero for unattempted and incorrect answer.
6. Any textual, printed or written material, mobile phones, calculator etc. is not allowed for the students appearing for the test.
7. All calculations / written work should be done in the rough sheet provided.

PHYSICS

PART-I (Multiple Choice Questions)

1. A solid cylinder rolls down an inclined plane of height 3 m and reaches the bottom of plane with angular velocity of $2\sqrt{2}$ rad.s^{-1}. The radius of cylinder must be (Take g = 10 ms^{-2})

(a) 5 cm (b) 0.5 cm

(c) $\sqrt{10}cm$ (d) $\sqrt{5}m$

2. In the figure shown, a particle of mass m is released from the position A on a smooth track. When the particle reaches at B, then normal reaction on it by the track is

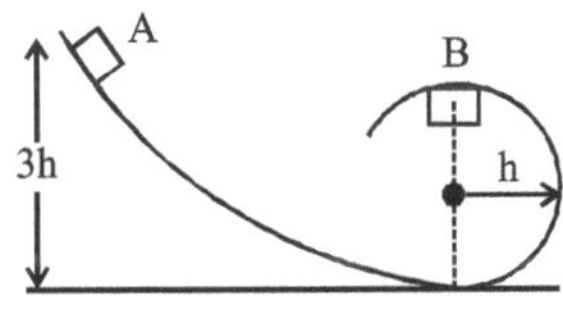

(a) mg (b) 2mg

(c) $\frac{2}{3}$mg (d) $\frac{m^2g}{h}$

3. The density ρ of water of bulk modulus B at a depth y in the ocean is related to the density at surface ρ_0 by the relation

(a) $\rho = \rho_0\left[1 - \frac{\rho_0 gy}{B}\right]$

(b) $\rho=\rho_0\left[1+\frac{\rho_0 gy}{B}\right]$

(c) $\rho=\rho_0\left[1+\frac{B}{\rho_0 hgy}\right]$

(d) $\rho=\rho_0\left[1-\frac{B}{\rho_0 hgy}\right]$

4. The electric field in a certain region is given by $\vec{E}=(5\hat{i}-3\hat{j})kV/m$. The potential difference $V_B - V_A$ between points A and B, having coordinates (4, 0, 3)m and (10, 3, 0)m respectively, is equal to

(a) 21 kV (b) –21 kV

(c) 39 kV (d) –39 kV

5. Two electric bulbs marked 25W – 220 V and 100W – 220V are connected in series to a 440 V supply. Which of the bulbs will fuse?

(a) Both (b) 100 W

(c) 25 W (d) Neither

6. Two long parallel wires P and Q are held perpendicular to the plane of the paper at a separation of 5 m. If P and Q carry currents of 2.5 A and 5 A respectively in the same direction, then the magnetic field at a point midway between P and Q is

(a) $\frac{\mu_0}{\pi}$ (b) $\sqrt{3}\frac{\mu_0}{\pi}$

(c) $\frac{\mu_0}{2\pi}$ (d) $\frac{3\mu_0}{2\pi}$

7. Two seconds after projection a projectile is travelling in a direction inclined at 30° to the horizontal. After one more second, it is travelling horizontally. The magnitude and direction of its initial velocity are-

(a) $2\sqrt{20}$ m/s 60°

(b) $20\sqrt{3}$ m/s 60°

(c) $6\sqrt{40}$ m/s 30°

(d) $40\sqrt{6}$ m/s 30°

8. A 40 kg slab rests on a frictionless floor as shown in the figure. A 10 kg block rests on the top of the slab. The static coefficient of friction between the block and slab is 0.60 while the coefficient of kinetic friction is 0.40. The 10 kg block is acted upon by a horizontal force 100 N. If g = 9.8 m/s^2, the resultaing acceleration of the slab will be

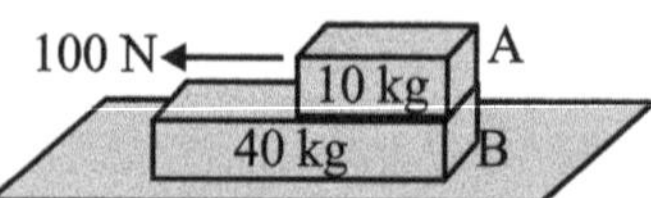

(a) 0.98 m/s^2 (b) 1.47 m/s^2

(c) 1.52 m/s^2 (d) 6.1 m/s^2

9. Two cars P and Q start from a point at the same time in a straight line and their positions are represented by $x_P(t) = at + bt^2$ and $x_Q(t) = ft - t^2$. At what time do the cars have the same velocity

(a) $\frac{f-a}{2(1+b)}$ (b) $\frac{a-1}{1+b}$

(c) $\frac{a+1}{2(b-1)}$ (d) $\frac{a+f}{2(1+b)}$

10. Ultraviolet light of wavelength 300 nm and intensity 1.0 watt/m^2 falls on the surface of a photosensitive material. If 1% of the incident photons produce photoelectrons, then find the number of photoelectrons emitted from an area of 1.0 cm^2 of the surface.
    (a) 9.61×10^{14} per sec
    (b) 4.12×10^{13} per sec
    (c) 1.51×10^{12} per sec
    (d) 2.13×10^{11} per sec
11. If the wavelength of the first line of the Balmer series of hydrogen is 6561 Å, find the wavelength of the second line of the series.
    (a) 13122 Å (b) 3280 Å
    (c) 4860 Å (d) 2187 Å
12. The concentration of hole - electron pairs in pure silicon at T = 300 K is 7×10^{15} per cubic meter. Antimony is doped into silicon in a proportion of 1 atom in 10^7 Si atoms. Assuming that half of the impurity atoms contribute electron in the conduction band, calculate the factor by which the number of charge carriers increases due to doping. The number of silicon atoms per cubic meter is 5×10^{28}
    (a) 2.8×10^5 (b) 3.1×10^2
    (c) 4.2×10^5 (d) 1.8×10^5
13. Shown below are the black body radiation curves at temperatures T_1 and T_2 ($T_2 > T_1$). Which one of the following plots is correct?

(a)
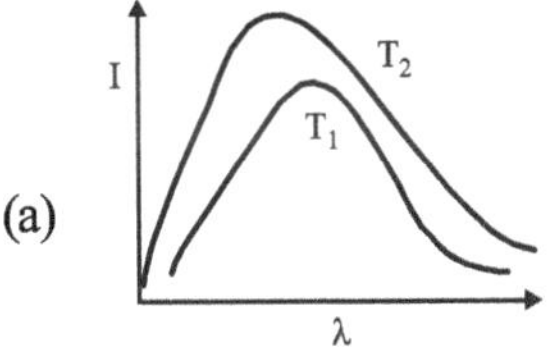

(b)
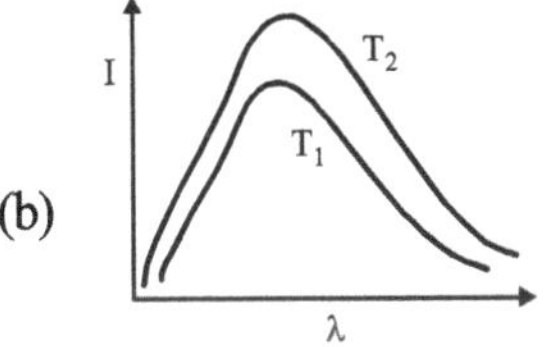

(c)
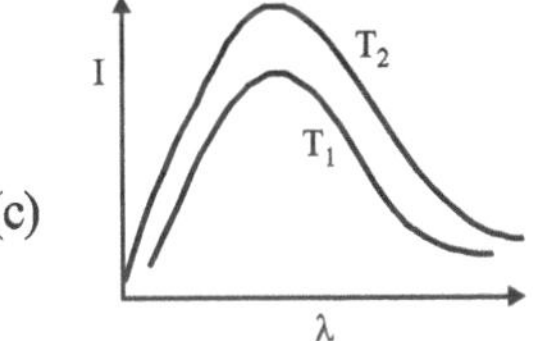

(d)
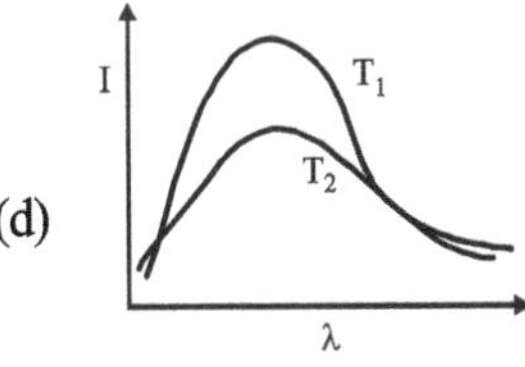

14. A forced oscillator is acted upon by a force $F = F_0 \sin \omega t$. The amplitude of oscillation is given by $\frac{55}{\sqrt{2\omega^2 - 36\omega + 9}}$.
    The resonant angular frequency is
    (a) 2 units (b) 9 units
    (c) 18 units (d) 36 units
15. Three closed vessels *A*, *B* and *C* are at the same temperature T and contain gases which obey the Maxwellian distribution of velocities. Vessel A contains only O_2, *B* only N_2 and *C* a mixture of

equal quantities of O_2 and N_2. If the average speed of the O_2 molecules in vessel A is V_1, that of the N_2 molecules in vessel B is V_2, the average speed of the O_2 molecules in vessel C is

(a) $(V_1 + V_2)/2$
(b) V_1
(c) $(V_1V_2)^{1/2}$
(d) $\sqrt{3kT/M}$

16. In the figure shown a source of sound of frequency 510 Hz moves with constant velocity $v_s = 20$ m/s in the direction shown. The wind is blowing at a constant velocity $v_w = 20$ m/s towards an observer who is at rest at point B. Corresponding to the sound emitted by the source at initial position A, the frequency detected by the observer is equal to (speed of sound relative to air = 330 m/s)

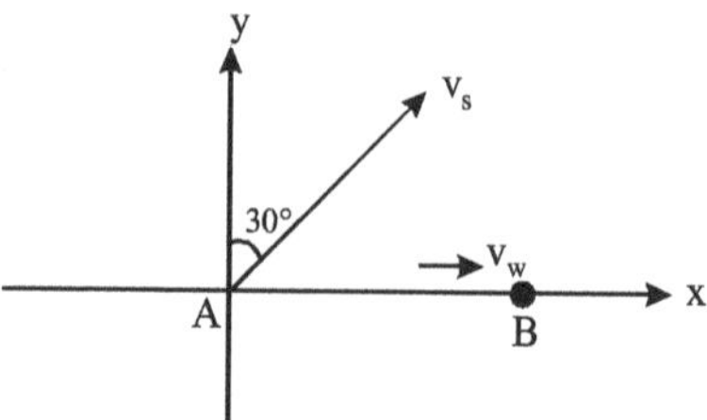

(a) 510 Hz (b) 500 Hz
(c) 525 Hz (d) 550 Hz

17. In fig, CODF is a semicircular loop of a conducting wire of resistance R and radius r. It is placed in a uniform magnetic field B, which is directed into the page (perpendicular to the plane of the loop).

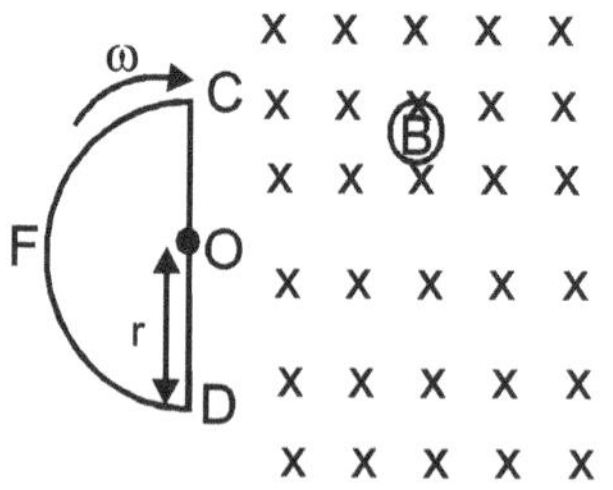

The loop is rotated with a constant angular speed ω about an axis passing through the centre O, and perpendicular to the page. Then the induced current in the wire loop is

(a) zero (b) $Br^2\omega/R$
(c) $Br^2\omega/2R$ (d) $B\pi r^2\omega/R$

18. If $E = 100 \sin(100t)$ volt and $I = 100 \sin\left(100t + \frac{\pi}{3}\right) mA$ are the instantaneous values of voltage and current, then the r.m.s. values of voltage and current are respectively

(a) 70.7V, 70.7 mA
(b) 70.7V, 70.7A
(c) 141.4V, 141.4mA
(d) 141.4V, 141.4A

19. A plane electromagnetic wave is incident on a plane surface of area A, normally and is perfectly reflected. If energy E strikes the surface in time t then average pressure exerted on the surface is (c = speed of light)

(a) zero (b) E/Atc
(c) 2E/Atc (d) E/c

20. A 2.0 cm tall object is placed 15 cm in front of a concave mirror of focal length 10 cm. What is the size and nature of the image
(a) 4 cm, real
(b) 4 cm, virtual
(c) 1.0 cm, real
(d) None of these

PART-II (Numerical Answer Questions)

21. An inclined plane making an angle of 30° with the horizontal is placed in a uniform electric field of intensity 100 V/m. A particle of mass 1 kg and charge 0.01 C is allowed to slide down from rest on the plane from a height of 1 m. If the coefficient of friction is 0.2, then find the time taken (in second) by the particle to reach the bottom.

22. A satellite is to be placed in equatorial geostationary orbit around earth for communication. The height (in metre) of such a satellite is
$[M_E = 6 \times 10^{24}$ kg, $R_E = 6400$ km, $T =$ 24 h, $G = 6.67 \times 10^{-11}$ N m^2 kg$^{-2}]$

23. A simple electric motor has an armature resistance of 1 Ω and runs from a dc source of 12 volt. When running unloaded it draws a current of 2 amp. When a certain load is connected, its speed becomes one-half of its unloaded value. What is the new value of current drawn (in ampere)?

24. A gas can be taken from A to B via two different processes ACB and ADB.

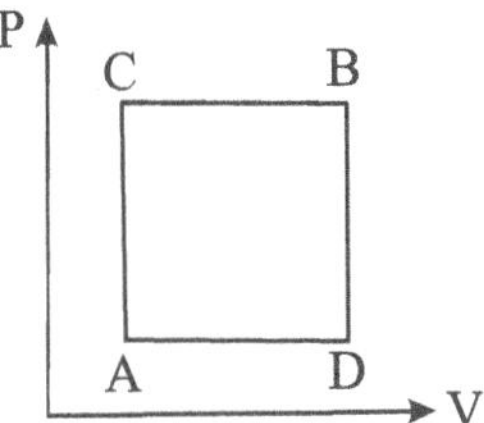

When path ACB is used 60 J of heat flows into the system and 30J of work is done by the system. If path ADB is used work done by the system is 10 J. The heat flow (in joule) into the system in path ADB is :

25. If 200 MeV energy is released per fission of U^{235} nuclei. Find the mass of U^{235} consumed (in mg) per day in a reactor of power 1MW assuming its efficiency is 80%.

26. The water is filled upto height of 12 m in a tank having vertical sidewalls. A hole is made in one of the walls at a depth 'h' below the water level. The value of 'h' for which the emerging stream of water strikes the ground at the maximum range is ___ m.

27. A fringe width of 6 mm was produced for two slits separated by 1 mm apart. The screen is placed 10 m away. The wavelength of light used is 'x' nm.
The value of 'x' to the nearest integer is _____.

28. A body of mass 2 kg is driven by an engine delivering a constant power of 1 J/s. The body starts from rest and moves in a straight line. After 9 seconds, the body has moved a distance (in m) ________.

29. The circuit shown below is working as a 8 V dc regulated voltage source. When 12 V is used as input, the power dissipated (in mW) in each diode is; (considering both zener diodes are identical) _____.

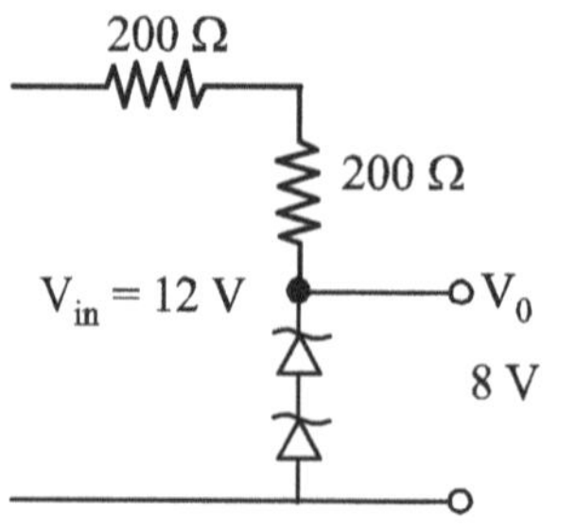

30. A rod CD of thermal resistance 10.0 KW^{-1} is joined at the middle of an identical rod AB as shown in figure, The end A, B and D are maintained at 200°C, 100°C and 125°C respectively. The heat current in CD is P watt. The value of P is ________.

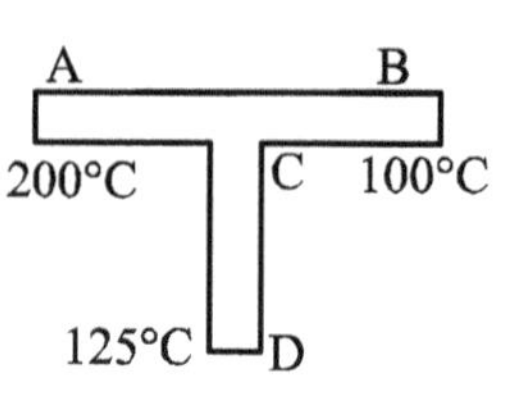

CHEMISTRY

PART-I (Multiple Choice Questions)

31. The reason for almost doubling the rate of reaction on increasing the temperature of the reaction system by 10 °C is
   (a) The value of threshold energy increases
   (b) Collision frequency increases
   (c) The fraction of the molecule having energy equal to threshold energy or more increases
   (d) Activation energy decreases

32. Which of the following factors may be regarded as the main cause of lanthanoid contraction?
   (a) Greater shielding of 5*d* electrons by 4*f* electrons.
   (b) Poorer shielding of 5*d* electrons by 4*f* electrons.
   (c) Effective shielding of one of 4*f* electrons by another in the subshell.
   (d) Poor shielding of one of 4*f* electron by another in the subshell.

33. Isobutyl magnesium bromide with dry ether and ethyl alcohol gives :
   (a) $CH_3CH(CH_3)CH_2OH$ & CH_3CH_2MgBr
   (b) $CH_3CH(CH_3)CH_3$ & $MgBr(OC_2H_5)$

(c) $CH_3CHCH=CH_2$ & $Mg(OH)Br$ (with CH_3 on the second carbon)

(d) CH_3CHCH_3 & CH_3CH_2OMgBr (with CH_3 on the second carbon)

34. The K_p/K_c ratio will be highest in case of

(a) $CO(g) + \frac{1}{2} O_2(g) \rightleftharpoons CO_2(g)$

(b) $H_2(g) + I_2(g) \rightleftharpoons 2HI(g)$

(c) $PCl_5(g) \rightleftharpoons PCl_3(g) + Cl_2(g)$

(d) $7H_2(g) + 2NO_2(g) \rightleftharpoons 2NH_3(g) + 4H_2O(g)$

35. Which of the following substances has the greatest ionic character ?

(a) Cl_2O (b) NCl_3

(c) $PbCl_2$ (d) $BaCl_2$

36. Given below are two Statements : One is labelled as **Assertion A** and the other is labelled as **Reason R** :

Assertion A : During the boiling of water having temporary hardness, $Mg(HCO_3)_2$ is converted to $MgCO_3$.

Reason R : The solubility product of $Mg(OH)_2$ is greater than that of $MgCO_3$.

In the light of the above statements, choose the **most appropriate** answer from the options given below:

(a) Both A and R are true but R is NOT the correct explanation of A

(b) A is true but R is false

(c) Both A and R are true and R is the correct explanation of A

(d) A is false but R is true

37. Consider the following transformations :

$$CH_3COOH \xrightarrow{CaCO_3} A \xrightarrow{heat} B \xrightarrow[NaOH]{I_2} C$$

The molecular formula of C is

(a) $CH_3-\underset{I}{\overset{OH}{C}}-CH_3$

(b) ICH_2-COCH_3

(c) CHI_3

(d) CH_3I

38. The values of ΔH and ΔS for the reaction,

$C(graphite) + CO_2(g) \rightarrow 2CO(g)$

are 170 kJ and 170 JK^{-1}, respectively. This reaction will be spontaneous at

(a) 910K (b) 1110K

(c) 510K (d) 710K

39. Containers A and B have same gases. Pressure, volume and temperature of A are all twice that of B, then the ratio of number of molecules of A and B are

(a) 1 : 2 (b) 2 : 1

(c) 1 : 4 (d) 4 : 1

40. Match List-I with List – II :

List-I (Name of ore /mineral)	**List-II (Chemical formula)**

(A) Calamine (i) Zns
(B) Malachite (ii) $FeCO_3$
(C) Siderite (iii) $ZnCO_3$
(D) Sphalerite (iv) $CuCO_3 . Cu(OH)_2$

Choose the **most appropriate** answer from the options given below:

(a) (A)-(iii), (B)-(iv), (C)-(ii), (D)-(i)
(b) (A)-(iii), (B)-(iv), (C)-(i), (D)-(ii)
(c) (A)-(iv), (B)-(iii), (C)-(i), (D)-(ii)
(d) (A)-(iii), (B)-(ii), (C)-(iv), (D)-(i)

41. Among the following four structures I to IV,

$C_2H_5 - CH(CH_3) - C_3H_7$, (I)

$CH_3 - C(=O) - CH(CH_3) - C_2H_5$, (II)

$H - C^+(H)(H)$, (III)

$C_2H_5 - CH(CH_3) - C_2H_5$ (IV)

it is true that

(a) only I and II are chiral compounds
(b) only III is a chiral compound
(c) only II and IV are chiral compounds
(d) all four are chiral compounds

42. Which is a dangerous radiological pollutant?

(a) C^{14} (b) S^{35}
(c) Sr^{90} (d) P^{32}

43. A compound of formula A_2B_3 has the *hcp* lattice. Which atom forms the *hcp* lattice and what fraction of tetrahedral voids is occupied by the other atoms:

(a) *hcp* lattice – A, $\frac{2}{3}$ Tetrahedral voids – B
(b) *hcp* lattice – A, $\frac{1}{3}$ Tetrahedral voids – B
(c) *hcp* lattice – B, $\frac{2}{3}$ Tetrahedral voids – A
(d) *hcp* lattice – B, $\frac{1}{3}$ Tetrahedral voids – A

44. Of the four isomeric hexanes, the isomer which can give two monochlorinated compounds is

(a) 2-methylpentane
(b) 2, 2-dimethylbutane
(c) 2, 3-dimethylbutane

40. The solubility product of $PbCl_2$ is 1.7×10^{-5}. The solubility in moles per litre would be :

(a) 1.62×10^{-4} (b) 1.62×10^{-8}
(c) 1.62×10^{-2} (d) 1.62×10^{-6}

46. Crystal field stabilization energy for high spin d^4 octahedral complex is:

(a) $-1.8\,\Delta_0$ (b) $-1.6\,\Delta_0 + P$
(c) $-1.2\,\Delta_0$ (d) $-0.6\,\Delta_0$

47. In the reaction sequence

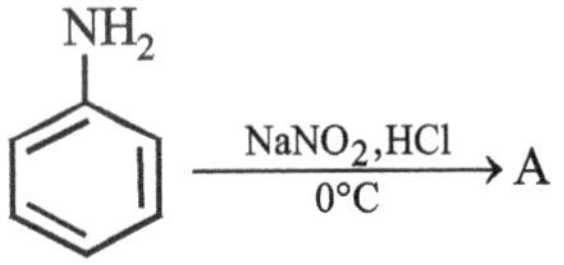

$$C_6H_5NH_2 \xrightarrow[0°C]{NaNO_2,HCl} A \xrightarrow{CuCN} B \xrightarrow{LiAlH_4} C$$, the product 'C' is:

(a) benzonitrile
(b) benzaldehyde
(c) benzoic acid
(d) benzylamine

48. Nylon threads are made of
(a) polyester polymer
(b) polyamide polymer
(c) polyethylene polymer
(d) polyvinyl polymer

49. In the reaction of oxalate with permanganate in acidic medium, the number of electrons involved in producing one molecule of CO_2 is:

(a) 1 (b) 10
(c) 2 (d) 5

50. Momentum of radiations of wavelength 0.33 nm is :
(a) 2.01×10^{-21} kg m sec^{-1}
(b) 2.01×10^{-24} g m sec^{-1}
(c) 2.01×10^{-21} g m sec^{-1}
(d) 2.01×10^{-24} kg m sec^{-1}

PART-II (Numerical Answer Questions)

51. Calculate the difference in the heat of formation (in calories) of carbon monoxide at constant pressure and at constant volume at 27 °C.

52. Calculate number of molecules of Grignard reagent consumed by 1 molecule of following compound.

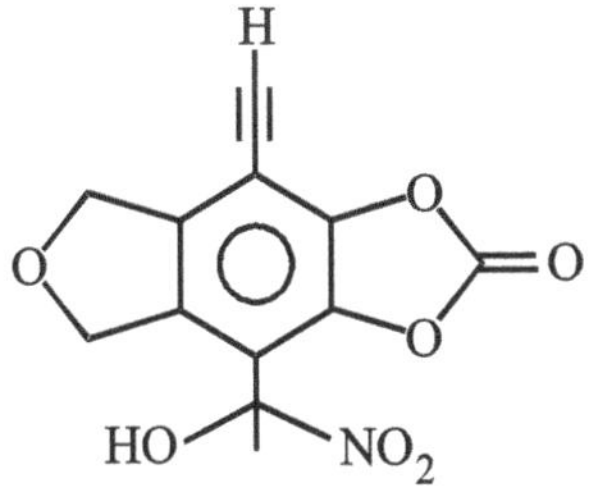

[Structure: benzene ring bearing an ethynyl group (C≡C–H) at top, a fused five-membered ring with O (dihydrofuran, CH₂–O–CH₂) on the left, a fused cyclic carbonate (O–C(=O)–O) on the right, and at the bottom a carbon bearing HO and NO_2.]

53. In a metal oxide, there is 20% oxygen by weight. What is its equivalent weight ?

54. Find the total number of possible isomers for the complex compound $[Cu^{II}(NH_3)_4][Pt^{II}Cl_4]$

55. Calculate the strength in % of labelled 10 volume H_2O_2 solution.

56. When 0.15 g of an organic compound was analyzed using Carius method for estimation of bromine, 0.2397 g of AgBr was obtained. The percentage of bromine in the organic compound is ______.
[Atomic mass : Silver = 108, Bromine = 80]

57. The value of magnetic quantum number of the outermost electron of Zn^+ ion is ________.

58. The reaction of sulphur in alkaline medium is given below:

$$S_8(s) + aOH^-(aq) \rightarrow bS^{2-}(aq) + cS_2O_3^{2-}(aq) + dH_2O(l)$$

The values of 'a' is ________.

59. At 363 K, the vapour pressure of A is 21 kPa and that of B is 18 kPa. One mole of A and 2 moles of B are mixed. Assuming that this solution is ideal, the vapour pressure of the mixture is ________ kPa.

60. The ratio of number of water molecules in Mohr's salt and potash alum is ________ $\times 10^{-1}$.

MATHEMATICS

PART-I (Multiple Choice Questions)

61. If $\left(7-4\sqrt{3}\right)^{x^2-4x+3}+\left(7+4\sqrt{3}\right)^{x^2-4x+3}=14,$

then the value of x is given by

(a) $2, 2\pm\sqrt{2}$

(b) $2\pm\sqrt{3}, 3$

(c) $3\pm\sqrt{2}, 2$

(d) None of these

62. The minimum value of the function

$f(x)=x^{3/2}+x^{-3/2}-4\left(x+\frac{1}{x}\right)$ for all permissible real x, is

(a) -10 (b) -6

(c) -7 (d) -8

63. In the expansion of $\left(\frac{x}{2}-\frac{3}{x^2}\right)^{10}$, the coefficient of x^4 is

(a) $\frac{405}{256}$ (b) $\frac{504}{259}$

(c) $\frac{450}{263}$

(d) None of these

64. If the plane $3x+y+2z+6=0$ is parallel to the line $\frac{3x-1}{2b}=3-y=\frac{z-1}{a}$, then the value of $3a+3b$ is

(a) $\frac{1}{2}$ (b) $\frac{3}{2}$

(c) 3 (d) 4

65. The domain of definition of the function

$f(x)=\sqrt{1+\log_e(1-x)}$ is

(a) $-\infty<x\le 0$

(b) $-\infty<x\le \frac{e-1}{e}$

(c) $-\infty<x\le 1$

(d) $x\ge 1-e$

66. The function $f(x)=[x]^2-[x^2]$ (where $[y]$ is the greatest integer less than or equal to y), is discontinuous at

(a) All integers

(b) All integers except 0 and 1

(c) All integers except 0

(d) All integers except 1

67. The line $y = mx$ bisects the area enclosed by lines $x=0$, $y=0$ and $x=3/2$ and the curve $y=1+4x-x^2$. Then the value of m is

(a) $\frac{13}{6}$ (b) $\frac{13}{2}$

(c) $\frac{13}{5}$ (d) $\frac{13}{7}$

Space for Rough Work

68. The sum of the series $3+33+333+......+n$ terms is

(a) $\frac{1}{27}(10^{n+1}+9n-28)$

(b) $\frac{1}{27}(10^{n+1}-9n-10)$

(c) $\frac{1}{27}(10^{n+1}+10n-9)$

(d) None of these

69. If $\int \frac{1}{1+\sin x}dx = \tan\left(\frac{x}{2}+a\right)+b$ then

(a) $a=-\frac{\pi}{4},\ b\in\mathbf{R}$

(b) $a=\frac{\pi}{4},\ b\in\mathbf{R}$

(c) $a=\frac{5\pi}{4},\ b\in\mathbf{R}$

(d) None of these

70. If $y=\tan^{-1}\left(\frac{2^x}{1+2^{2x+1}}\right)$, then $\frac{dy}{dx}$ at $x=0$ is

(a) $\frac{3}{5}\log 2$ (b) $\frac{2}{5}\log 2$

(c) $-\frac{3}{2}\log 2$

(d) None of these

71. The value of $\cos\frac{2\pi}{7}+\cos\frac{4\pi}{7}+\cos\frac{6\pi}{7}$ is

(a) 0 (b) 1

(c) $\frac{1}{2}$ (d) $-\frac{1}{2}$

72. An integrating factor of the differential equation $\frac{dy}{dx}=y\tan x-y^2\sec x$ is equal to:

(a) $\tan x$ (b) $\sec x$

(c) $\operatorname{cosec} x$ (d) $\cot x$

73. If $y = 2x$ is a chord of the circle $x^2+y^2=10x$, then the equation of the circle whose diameter is this chord, is -

(a) $x^2+y^2+2x+4y=0$

(b) $x^2+y^2+2x-4y=0$

(c) $x^2+y^2-2x-4y=0$

(d) None of these

74. Magnitudes of vectors $\vec{a},\vec{b},\vec{c}$ are 3, 4, 5 respectively. If $\vec{a}$ and $\vec{b}+\vec{c}$, $\vec{b}$ and $\vec{c}+\vec{a}$, $\vec{c}$ and $\vec{a}+\vec{b}$ are mutually perpendicular, then magnitude of $\vec{a}+\vec{b}+\vec{c}$ is

(a) $4\sqrt{2}$ (b) $3\sqrt{2}$

(c) $5\sqrt{2}$ (d) $3\sqrt{3}$

75. If $a+b+c=0$, then the solution of the equation

$$\begin{vmatrix} a-x & c & b \\ c & b-x & a \\ b & a & c-x \end{vmatrix}=0 \text{ is}$$

(a) 0

(b) $\pm\frac{3}{2}(a^2+b^2+c^2)$

(c) $0, \pm\sqrt{\frac{3}{2}(a^2+b^2+c^2)}$

(d) $0, \pm\sqrt{(a^2+b^2+c^2)}$

76. If $I_1 = \int_0^1 2^{x^2} dx$, $I_2 = \int_0^1 2^{x^3} dx$, $I_3 = \int_1^2 2^{x^2} dx$ and $I_4 = \int_1^2 2^{x^3} dx$ then

(a) $I_2 > I_1$ (b) $I_1 > I_2$

(c) $I_3 = I_4$ (d) $I_3 > I_4$

77. If $f: R \to R$ and $g: R \to R$ are defined by $f(x) = |x|$ and $g(x) = [x-3]$ for $x \in R$, then $\left\{g(f(x)) : -\frac{8}{5} < x < \frac{8}{5}\right\}$ is equal to

(a) $\{0,1\}$ (b) $\{1,2\}$

(c) $\{-3,-2\}$ (d) $\{2,3\}$

78. If A and B are two events such that $P(A) = \frac{1}{2}$ and $P(B) = \frac{2}{3}$, then

(a) $P(A \cup B) \geq \frac{2}{3}$

(b) $\frac{1}{6} \leq P(A \cap B) \leq \frac{1}{2}$

(c) $\frac{1}{6} \leq P(A' \cap B) \leq \frac{1}{2}$

(d) All of these

79. If PQ is a double ordinate of hyperbola $\frac{x^2}{a^2} - \frac{y^2}{b^2} = 1$ such that OPQ is an equilateral triangle, O being the centre of the hyperbola. Then the eccentricity e of the hyperbola satisfies

(a) $1 < e < 2/\sqrt{3}$ (b) $e = 2/\sqrt{3}$

(c) $e = \sqrt{3}/2$ (d) $e > 2/\sqrt{3}$

80. The equation of the lines on which the perpendiculars from the origin make 30° angle with x-axis and which form a triangle of area $\frac{50}{\sqrt{3}}$ with axes, are

(a) $x + \sqrt{3}y \pm 10 = 0$

(b) $\sqrt{3}x + y \pm 10 = 0$

(c) $x \pm \sqrt{3}y - 10 = 0$

(d) None of these

PART-II (Numerical Answer Questions)

81. The number of pairs (x, y) satisfying the equations $\sin x + \sin y = \sin(x+y)$ and $|x| + |y| = 1$ is ________.

82. The value of ________.

$$\lim_{x \to 0} \left\{ \frac{\sin x - x + \frac{x^3}{6}}{x^5} \right\} \text{ is } \frac{1}{k},$$

then k is ________.

83. An edge of a variable cube is increasing at the rate cm/sec. Then, the state of increase in volume of the cube when the edge is 5 cm long, is ________.

84. If $2x = -1 + \sqrt{3}i$, then the value of $(1 - x^2 + x)^6 - (1 - x + x^2)^6$ is ________.

85. Sum of all three digit numbers (no digit being zero) having the property that all digits are perfect squares, is ________.

86. Let z be those complex numbers which satisfy $|z+5| \le 4$ and $z(1+i)+\bar{z}(1-i) \ge -10,\ i=\sqrt{-1}$. If the maximum value of $|z+1|^2$ is $\alpha+\beta\sqrt{2}$, then the value of $(\alpha+\beta)$ is ________.

87. There are 15 players in a cricket team, out of which 6 are bowlers, 7 are batsmen and 2 are wicketkeepers. The number of ways, a team of 11 players be selected from them so as to include at least 4 bowlers, 5 batsmen and 1 wicketkeeper, is ________.

88. Let the domain of the function $f(x) = \log_4(\log_5(\log_3(18x - x^2 - 77)))$ be (a, b). Then the value of the integral

$$\int_a^b \frac{\sin^3 x}{\left(\sin^3 x + \sin^3(a+b-x)\right)} dx$$ is

equal to ________.

89. Let $(\lambda, 2, 1)$ be a point on the plane which passes through the point $(4, -2, 2)$. If the plane is perpendicular to the line joining the points $(-2, -21, 29)$ and $(-1, -16, 23)$, then $\left(\frac{\lambda}{11}\right)^2 - \frac{4\lambda}{11} - 4$ is equal to ________.

90. If the minimum area of the triangle formed by a tangent to the ellipse $\frac{x^2}{b^2} + \frac{y^2}{4a^2} = 1$ and the co-ordinate axis is kab, then k is equal to ________.

RESPONSE SHEET

PHYSICS		CHEMISTRY		MATHEMATICS	
1.	ⓐⓑⓒⓓ	31.	ⓐⓑⓒⓓ	61.	ⓐⓑⓒⓓ
2.	ⓐⓑⓒⓓ	32.	ⓐⓑⓒⓓ	62.	ⓐⓑⓒⓓ
3.	ⓐⓑⓒⓓ	33.	ⓐⓑⓒⓓ	63.	ⓐⓑⓒⓓ
4.	ⓐⓑⓒⓓ	34.	ⓐⓑⓒⓓ	64.	ⓐⓑⓒⓓ
5.	ⓐⓑⓒⓓ	35.	ⓐⓑⓒⓓ	65.	ⓐⓑⓒⓓ
6.	ⓐⓑⓒⓓ	36.	ⓐⓑⓒⓓ	66.	ⓐⓑⓒⓓ
7.	ⓐⓑⓒⓓ	37.	ⓐⓑⓒⓓ	67.	ⓐⓑⓒⓓ
8.	ⓐⓑⓒⓓ	38.	ⓐⓑⓒⓓ	68.	ⓐⓑⓒⓓ
9.	ⓐⓑⓒⓓ	39.	ⓐⓑⓒⓓ	69.	ⓐⓑⓒⓓ
10.	ⓐⓑⓒⓓ	40.	ⓐⓑⓒⓓ	70.	ⓐⓑⓒⓓ
11.	ⓐⓑⓒⓓ	41.	ⓐⓑⓒⓓ	71.	ⓐⓑⓒⓓ
12.	ⓐⓑⓒⓓ	42.	ⓐⓑⓒⓓ	72.	ⓐⓑⓒⓓ
13.	ⓐⓑⓒⓓ	43.	ⓐⓑⓒⓓ	73.	ⓐⓑⓒⓓ
14.	ⓐⓑⓒⓓ	44.	ⓐⓑⓒⓓ	74.	ⓐⓑⓒⓓ
15.	ⓐⓑⓒⓓ	45.	ⓐⓑⓒⓓ	75.	ⓐⓑⓒⓓ
16.	ⓐⓑⓒⓓ	46.	ⓐⓑⓒⓓ	76.	ⓐⓑⓒⓓ
17.	ⓐⓑⓒⓓ	47.	ⓐⓑⓒⓓ	77.	ⓐⓑⓒⓓ
18.	ⓐⓑⓒⓓ	48.	ⓐⓑⓒⓓ	78.	ⓐⓑⓒⓓ
19.	ⓐⓑⓒⓓ	49.	ⓐⓑⓒⓓ	79.	ⓐⓑⓒⓓ
20.	ⓐⓑⓒⓓ	50.	ⓐⓑⓒⓓ	80.	ⓐⓑⓒⓓ
21.		51.		81.	
22.		52.		82.	
23.		53.		83.	
24.		54.		84.	
25.		55.		85.	
26.		56.		86.	
27.		57.		87.	
28.		58.		88.	
29.		59.		89.	
30.		60.		90.	

5 Mock Test

INSTRUCTIONS

1. This test will be a 3 hours Test.
2. This test consists of Physics, Chemistry and Mathematics questions with equal weightage of 100 marks.
3. Each question is of 4 marks.
4. There are three sections in the question paper consisting of Physics (Q.no.1 to 30), Chemistry (Q.no.31 to 60) and Mathematics (Q. no.61 to 90). Each section is divided into two parts, Part I consists of 20 multiple choice questions & Part II consists of 10 Numerical value type Questions, attempt any 5 questions out of 10.
5. There will be only one correct choice in the given four choices in Part I. For each question 4 marks will be awarded for correct choice, 1 mark will be deducted for incorrect choice for Part I Questions and zero mark will be awarded for not attempted question. For Part II Questions 4 marks will be awarded for correct answer and zero for unattempted and incorrect answer.
6. Any textual, printed or written material, mobile phones, calculator etc. is not allowed for the students appearing for the test.
7. All calculations / written work should be done in the rough sheet provided.

PHYSICS

PART-I (Multiple Choice Questions)

1. A sphericla ball A of mass 4 *kg*, moving along a straight line strikes another spherical ball *B* of mass 1*kg* at rest. After the collision, *A* and *B* move with velocities $\upsilon_1\, ms^{-1}$ and $\upsilon_2\, ms^{-1}$ respectively making angles of 30° and 60° with respect to the original direction of motion of *A*.

The ratio $\frac{\upsilon_1}{\upsilon 2}$ will be

(a) $\sqrt{3}/4$ (b) $4/\sqrt{3}$

(c) $1/\sqrt{3}$ (d) $\sqrt{3}$

2. A thin wire of length L and uniform linear mass density ρ is bent into a circular loop with centre at O as shown. The moment of inertia of the loop about the axis XX′ is

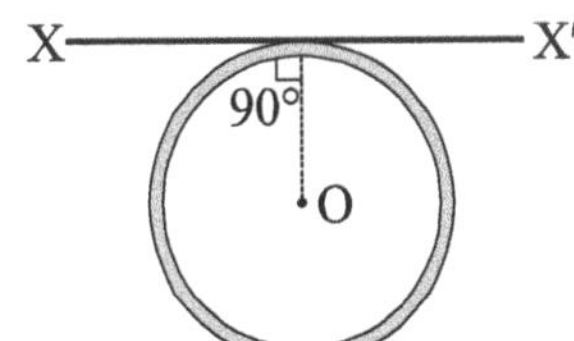

(a) $\frac{\rho L^3}{8\pi^2}$ (b) $\frac{\rho L^3}{16\pi^2}$

(c) $\frac{5\rho L^3}{16\pi^2}$ (d) $\frac{3\rho L^3}{8\pi^2}$

3. The diagram showing the variation of gravitational potential of earth with distance from the centre of earth is

(a)

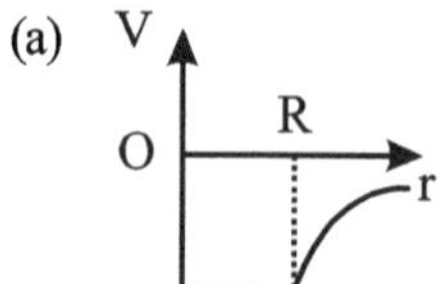

(b)

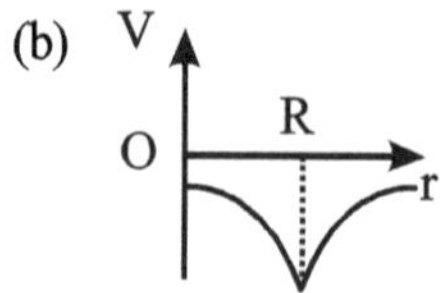

(c)

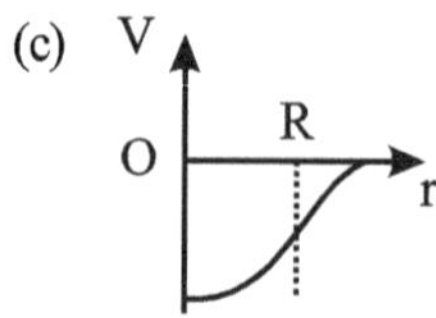

(d)

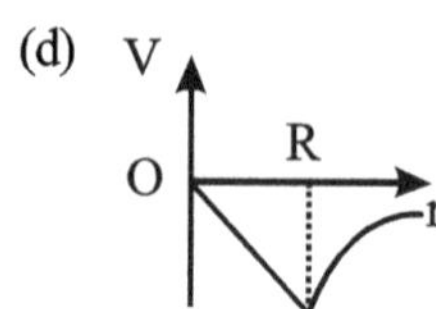

4. Two thin dielectric slabs of dielectric constants K_1 and K_2 ($K_1 < K_2$) are inserted between plates of a parallel plate capacitor, as shown in the figure. The variation of electric field 'E' between the plates with distance 'd' as measured from plate P is correctly shown by :

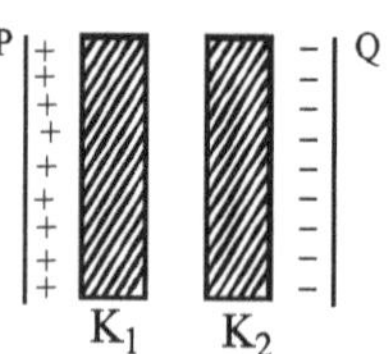

(a)

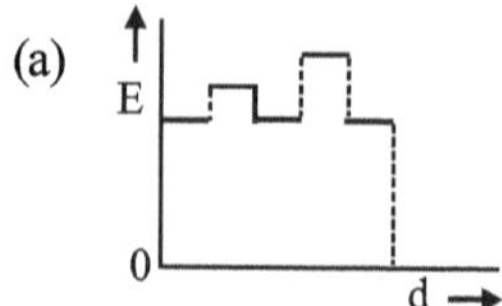

(b)

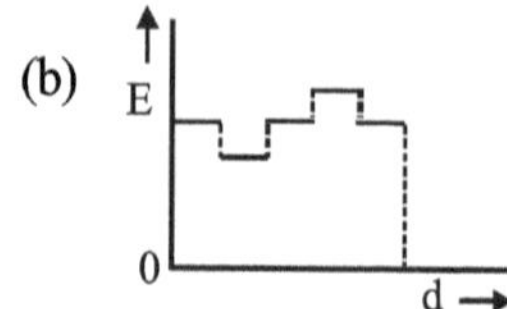

(c)

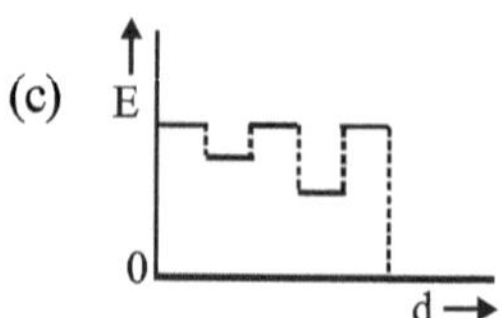

(d)

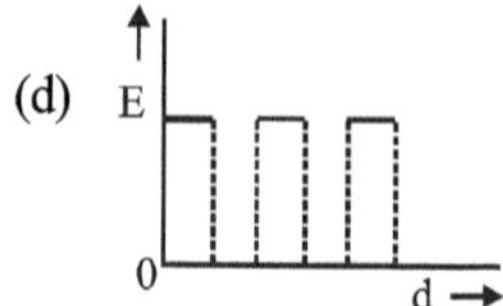

5. Two identical capacitors having plate separation d_0 are connected parallel to each other across points A and B as shown in figure. A charge Q is imparted to the

system by connecting a battery across A and B and battery is removed. Now first plate of first capacitor and second plate of second capacitor starts moving with constant velocity u_0 towards left. Find the magnitude of current flowing in the loop during the process.

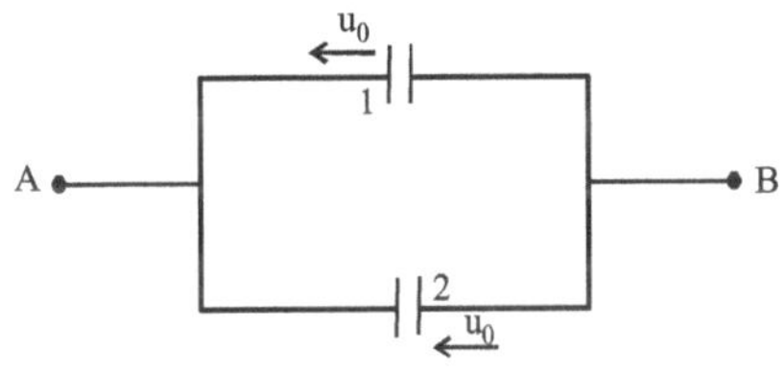

(a) $\frac{Q}{2d_0}u_0$ (b) $\frac{Q}{d_0}u_0$

(c) $\frac{2Q}{d_0}u_0$ (d) $\frac{Q}{3d_0}u_0$

6. Two long parallel wires are at a distance 2d apart. They carry steady equal currents flowing out of the plane of the paper as shown. The variation of the magnetic field B along the line XX' is given by

(a)
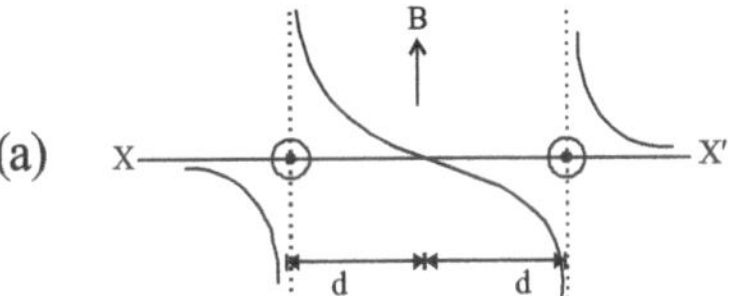

(b)
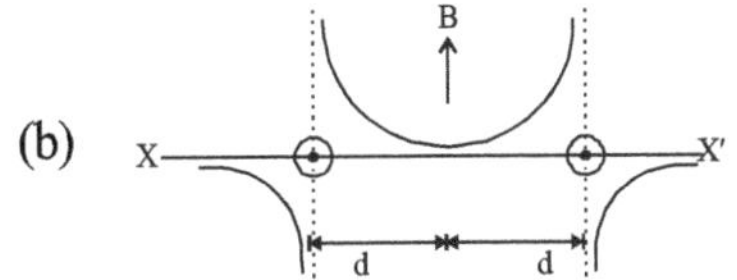

(c)
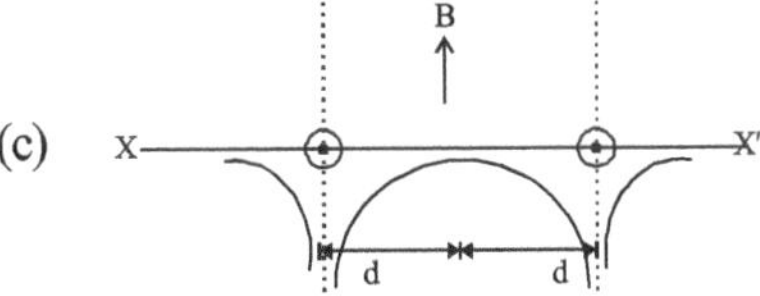

(d)
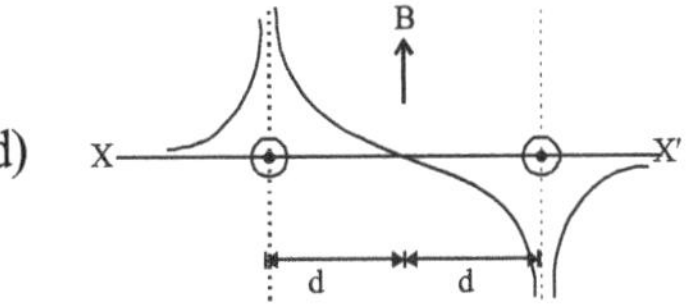

7. If dimensions of critical velocity υ_c of a liquid flowing through a tube are expressed as $[\eta^x \rho^y r^x]$, where η, ρ and r are the coefficient of viscosity of liquid, density of liquid and radius of the tube respectively, then the values of x, y and z are given by :

(a) $-1, -1, 1$ (b) $-1, -1, -1$

(c) $1, 1, 1$ (d) $1, -1, -1$

8. A car accelerates from rest at a constant rate α for some time, after which it decelerates at a constant rate β and comes to rest. If the total time elapsed is t, then the maximum velocity acquired by the car is

(a) $\left(\frac{\alpha^2+\beta^2}{\alpha\beta}\right)t$

(b) $\left(\frac{\alpha^2-\beta^2}{\alpha\beta}\right)t$

(c) $\frac{(\alpha+\beta)t}{\alpha\beta}$

(d) $\frac{\alpha\beta t}{\alpha+\beta}$

9. The speed of a projectile at its maximum height is $\frac{\sqrt{3}}{2}$ times its initial speed. If the range of the projectile is 'P' times the maximum height attained by it. P is-

(a) $\frac{4}{3}$ (b) $2\sqrt{3}$

(c) $4\sqrt{3}$ (d) $\frac{3}{4}$

10. All electrons ejected from a surface by incident light of wavelength 200nm can be stopped before travelling 1m in the direction of uniform electric field of 4N/C. The work function of the surface is

(a) 4 eV (b) 6.2 eV

(c) 2 eV (d) 2.2 eV

11. Find the ratio of longest wavelength and the shortest wavelength observed in the five spectral series of emission spectrum of hydrogen.

(a) $\frac{4}{3}$ (b) $\frac{525}{376}$

(c) 25 (d) $\frac{900}{11}$

12. The energy spectrum of β-particles [Number N(E) as a function of β-energy E] emitted from a radioactive source is

(a)

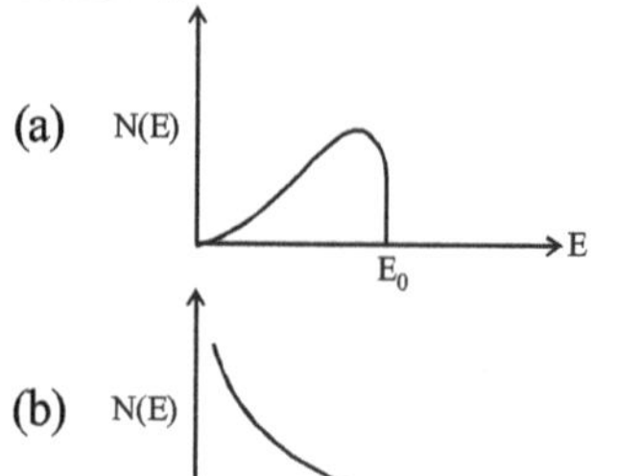

(b) N(E) E E_0

(c) N(E) E E_0

(d) N(E) E E_0

13. If a piece of metal is heated to temperature θ and then allowed to cool in a room which is at temperature θ_0, the graph between the temperature T of the metal and time t will be closest to

(a)

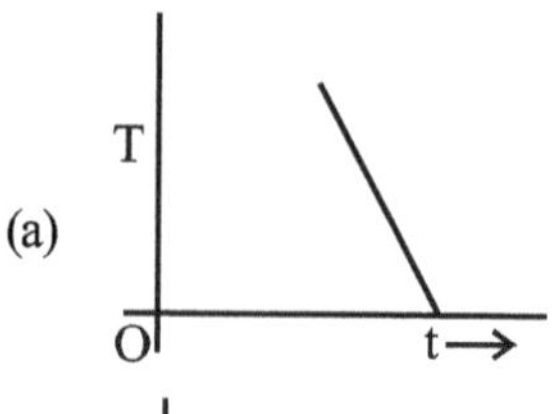

(b)

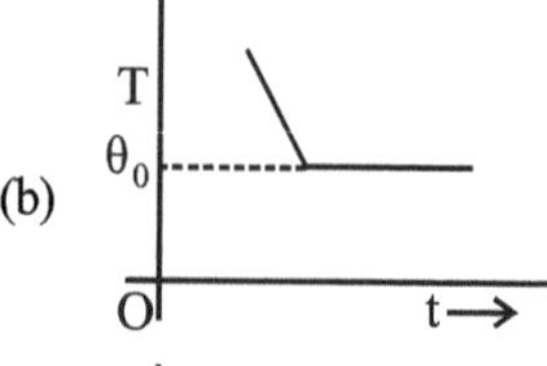

(c)

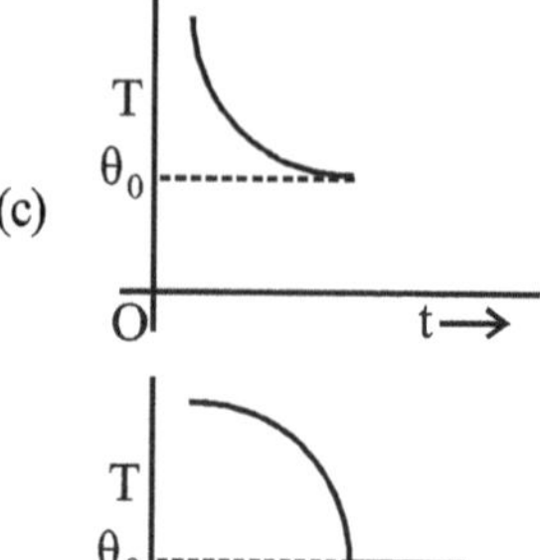

(d) T θ_0 O t→

14. 'n' moles of an ideal gas undergoes a process A $\rightarrow$ B as shown in the figure. The maximum temperature of the gas during the process will be :

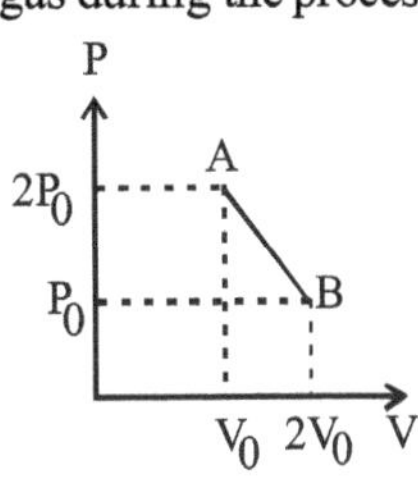

(a) $\frac{9P_0V_0}{2nR}$ (b) $\frac{9P_0V_0}{nR}$

(c) $\frac{9P_0V_0}{4nR}$ (d) $\frac{3P_0V_0}{2nR}$

15. In the given (V – T) diagram, what is the relation between pressure P_1 and P_2 ?

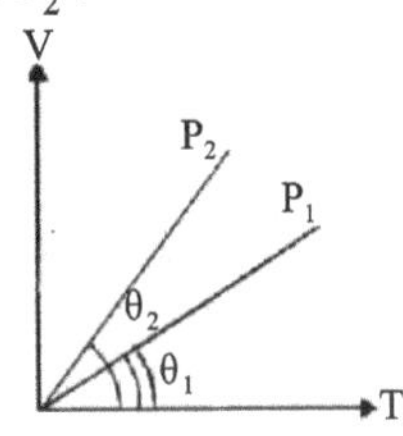

(a) $P_2 > P_1$

(b) $P_2 < P_1$

(c) Cannot be predicted

(d) $P_2 = P_1$

16. A particle executes simple harmonic motion with a time period of 16s. At time t = 2s, the particle crosses the mean position while at t = 4s, its velocity is 4 m/s^{-1}. The amplitude of motion in metre is

(a) $\sqrt{2}\pi$ (b) $16\sqrt{2}\pi$

(c) $24\sqrt{2}\pi$ (d) $\frac{32\sqrt{2}}{\pi}$

17. A metallic rod of length 'ℓ' is tied to a string of length 2ℓ and made to rotate with angular speed ω on a horizontal table with one end of the string fixed. If there is a vertical magnetic field 'B' in the region, the e.m.f. induced across the ends of the rod is

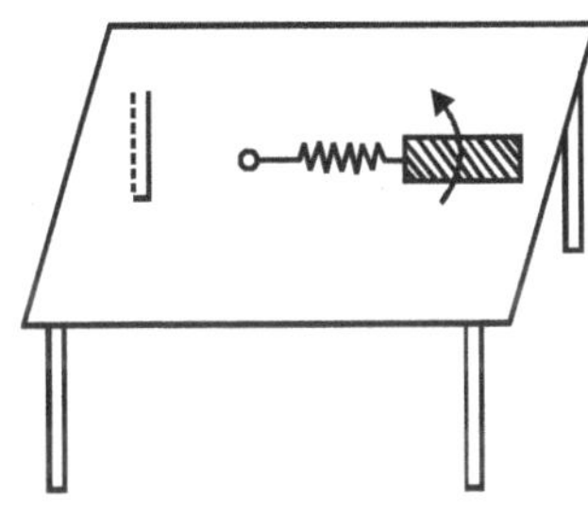

(a) $\frac{2B\omega\ell^2}{2}$ (b) $\frac{3B\omega\ell^2}{2}$

(c) $\frac{4B\omega\ell^2}{2}$ (d) $\frac{5B\omega\ell^2}{2}$

18. In an LCR circuit as shown below both switches S_1 and S_2 are open initially. Now switch S_1 is closed, S_2 kept open. (q is charge on the capacitor and $\tau = RC$ is capacitive time constant). Which of the following statements is correct ?

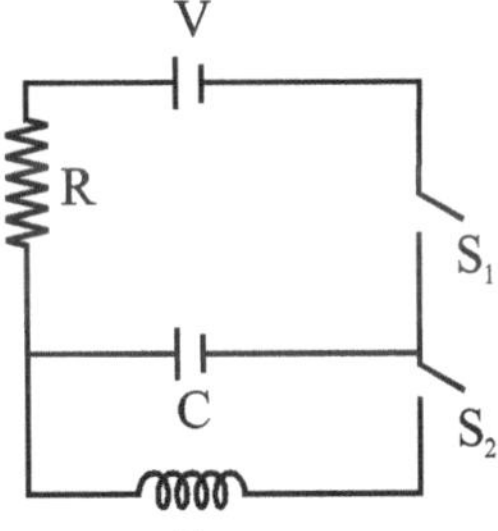

(a) Work done by the battery is half of the energy dissipated in the resistor

(b) At $t=\tau, q=CV/2$

(c) At $t=2\tau, q=CV(1-e^{-2})$

(d) At $t=\frac{\tau}{2}$, $q=CV(1-e^{-1})$

19. An electromagnetic wave in vacuum has the electric and magnetic field $\vec{E}$ and $\vec{B}$, which are always perpendicular to each other. The direction of polarization is given by $\vec{X}$ and that of wave propagation by $\vec{k}$. Then

(a) $\vec{X} \parallel \vec{B}$ and $\vec{k} \parallel \vec{B}\times\vec{E}$

(b) $\vec{X} \parallel \vec{E}$ and $\vec{k} \parallel \vec{E}\times\vec{B}$

(c) $\vec{X} \parallel \vec{B}$ and $\vec{k} \parallel \vec{E}\times\vec{B}$

(d) $\vec{X} \parallel \vec{E}$ and $\vec{k} \parallel \vec{B}\times\vec{E}$

20. Two blocks each of mass m lie on a smooth table. They are attached to two other masses as shown in the figure. The pulleys and strings are light. An object O is kept at rest on the table. The sides AB and CD of the two blocks are made reflecting. The acceleration of two images formed in these two reflecting surfaces w.r.t. each other is 17g/A then find the value of

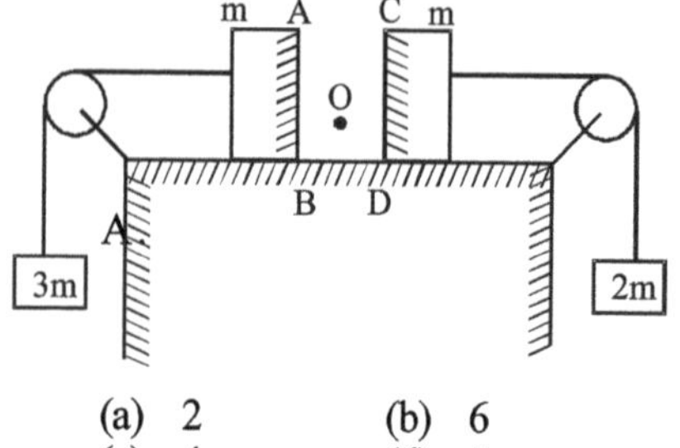

(a) 2 (b) 6

(c) 4 (d) 5

PART-II (Numerical Answer Questions)

21. Combination of two identical capacitors, a resistor R and a DC voltage source of voltage 6 V is used in an experiment on C-R circuit. It is found that for a parallel combination of the capacitor the time in which the voltage of the fully charged combination reduces to half its original voltage is 10 s. For series combination the time (in sec) needed for reducing the voltage of the fully charged series combination by half is

22. Escape velocity for earth surface is 11 km/s. If the radius of any planet is two times the radius of the earth but average density is same as that of earth. Then the escape velocity (in km/s) at the planet will be

23. Two identical glass rods S_1 and S_2 (refractive index = 1.5) have one convex end of radius of curvature 10 cm. They are placed with the curved surfaces at a distance d as shown in the figure, with their axes (shown by the dashed line) aligned. When a point source of light P is placed inside rod S_1 on its axis at a distance of 50 cm from the curved face, the light rays emanating from it are found to be parallel to the axis inside S_2. The distance d (in cm) is

S_2 P 50 cm d S_2

24. The displacement of a particle executing SHM is given by $y = 5\sin\left(4t + \frac{\pi}{3}\right)$. If T is the time period and mass of the particle is 2g, the kinetic energy (in joule) of the particle when $t = \frac{T}{4}$ is given by

25. A zener diode of voltage $V_Z (= 6V)$ is used to maintain a constant voltage across a load resistance R_L (= 1000 Ω) by using a series resistance R_s (= 100Ω). If the e.m.f. of source is E (= 9 V), what is the power (in watt) being dissipated in Zener diode ?

26. A stone of mass 20 g is projected from a rubber catapult of length 0.1 m and area of cross section 10^{-6} m^2 stretched by an amount 0.04 m. The velocity of the projected stone is __________ m/s.
(Young's modulus of rubber = 0.5 × 10^9 N/m^2)

27. A body of mass 1 kg rests on a horizontal floor with which it has a coefficient of static friction $\frac{1}{\sqrt{3}}$. It is desired to make the body move by applying the minimum possible force F N. The value of F will be _________. (Round off to the Nearest integer) [Take g = 10 ms^{-2}]

28. A circular conducting coil of radius 1 m is being heated by the change of magnetic field $\vec{B}$ passing perpendicular to the plane in which the coil is laid. The resistance of the coil is 2 μΩ. The magnetic field is slowly switched off such that its magnitude changes in time as

$$B = \frac{4}{\pi} \times 10^{-3} T\left(1 - \frac{t}{100}\right)$$

The energy dissipated by the coil before the magnetic field is switched off completely is E = ________ mJ.

29. The centre of mass of a solid hemi-sphere of radius 8 cm is x cm from the centre of the flat surface. Then value of x is ______.

30. An ac circuit has an inductor and a resistor of resistance R in series, such that $X_L = 3R$. Now, a capacitor is added in series such that X_C = 2R. The ratio of new power factor with the old power factor of the circuit is $\sqrt{5} : x$. The value of x is __________.

CHEMISTRY

PART-I (Multiple Choice Questions)

31. The compound that does not produce nitrogen gas by the thermal decomposition is :
(a) $Ba(N_3)_2$ (b) $(NH_4)_2Cr_2O_7$
(c) NH_4NO_2 (d) $(NH_4)_2SO_4$

32. The following compound is used as

$$\text{C}_6\text{H}_4(\text{O—}\overset{\text{O}}{\overset{\|}{\text{C}}}\text{—CH}_3)(\text{COOH})$$

(a) an anti-inflammatory compound
(b) analgesic
(c) hypnotic
(d) antiseptic

33. In a reversible reaction the energy of activation of the forward reaction is 50 kcal. The energy of activation for the reverse reaction will be

(a) < 50 kcal
(b) either greater than or less than 50 kcal
(c) 50 kcal
(d) > 50 kcal

34. The method not used in metallurgy to refine the impure metal is

(a) Mond's process
(b) van–Arkel process
(c) Amalgamation process
(d) Liquation

35. Match List-I with List-II :

List-I Name of oxo acid	**List-II** Oxidation state of 'P'
(A) Hypophosphorous acid	(I) +5
(B) Orthophosphoric acid	(II) +4
(C) Hypophosphoric acid	(III) +3
(D) Orthophosphorous acid	(IV) +2
	(V) +1

Choose the correct answer from the options given below:

(a) (A)-(IV), (B)-(V), (C)-(II), (D)-(III)
(b) (A)-(V), (B)-(IV), (C)-(II), (D)-(III)
(c) (A)-(V), (B)-(I), (C)-(II), (D)-(III)
(d) (A)-(IV), (B)-(I), (C)-(II), (D)-(III)

36. Soap helps in cleaning clothes, because

(a) chemical of soap change
(b) it increases the surface tension of the solution
(c) it absorbs the dirt
(d) it lowers the surface tension of the solution

37. Orthoboric acid –

(a) donate proton to form $H_2BO_3^-$
(b) accept proton of form $H_4BO_3^+$
(c) donate OH^- to form $H_2BO_2^+$
(d) accept OH^- to form $[B(OH)_4]^-$

38. Consider the reaction

$$N_2(g) + 3H_2(g) \rightleftharpoons 2NH_3(g)$$

The equilibrium constant of the above reaction is K_P. If pure ammonia is left to dissociate, the partial pressure of ammonia at equilibrium is given by (Assume that $P_{NH_3} << P_{total}$ at equilibrium)

(a) $\frac{3^{3/2} K_P^{1/2} P^2}{16}$

(b) $\frac{K_P^{1/2} P^2}{16}$

(c) $\frac{K_P^{1/2} P^2}{4}$

(d) $\frac{3^{3/2} K_P^{1/2} P^2}{4}$

39. The property which distinguishes formic acid from acetic acid is
- (a) only ammonium salt of formic acid on heating gives amide.
- (b) when heated with alcohol/ H_2SO_4 only acetic acid forms ester.
- (c) only acetic acid forms salts with alkali.
- (d) only formic acid reduces Fehling's solution.

40. The standard emf of a cell, involving one electron change is found to be 0.591 V at 25°C. The equilibrium constant of the reaction is (F = 96500 C mol^{-1})
- (a) 1.0×10^1 (b) 1.0×10^5
- (c) 1.0×10^{10} (d) 1.0×10^{30}

41. Calomel (Hg_2Cl_2) on reaction with ammonium hydroxide gives
- (a) HgO
- (b) Hg_2O
- (c) $NH_2 - Hg - Hg - Cl$
- (d) Hg_2NH_2Cl

42. Given below are two statements :

Statement I : The E° value for Ce^{4+}/Ce^{3+} is + 1.74 V.

Statement II : Ce is more stable in Ce^{4+} state than Ce^{3+} state.

In the light of the above statements, choose the **most appropriate** answer from the options given below.
- (a) Both statement I and statement II are correct
- (b) Statement I is correct but statement II is incorrect
- (c) Both statement I and statement II are incorrect
- (d) Statement I is incorrect but statement II is correct

43. Bromination of toluene gives
- (a) only *m*-substituted product
- (b) only *p*-substituted product
- (c) mixture of *o*-and *p*-substituted products
- (d) mixture of *o*-and *m*-substituted products

44. In sodium fusion test of organic compounds, the nitrogen of the organic compound is converted into
- (a) sodamide
- (b) sodium cyanide
- (c) sodium nitrite
- (d) sodium nitrate

45. What happens when magnesium is burnt in air and the products X and Y are treated with water?

$$\text{Mg} \xrightarrow{\text{Air}} \text{X} + \text{Y}; \quad \text{X} \xrightarrow{H_2O} \text{P}; \quad \text{Y} \xrightarrow{H_2O} \text{P} + \text{Q}$$

	X	Y	P	Q
(a)	MgO	$Mg(OH)_2$	$Mg(OH)_2$	N_2
(b)	MgO	Mg_3N_2	$Mg(OH)_2$	NH_3
(c)	MgO	Mg_3N_2	$Mg(OH)_2$	N_2
(d)	MgO	$MgCO_3$	$Mg(OH)_2$	CO_2

46. When a small quantity of $FeCl_3$ solution is added to the fresh precipitate of $Fe(OH)_3$, a colloidal sol is obtained.
The process through which this sol is formed is known as
(a) exchange of solvent
(b) chemical double decomposition
(c) peptization
(d) electrophoresis

47. The molal elevation constant of water = 0.52 °C kg mol^{-1}. The boiling point of 1.0 molal aqueous KCl solution (assuming complete dissociation of KCl), therefore should be
(a) 100.52 °C (b) 101.04 °C
(c) 99.48 °C (d) 98.96 °C

48. The oxidation state of Cr in $[Cr(NH_3)_4Cl_2]^+$ is
(a) 0 (b) +1
(c) +2 (d) +3

49. Standard reduction potentials of the half reactions are given below:

$F_2(g) + 2e^- \rightarrow 2F^-(aq)$; $E^\circ = +2.85$ V

$Cl_2(g) + 2e^- \rightarrow 2Cl^-(aq)$; $E^\circ = +1.36$ V

$Br_2(l) + 2e^- \rightarrow 2Br^-(aq)$; $E^\circ = +1.06$ V

$I_2(s) + 2e^- \rightarrow 2I^-(aq)$; $E^\circ = +0.53$ V

The strongest oxidising and reducing agents respectively are :
(a) F_2 and I^- (b) Br_2 and Cl^-
(c) Cl_2 and Br^- (d) Cl_2 and I_2

50. Cyclopropane rearranges to form propene

$$\triangle \longrightarrow CH_3 - CH = CH_2$$

This follows first order kinetics. The rate constant is 2.714×10^{-3} s^{-1}. The initial concentration of cyclopropane is 0.29 M. What will be the concentration of cyclopropane after 100 s?
(a) 0.035 M (b) 0.22 M
(c) 0.145 M (d) 0.0018 M

PART-II (Numerical Answer Questions)

51. What is the order of reaction of the formation of gas at the surface of tungsten due to adsorption?

52. 1.0 g of metal nitrate gave 0.86 g of metal sulphate. Calculate equivalent wt. of metal in grams.

53. How many isomeric naphthylamines are expected in the following reaction ?

2-Bromonaphthalene (Br) $\xrightarrow[-33°C]{NaNH_2,\ NH_3}$

54. At infinite dilution, the molar conductance of Ba^{2+} and Cl^- are 127 and 76 S cm^2 mol^{-1}. What is the molar conductivity of $BaCl_2$ at indefinite dilution?

55. The enthalpy of hydrogenation of cyclohexene is – 119.5 kJ mol^{-1}. If resonance energy of benzene is – 150.4 kJ mol^{-1}, calculate its enthalpy of hydrogenation in kJ.

56. AB_3 is an interhalogen T-shaped molecule. The number of lone pairs of electrons on A is ______.

57. The number of sigma bonds in

$$H_3C-\underset{\underset{H}{|}}{C}=CH-C\equiv C-H$$

is ______.

58. Potassium chlorate is prepared by electrolysis of KCl in basic solution as shown by following equation.

$$6OH^- + Cl^- \rightarrow ClO_3^- + 3H_2O + 6e^-$$

A current of xA has to be passed for 10h to produce 10.0g of potassium chlorate. The value of x is _____. (Nearest integer)
(Molar mass of $KClO_3$ = 122.6 g mol^{-1}, F = 96500 C)

59. The reaction of white phosphorus on boiling with alkali in inert atmosphere resulted in the formation of product 'A'. The reaction of 1 mol of 'A' with excess of $AgNO_3$ in aqueous medium gives ________ mol(s) of Ag. (Round off to the Nearest Integer).

60. A certain gas obeys $P(V_m - b) = RT$. The value of $\left(\frac{\partial Z}{\partial P}\right)_T$ is $\frac{xb}{RT}$. The value of x is ________.
(Integer answer) (Z : compressibility factor)

MATHEMATICS

PART-I (Multiple Choice Questions)

61. If one root is square of the other root of the equation $x^2 + px + q = 0$, then the relation between p and q is
(a) $p^3 - (3p-1)q + q^2 = 0$
(b) $p^3 - q(3p+1) + q^2 = 0$
(c) $p^3 + q(3p-1) + q^2 = 0$
(d) $p^3 + q(3p+1) + q^2 = 0$

62. A chord AB drawn from the point $A(0, 3)$ on circle $x^2 + 4x + (y-3)^2 = 0$ meets to M in such a way that $AM = 2AB$, then the locus of point M will be
(a) Straight line
(b) Circle
(c) Parabola
(d) None of these

63. Let $f(x) = \begin{cases} (x-1)\sin\frac{1}{x-1} & \text{if } x \neq 1 \\ 0 & \text{if } x = 1 \end{cases}$

Then which one of the following is true?

(a) f is differentiable at $x=0$ and $x=1$
(b) f is differentiable at $x=0$ but not at $x=1$
(c) f is differentiable at $x=1$ but not at $x=0$
(d) f is neither differentiable at $x=0$ nor at $x=1$

64. In a town of 10,000 families it was found that 40% family buy newspaper A, 20% buy newspaper B and 10% families buy newspaper C, 5% families buy A and B, 3% buy B and C and 4% buy A and C. If 2% families buy all the three newspapers, then number of families which buy A only is
(a) 3100 (b) 3300
(c) 2900 (d) 1400

65. The numbers P, Q and R for which the function

$f(x)=Pe^{2x}+Qe^{x}+Rx$ satisfies the conditions

$f(0)=-1, f'(\log 2)=31$ and

$\int_0^{\log 4}[f(x)-Rx]dx=\frac{39}{2}$

are given by
(a) $P=2, Q=-3, R=4$
(b) $P=-5, Q=2, R=3$
(c) $P=5, Q=-2, R=3$
(d) $P=5, Q=-6, R=3$

66. The value of $\lim\limits_{x\to 0^+} x^m(\log x)^n$, m, $n \in N$ is
(a) 0
(b) $\frac{m}{n}$
(c) mn
(d) None of these

67. The value of a in order that $f(x) = \sin x - \cos x - ax + b$ decreases for all real values is given by
(a) $a \geq \sqrt{2}$ (b) $a < \sqrt{2}$
(c) $a \geq 1$ (d) $a < 1$

68. If in ΔABC, $2b^2 = a^2 + c^2$, then

$\frac{\sin 3B}{\sin B} =$

(a) $\frac{c^2-a^2}{2ca}$

(b) $\frac{c^2-a^2}{ca}$

(c) $\left(\frac{c^2-a^2}{ca}\right)^2$

(d) $\left(\frac{c^2-a^2}{2ca}\right)^2$

69. The equation of the normal to the curve

$y=(1+x)^y+\sin^{-1}(\sin^2 x)$ at $x=0$ is
(a) $x+y=1$
(b) $x+y+1=0$

(c) $2x-y+1=0$

(d) $x+2y+2=0$

70. If a circles $x^2+y^2=a^2$ and the rectangular hyperbola $xy=c^2$ intersect in four points, $\left(ct_r, \frac{c}{t_r}\right)$, $r=1,2,3,4$ then $t_1t_2t_3t_4$ is equal to

(a) -1 (b) 1

(c) c^4 (d) $-c^4$

71. $\int\left(32x^3(\log x)^2 dx\right)$ is equal to :

(a) $8x^4(\log x)^2+C$

(b) $x^4\{8(\log x)^2-4(\log x)+1\}+C$

(c) $x^4\{8(\log x)^2-4(\log x)\}+C$

(d) $x^3\{(\log x)^2-2\log x\}+C$

72. Differential coefficient of $\tan^{-1}\frac{2x}{1-x^2}$ with respect to $\sin^{-1}\frac{2x}{1+x^2}$ will be

(a) 1 (b) -1

(c) $-1/2$ (d) x

73. The area of the plane region bounded by the curves $x+2y^2=0$ and $x+3y^2=1$ is equal to

(a) 1/3 (b) 2/3

(c) 4/3 (d) 5/3

74. The inverse of the statement $(p\wedge\sim q)\to r$ is

(a) $\sim(p\vee\sim q)\to\sim r$

(b) $(\sim p\wedge q)\to\sim r$

(c) $(\sim p\vee q)\to\sim r$

(d) None of these

75. The coefficient of the term independent of x in the expansion of $(1+x+2x^3)\left(\frac{3}{2}x^2-\frac{1}{3x}\right)^9$ is

(a) $\frac{1}{3}$ (b) $\frac{19}{54}$

(c) $\frac{17}{54}$ (d) $\frac{1}{4}$

76. The solution to the differential equation $\frac{dy}{dx}=\frac{yf'(x)-y^2}{f(x)}$ where $f(x)$ is a given function is

(a) $f(x)=y(x+c)$

(b) $f(x)=cxy$

(c) $f(x)=c(x+y)$

(d) $yf(x)=cx$

77. Two fixed points are $A(a, 0)$ and $B(-a, 0)$. If $\angle A-\angle B=\theta$, then the locus of point C of triangle ABC will be

(a) $x^2+y^2+2xy\tan\theta=a^2$

(b) $x^2-y^2+2xy\tan\theta=a^2$

(c) $x^2+y^2+2xy\cot\theta=a^2$

(d) $x^2-y^2+2xy\cot\theta=a^2$

78. The equation of the planes passing through the line of intersection of the planes $3x-y-4z=0$ and $x+3y+6=0$ whose distance from the origin is 1, are

(a) $x-2y-2z-3=0$,
$2x+y-2z+3=0$

(b) $x-2y+2z-3=0$,
$2x+y+2z+3=0$

(c) $x+2y-2z-3=0$,
$2x-y-2z+3=0$

(d) None of these

79. In a triangle the length of the two larger sides are 10 and 9, respectively. If the angles are in A.P., then the length of the third side can be :

(a) $\sqrt{91}$

(b) $3\sqrt{3}$

(c) 5

(d) None of these

80. If $\vec{a}=(1,-1,2)$, $\vec{b}=(-2,3,5)$, $\vec{c}=(2,-2,4)$ and $\hat{i}$ is the unit vector in the x-direction, then $(\vec{a}-2\vec{b}+3\vec{c})\hat{i}=$

(a) 11
(b) 15
(c) 18
(d) 36

PART-II (Numerical Answer Questions)

81. Find the greatest angle of a triangle whose sides are $a, b, \sqrt{a^2+b^2+ab}$.

82. How many 3 × 3 matrices M with entries from {0, 1, 2} are there, for which the sum of the diagonal entries of $M^T M$ is 5

83. For all complex numbers z_1, z_2 satisfying $|z_1|=12$ and $|z_2-3-4i|=5$, the minimum value of $|z_1-z_2|$ is ________.

84. The number of positive integral solution of the equation $x_1x_2x_3x_4x_5=1050$ is

85. Two numbers are selected at random from 1, 2, 3..... 100 and are multiplied, then the probability correct to two places of decimals that the product thus obtained is divisible by 3, is ________

86. If the least and the largest real values of α, for which the equation $z+\alpha|z-1|+2i=0$ ($z \in C$ and $i=\sqrt{-1}$) has a solution, are p and q respectively, then $4(p^2+q^2)$ is equal to ________

87. The students $S_1, S_2, \ldots\ldots, S_{10}$ are to be divided into 3 groups A, B and C such that each group has at least one student and the group C has at most 3 students. Then the total number of possibilities of forming such groups is ________

88. If $\int_0^{\pi}(\sin^3 x)e^{-\sin^2 x}\,dx = \alpha - \frac{\beta}{e}\int_0^1 \sqrt{t}\,e^t\,dt$, then $\alpha + \beta$ is equal to ______.

89. If the shortest distance between the lines

$\vec{r_1} = \alpha\hat{i} + 2\hat{j} + 2\hat{k} + \lambda(\hat{i} - 2\hat{j} - 2\hat{k})$,

$\lambda \in R, \alpha > 0$ and

$\vec{r_2} = -4\hat{i} - \hat{k} + \mu(3\hat{i} - 2\hat{j} - 2\hat{k}), \mu \in R$ is 9, then α is equal to _____.

90. The minimum value of α for which the equation $\frac{4}{\sin x} + \frac{1}{1 - \sin x} = \alpha$ has at least one solution in $\left(0, \frac{\pi}{2}\right)$ is ________.

RESPONSE SHEET

PHYSICS		CHEMISTRY		MATHEMATICS	
1.	ⓐⓑⓒⓓ	31.	ⓐⓑⓒⓓ	61.	ⓐⓑⓒⓓ
2.	ⓐⓑⓒⓓ	32.	ⓐⓑⓒⓓ	62.	ⓐⓑⓒⓓ
3.	ⓐⓑⓒⓓ	33.	ⓐⓑⓒⓓ	63.	ⓐⓑⓒⓓ
4.	ⓐⓑⓒⓓ	34.	ⓐⓑⓒⓓ	64.	ⓐⓑⓒⓓ
5.	ⓐⓑⓒⓓ	35.	ⓐⓑⓒⓓ	65.	ⓐⓑⓒⓓ
6.	ⓐⓑⓒⓓ	36.	ⓐⓑⓒⓓ	66.	ⓐⓑⓒⓓ
7.	ⓐⓑⓒⓓ	37.	ⓐⓑⓒⓓ	67.	ⓐⓑⓒⓓ
8.	ⓐⓑⓒⓓ	38.	ⓐⓑⓒⓓ	68.	ⓐⓑⓒⓓ
9.	ⓐⓑⓒⓓ	39.	ⓐⓑⓒⓓ	69.	ⓐⓑⓒⓓ
10.	ⓐⓑⓒⓓ	40.	ⓐⓑⓒⓓ	70.	ⓐⓑⓒⓓ
11.	ⓐⓑⓒⓓ	41.	ⓐⓑⓒⓓ	71.	ⓐⓑⓒⓓ
12.	ⓐⓑⓒⓓ	42.	ⓐⓑⓒⓓ	72.	ⓐⓑⓒⓓ
13.	ⓐⓑⓒⓓ	43.	ⓐⓑⓒⓓ	73.	ⓐⓑⓒⓓ
14.	ⓐⓑⓒⓓ	44.	ⓐⓑⓒⓓ	74.	ⓐⓑⓒⓓ
15.	ⓐⓑⓒⓓ	45.	ⓐⓑⓒⓓ	75.	ⓐⓑⓒⓓ
16.	ⓐⓑⓒⓓ	46.	ⓐⓑⓒⓓ	76.	ⓐⓑⓒⓓ
17.	ⓐⓑⓒⓓ	47.	ⓐⓑⓒⓓ	77.	ⓐⓑⓒⓓ
18.	ⓐⓑⓒⓓ	48.	ⓐⓑⓒⓓ	78.	ⓐⓑⓒⓓ
19.	ⓐⓑⓒⓓ	49.	ⓐⓑⓒⓓ	79.	ⓐⓑⓒⓓ
20.	ⓐⓑⓒⓓ	50.	ⓐⓑⓒⓓ	80.	ⓐⓑⓒⓓ
21.		51.		81.	
22.		52.		82.	
23.		53.		83.	
24.		54.		84.	
25.		55.		85.	
26.		56.		86.	
27.		57.		87.	
28.		58.		88.	
29.		59.		89.	
30.		60.		90.	

HINTS & SOLUTIONS

MOCK TEST-1

PHYSICS

1. (b) Since the speeds of the stars are negligible when they are at a distance r, hence the initial kinetic energy of the system is zero. Therefore, the initial total energy of the system is

$$E_i = KE + PE = 0 + \left(-\frac{GMM}{r}\right) = -\frac{GM^2}{r}$$

where M represents the mass of each star and r is initial separation between them.

When two stars collide their centres will be at a distance twice the radius of a star *i.e.* $2R$.

Let v be the speed with which two stars collide. Then total energy of the system at the instant of their collision is given by

$$E_f = 2\times\left(\frac{1}{2}Mv^2\right) + \left(-\frac{GMM}{2R}\right) = Mv^2 - \frac{GM^2}{2R}$$

According to law of conservation of mechanical energy,

$E_f = E_i$

$$Mv^2 - \frac{GM^2}{2R} = -\frac{GM^2}{r} \text{ or } v^2 = GM\left(\frac{1}{2R} - \frac{1}{r}\right)$$

$$\text{or } v = \sqrt{GM\left(\frac{1}{2R} - \frac{1}{r}\right)}$$

2. (b)

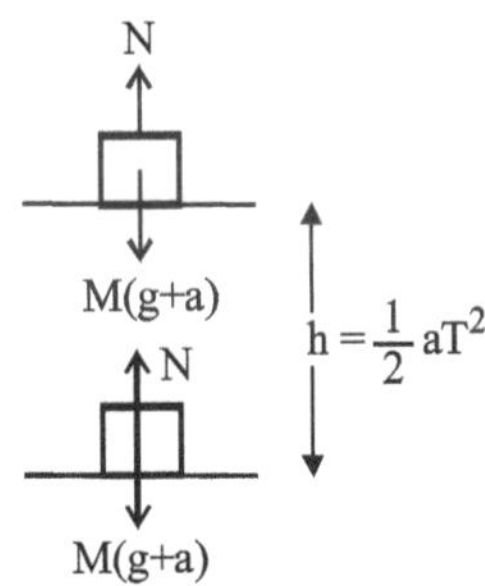

Work done by normal reaction

$$= Nh = M(g+a)\frac{1}{2}aT^2 = \frac{1}{2}M(g+a)aT^2$$

3. (c) Rise in temperature, $\Delta\theta = \frac{3T}{JSd}\left(\frac{1}{r} - \frac{1}{R}\right)$

$$\therefore \Delta\theta = \frac{3T}{J}\left(\frac{1}{r} - \frac{1}{R}\right) \quad \text{(For water S = 1 and d = 1)}$$

4. (c) $\left|\vec{F_B}\right| = \left|\vec{F_C}\right| = k \cdot \frac{Q^2}{a^2}$

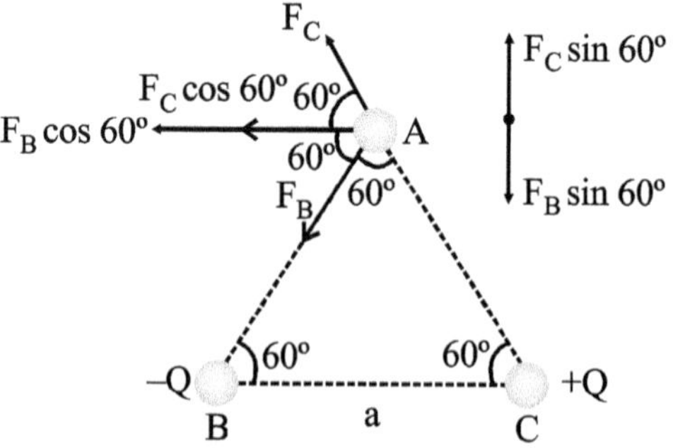

Hence force experienced by the charge at A in the direction normal to BC is zero.

5. (a) The magnitude of magnetic field at P $\left(\frac{R}{2}, y, \frac{R}{2}\right)$ is

$$B = \frac{\mu_0 Jr}{2} = \frac{\mu_0 i}{2\pi R^2} \times \frac{R}{\sqrt{2}} = \frac{\mu_0 i}{2\sqrt{2}\pi R}$$

(independent on y-coordinate)

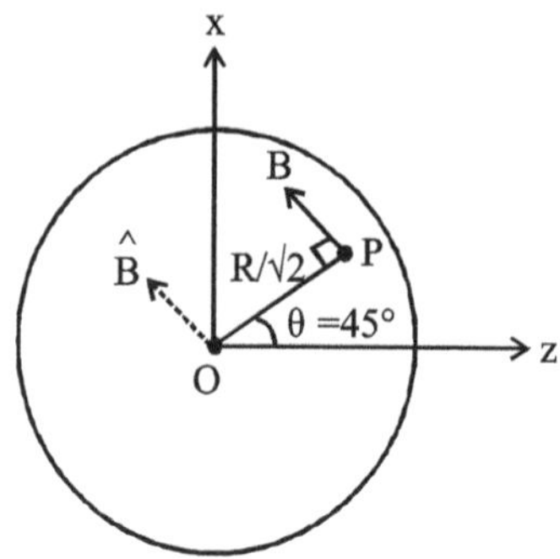

Unit vector in direction of magnetic field is

$\hat{B} = \frac{\hat{i} - \hat{k}}{\sqrt{2}}$ (shown by dotted lines)

$\therefore \ \vec{B} = B\hat{B} = \frac{\mu_0 i}{4\pi R}(\hat{i} - \hat{k})$

6. (d) ① S N B_2 P B_1 S N ②

0.1m 0.1m

From figure $B_{net} = \sqrt{B_a^2 + B_e^2}$

$= \sqrt{\left(\frac{\mu_0}{4\pi} \cdot \frac{2M}{d^3}\right)^2 + \left(\frac{\mu_0}{4\pi} \cdot \frac{M}{d^3}\right)^2}$

$= \sqrt{5} \cdot \frac{\mu_0}{4\pi} \cdot \frac{M}{d^3} = \sqrt{5} \times 10^{-7} \times \frac{10}{(0.1)^3} = \sqrt{5} \times 10^{-3}$ tesla

7. (d)

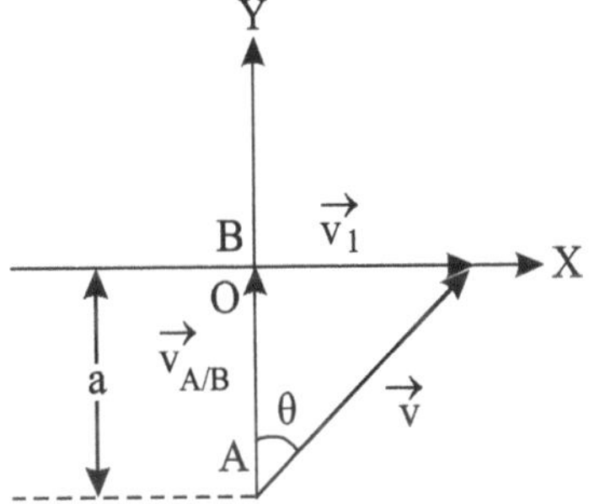

Velocity of A relative to B is given by

$\vec{v}_{A/B} = \vec{v}_A - \vec{v}_B = \vec{v} - \vec{v}_1$ ....(1)

By taking x-components of equation (1), we get

$0 = v \sin\theta - v_1 \Rightarrow \sin\theta = \frac{v_1}{v}$ ....(2)

By taking Y-components of equation (1), we get

$v_y = v\cos\theta$ .....(3)

Time taken by boy at A to catch the boy at B is given by

$$t=\frac{\text{Relative displacement along Y - axis}}{\text{Relative velocity along Y - axis}}$$

$$=\frac{a}{v\cos\theta}=\frac{a}{v.\sqrt{1-\sin^2\theta}}=\frac{a}{v.\sqrt{1-\left(\frac{v_1}{v}\right)^2}}$$ [From equation (1)]

$$=\frac{a}{v.\sqrt{\frac{v^2-v_1^2}{v^2}}}=\frac{a}{\sqrt{v^2-v_1^2}}=\sqrt{\frac{a^2}{v^2-v_1^2}}$$

8. **(c)**

9. **(b)** Joule is a unit of ernergy.

SI	**New system**
$n_1=5$	$n_2=?$
$M_1=1\text{ kg}$	$M^2=\alpha\text{ kg}$
$L_1=1\text{ m}$	$L^2=\beta\text{ m}$
$T_1=1\text{ s}$	$T^2=\gamma\text{ s}$

Dimensional formula of energy is comparing with, $[M^aL^bT^c]$, we get $a=1, b=2, c=-2$

$$\text{As } n_2=n_1\left(\frac{M^1}{M^2}\right)^a\left(\frac{L^1}{L^2}\right)^b\left(\frac{T_1}{T_2}\right)^c$$

$$=5\left(\frac{1kg}{\alpha kg}\right)^1\left(\frac{1m}{\beta m}\right)^2\left(\frac{1s}{\gamma s}\right)^{-2}=\frac{5\gamma^2}{\alpha\beta^2}=\frac{5\gamma^2}{\alpha\beta^2}=5\alpha^{-1}\beta^{-2}\gamma^2$$

10. **(d)**

11. **(a)** $I_m=\frac{V_m}{R_f+R_L}=\frac{25}{(10+1000)}=24.75\text{ mA}$

$$I_{dc}=\frac{I_m}{\pi}=\frac{24.75}{3.14}=7.87\text{ mA}$$

$$I_{rms}=\frac{I_m}{2}=\frac{24.75}{2}=12.37\text{ mA}$$

$P_{dc}=I_{dc}{}^2\times R_L=(7.87\times10^{-3})^2\times10^3=61.9\text{ mW}$

$P_{ac}=I_{rms}{}^2(R_f+R_L)=(12.37\times10^{-3})^2\times(10+1000)$

$=154.54\text{ mW}$

Rectifier efficiency

$$\eta = \frac{P_{dc}}{P_{ac}} \times 100 = \frac{61.9}{154.54} \times 100 = 40.05\%$$

12. **(c)** $K_{max} = E - W_0$

$\therefore \quad T_A = 4.25 - (W_0)_A$

$T_B = (T_A - 1.5) = 4.70 - (W_0)_B$

Equation (i) and (ii) gives $(W_0)_B - (W_0)_A = 1.95\, eV$

De Broglie wave length $\lambda = \dfrac{h}{\sqrt{2mK}} \Rightarrow \lambda \propto \dfrac{1}{\sqrt{K}}$

$$\Rightarrow \frac{\lambda_B}{\lambda_A} = \sqrt{\frac{K_A}{K_B}} \Rightarrow 2 = \sqrt{\frac{T_A}{T_B - 1.5}} \Rightarrow T_A = 2eV$$

From equation (i) and (ii)

$W_A = 2.25\, eV$ and $W_B = 4.20\, eV$.

13. **(c)** $PV = \mu RT = \dfrac{m}{M} RT,$

where m = mass of the gas

and $\dfrac{m}{M} = \mu$ = number of moles.

$\dfrac{PV}{T} = \mu R =$ a constant for all values of P.

That is why, ideally it is a straight line.

$$\therefore \quad \frac{PV}{T} = \frac{1\text{g}}{32\text{g mol}^{-1}} \times 8.31\ \text{J mol}^{-1}\text{K}^{-1} = 0.259\ \text{J K}^{-1}$$

Also, $T_1 > T_2$

14. **(c)** $f_{apparent} = \left(\dfrac{u + u/5}{u}\right) f = \dfrac{6}{5} f = 1.2f$

Wavelength remains constant (unchanged) in this case.

15. **(d)** Consider a shell of thickness (dr) and of radii (r) and the temperature of inner and outer surfaces of this shell be T, $(T - dT)$

$\dfrac{dQ}{dt}$ = rate of flow of heat through it

$$= \frac{KA[(T - dT) - T]}{dr} = \frac{-KAdT}{dr}$$

$$= -4\pi Kr^2 \frac{dT}{dr} \quad (\because\ A = 4\pi r^2)$$

To measure the radial rate of heat flow, integration technique is used, since the area of the surface through which heat will flow is not constant.

Then, $\left(\frac{dQ}{dt}\right)\int_{r_1}^{r_2} \frac{1}{r^2} dr = -4\pi K \int_{T_1}^{T_2} dT$

$$\frac{dQ}{dt}\left[\frac{1}{r_1} - \frac{1}{r_2}\right] = -4\pi K\left[T_2 - T_1\right]$$

or $\quad \frac{dQ}{dt} = \frac{-4\pi K r_1 r_2 (T_2 - T_1)}{(r_2 - r_1)} \quad \therefore \quad \frac{dQ}{dt} \propto \frac{r_1 r_2}{(r_2 - r_1)}$

16. **(b)** W_{ext} = negative of area with volume-axis
W(adiabatic) > W(isothermal)

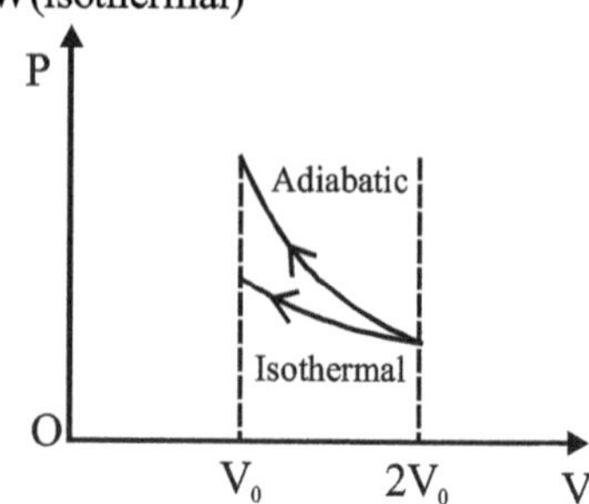

17. **(a)**

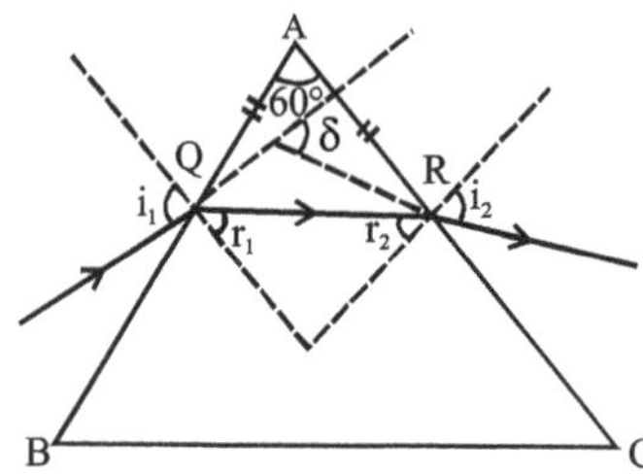

Given AQ = AR and $\angle A = 60°$

$\therefore \quad \angle AQR = \angle ARQ = 60°$

$\therefore \quad r_1 = r_2 = 30°$

Applying Snell's law on face AB.

$1. \sin i_1 = \mu \sin r_1$

$\Rightarrow \sin i_1 = \sqrt{3} \sin 30° = \sqrt{3} \times \frac{1}{2} = \frac{\sqrt{3}}{2}$

$\therefore \quad i_1 = 60°$

Similarly, $i_2 = 60°$

In a prism, deviation

$\delta = i_1 + i_2 - A = 60° + 60° - 60° = 60°$

18. **(a)** Both magnetic and electric fields have zero average value in a plane e.m. wave.

19. **(a)** At t = 0, current will flow only in 12Ω resistance

$\therefore I_{min} = \frac{5}{12}$

At $t \to \infty$ both L_1 and $_2$ behave as conductign wires

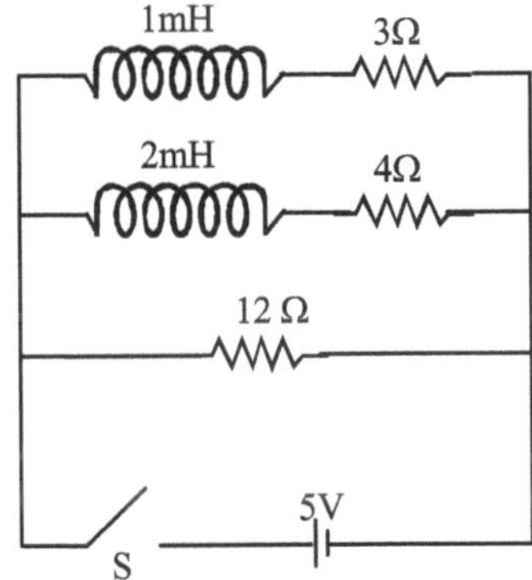

$\therefore R_{eff} = \frac{3}{2}, \; I_{max} = \frac{10}{3}$

$\frac{I_{max}}{I_{min}} = 8$

20. **(d)** For the first minima,

$\theta = \frac{\eta\lambda}{a} \quad \Rightarrow \quad \sin 30° = \frac{\lambda}{a} = \frac{1}{2}$

First secondary maxima will be at,

$\sin\theta = \frac{3\lambda}{2a} = \frac{3}{2}\left(\frac{1}{2}\right) \quad \Rightarrow \quad \theta = \sin^{-1}\left(\frac{3}{4}\right)$

21. **(11.75)** Let E_1 and E_2 be potential drops across R and X so

$$\frac{E_2}{E_1} = \frac{IX}{IR} = \frac{X}{R} \text{ or } X = \frac{E_2}{E_1}R$$

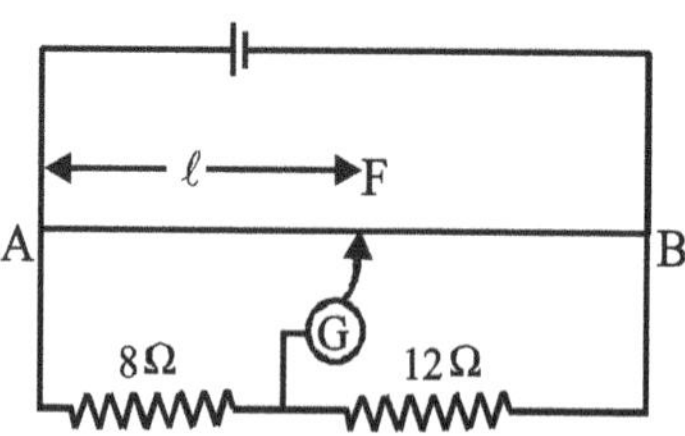

But $\frac{E_2}{E_1} = \frac{\ell_2}{\ell_1}$

so $$X = \frac{\ell_2}{\ell_1}R = \frac{68.5}{58.3} \times 10 = 11.75\Omega$$

22. **(6.66) Given :** Speed $V = 54 \text{ kmh}^{-1} = 15 \text{ ms}^{-1}$

Moment of inertia, $I = 3 \text{ kgm}^2$

Time $t = 15\text{s}$

$$\omega_i = \frac{V}{r} = \frac{15}{0.45} = \frac{100}{3} \quad \omega_f = 0$$

$$\omega_f = \omega_i + \alpha t$$

$$0 = \frac{100}{3} + (-\alpha)(15) \qquad \Rightarrow \quad \alpha = \frac{100}{45}$$

Average torque transmitted by brakes to the wheel

$$\tau = (I)(\alpha) = 3 \times \frac{100}{45} = 6.66 \text{ kgm}^2\text{s}^{-2}$$

23. **(0.05)** Given : $A = 4 \text{ m}^2$, $e = 0.32$ V, $dt = 0.5$sec.

B_1 is the initial magnetic induction and when it is reduced to 20%

$B_2 = 0.2 B_1$

$$e = \frac{d\phi}{dt} = \frac{A(B_1 - B_2)}{\Delta t} \text{ or } 0.32 = \frac{4(B_1 - 0.2B_1)}{0.5}$$

Magnetic induction $B_1 = \frac{0.16}{3.2} = 0.05 \text{ Wb/m}^2$

24. **(0.94)** Time period of a physical pendulum is

$$T = 2\pi\sqrt{\frac{I}{mgh}}$$

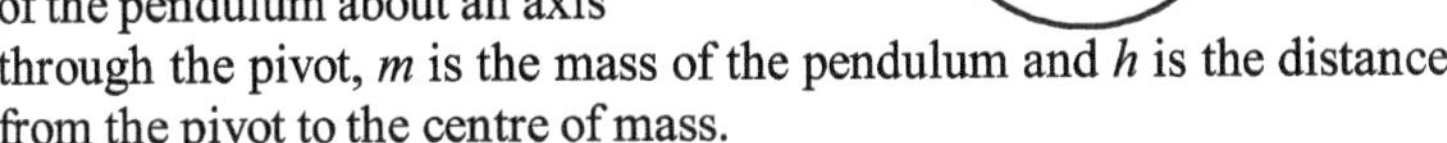

where I is the moment of inertia of the pendulum about an axis through the pivot, m is the mass of the pendulum and h is the distance from the pivot to the centre of mass.

In this case, a solid disc of R oscillates as a physical pendulum about an axis perpendicular to the plane of the disc at a distance r from its centre.

$$\therefore\ I = \frac{mR^2}{2} + mr^2 = \frac{mR^2}{2} + m\left(\frac{R}{4}\right)^2 = \frac{mR^2}{2} + \frac{mR^2}{16}$$

$$= \frac{9mR^2}{16} \qquad \left(\because r = \frac{R}{4}\right)$$

Here, $R = 10$ cm $= 0.1$ m, $h = \frac{R}{4}$

$$\therefore\ T = 2\pi\sqrt{\frac{\frac{9mR^2}{16}}{\frac{mgR}{4}}} = 2\pi\sqrt{\frac{9R}{4g}}$$

$$= 2\pi\sqrt{\frac{9\times0.1}{4\times10}} = 2\pi\times\frac{3}{2}\times\frac{1}{10} = 0.94\,\text{s}$$

25. **(488.9)** $\frac{1}{\lambda_1} = R\left(\frac{1}{2^2} - \frac{1}{3^2}\right) = \frac{5R}{36}$

$$\frac{1}{\lambda_2} = R\left(\frac{1}{2^2} - \frac{1}{4^2}\right) = \frac{3R}{16}$$

$$\therefore \frac{\lambda_2}{\lambda_1} = \frac{80}{108}$$

$$\lambda_2 = \frac{80}{108}\lambda_1 = \frac{80}{108}\times 660 = 488.9\text{nm}.$$

26. **(34)** Volume of sphere, $V = \frac{4}{3}\pi R^3$

Percentage error in volume

$$\frac{\Delta V}{V} \times 100 = (3) \times \frac{\Delta R}{R} \times 100$$

$$= (3) \times \frac{0.85}{7.5} \times 100 = 34$$

Hence $x = 34$

27. (16.00)

Using law of conservation of energy
Total energy at height 10 R = total energy at earth

$$-\frac{GM_E m}{10R} + \frac{1}{2}mV_0^2 = -\frac{GM_E m}{R} + \frac{1}{2}mV^2$$

$$\left[\because \text{Gravitational potential energy} = -\frac{GMm}{r}\right]$$

$$\Rightarrow \frac{GM_E}{R}\left(1 - \frac{1}{10}\right) + \frac{V_0^2}{2} = \frac{V^2}{2} \Rightarrow V^2 = V_0^2 + \frac{9}{5}gR$$

$$\Rightarrow V = \sqrt{V_0^2 + \frac{9}{5}gR} \approx 16\ km/s$$

[$\because$ $V_0 = 12$ km/s given]

28. (0.1) Magnetic field, $B = \dfrac{\mu_0 NIR^2}{2(R^2 + x^2)^{3/2}}$

or, $B \propto \dfrac{1}{(R^2 + x^2)^{3/2}}$

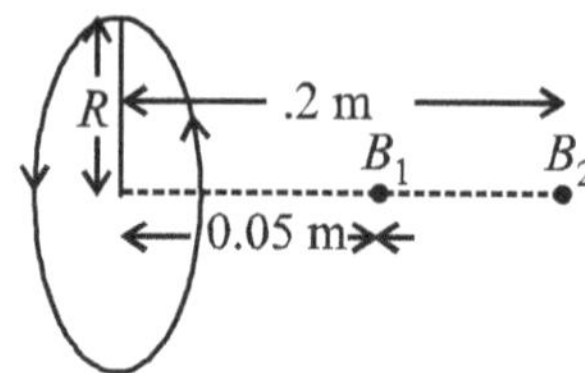

$$\therefore \frac{B_1}{B_2} = \frac{[R^2 + (0.2)^2]^{3/2}}{[R^2 + (0.05)^2]^{3/2}} = \frac{8}{1}$$

$$\Rightarrow \left(\frac{8}{1}\right)^{2/3} = \frac{[R^2+(0.2)^2]}{[R^2+(0.05)^2]}$$

$$\Rightarrow \frac{R^2+0.04}{R^2+0.0025} = \frac{4}{1}$$

$$\Rightarrow R^2+0.04 = 4R^2+0.01 \Rightarrow 3R^2 = 0.03$$

$$\therefore R = 0.1 \text{ m}$$

29. (2.8) de-Broglie wavelength, $\lambda = \frac{h}{P}$

$$\lambda_P = \frac{h}{\sqrt{2m_P \times (e \times V)}} \text{ and } \lambda_\alpha = \frac{h}{\sqrt{2m_\alpha \times (2e \times V)}}$$

$$\therefore \frac{\lambda_P}{\lambda_\alpha} = \sqrt{\frac{m_\alpha}{m_P} \times 2} = \sqrt{4 \times 2} = 2\sqrt{2} = 2.8.$$

30. (03.00) Maximum speed $= a\omega$

$$V = \omega\sqrt{a^2 - y^2}$$

or, $$\frac{a\omega}{2} = \omega\sqrt{a^2 - y^2}$$

$$\Rightarrow \frac{a^2}{4} = a^2 - y^2$$

$$\Rightarrow y^2 = \frac{3a^2}{4}$$

or, $$y = \frac{a\sqrt{3}}{2}$$

$$\therefore x = 3$$

CHEMISTRY

31. (a) Nitrogen due to small size is able to show $p\pi$-$p\pi$ lateral overlap forming $N \equiv N$, rest elements due to bigger size are not able to show $p\pi$-$p\pi$ lateral overlap.

32. (b) CuF_2 is both paramagnetic and coloured.

33. (c) s-character $\propto$ bond angle

For 25% s character (as in sp^3 hybrid orbital), bond angle is 109.5°, for

33.3% s character (as in sp^2 hybrid orbital), bond angle is 120° and for 50% s character (as in sp hybrid orbital), bond angle is 180°.

Similarly, when the bond angle decreases below 109.5°, the s-character will decrease accordingly.

Decrease in angle $= 120° - 109.5° = 10.5°$

Decrease in s-character $= 33.3 - 25 = 8.3$

Actual decrease in bond angle $= 109.5° - 105° = 4.5°$

Expected decrease in s-character

$$= \frac{8.3}{10.5} \times 4.5 = 3.56\%$$

Thus, the s-character should decrease by about 3.56% i.e., s-character $= 25 - 3.56 = 21.44\%$

34. **(d)** $CH_3 - COONH_4 \xrightarrow{\Delta} \underset{(X)}{CH_3 - CONH_2}$

$$\xrightarrow{\Delta / P_2O_5} \underset{(Y)}{CH_3 - CN} \xrightarrow{H_3O^{\oplus}} \underset{(Z)}{CH_3 - COOH}$$

35. **(a)** $Be - 1s^2 2s^2$; $B - 1s^2 2s^2 2p^1$; $C - 1s^2 2s^2 2p^2$; $N - 1s^2 2s^2 2p^3$; $O - 1s^2 2s^2 2p^4$. IP increases along the period. But IP of Be > B. Further IP of O < N because atoms with fully or partly filled orbitals are most stable and hence have high ionisation energy.

36. **(a)** From data 1 and 3, it is clear that keeping (B) const, [A] is doubled, rate remains unaffected. Hence rate is independent of [A]. From 1 and 4, keeping [A] constant, [B] is doubled, rate become 8 times. Hence rate $\propto [B]^3$.

37. **(b)** (i) HCl is a strong acid. Hence its pH is lowest among the others.

(ii) NaCl is a salt of strong acid and strong base so it is not hydrolysed and hence its pH is 7.

(iii) $NH_4Cl + H_2O \rightleftharpoons NH_4OH + HCl$

$\therefore$ The solution is acidic and pH is less than that of 0.1 M HCl.

(iv) $NaCN + H_2O \rightleftharpoons NaOH + HCN$

$\therefore$ The solution is basic and pH is more than that of 0.1 M HCl.

$\therefore$ Correct order for increase in pH is

$HCl < NH_4Cl < NaCl < NaCN$.

38. **(b)** Tollen's reagent is ammonical $AgNO_3$. Aldehydes form silver mirror with it and ketones do not show any change. So Tollen's reagent is used to distinguish between aldehydes and ketones.

39. **(b)** All proteins are not found in L-form but they may be present in form of D or L

40. **(a)** $2CuSO_4 + 2Na_2CO_3 + H_2O \longrightarrow CuCO_3.Cu(OH)_2 + 2Na_2SO_4 + CO_2$

41. (c) For metal, as temperature increases, resistance increases and hence conductivity decreases.

42. (c) Frenkel defects exhibit both vacancy and interstitial defects. When smaller ion, generally cation is dislocated from its normal lattice site to an interstitial site, the vacancy defect is produced at its lattice site and an interstitial defect at its lattice interstitial site. Schottky defect leads to colour in ionic solid due to presence of F- centre, which is produced in metal excess defect. Therefore, statement-I is correct and II is wrong.

43. (d) With Br_2 water, phenol gives 2, 4, 6- tribromophenol.

$$C_6H_5OH + 3Br_2\,(\text{excess}) \xrightarrow{H_2O} C_6H_2Br_3OH + 3HBr$$

2, 4, 6-Tribromophenol

44. (c) V_2O_5 is used as catalyst in contact process of manufacturing H_2SO_4

45. (d) (A) - (III); (B) - (IV); (C) - (I); (D) - (II)

Molecule	Bond order
Ne_2	0
N_2	3
F_2	1
O_2	2

46. (a) $NaCl(s) \rightarrow NaCl(l)$

Given that : $\Delta H = 30.5\ kJ\ mol^{-1}$

$\Delta S = 28.8\ JK^{-1}mol^{-1} = 28.8 \times 10^{-3}\ kJ\ K^{-1}\ mol^{-1}$

By using $\Delta S = \frac{\Delta H}{T} = \frac{30.5}{28.8 \times 10^{-3}} = 1059\,K.$

47. (a)

$$CH_3-CH_2-\overset{H}{C}=\underset{CH_3}{\overset{CH_3}{C}} \xrightarrow{O_3} CH_3-CH_2-\text{(ozonide: } \overset{H}{C}\text{–O–}C(CH_3)_2\text{, O–O)}$$

$$\xrightarrow{(-H_2O)} CH_3-\overset{O}{\overset{||}{C}}-CH_3 + CH_3-CH_2-CHO$$

48. (a) In acidic medium MnO_4^- changes to Mn^{2+}, hence O.N. changes from +7 to +2.

49. (b) Radioactive decay follows first order kinetics. therefore,

Decay constant $(\lambda) = \frac{0.693}{t_{1/2}} = \frac{0.693}{5730}$

Given, $R_0 = 100$ $\quad\therefore\quad R = 80$

and $t = \frac{2.303}{\lambda}\log\frac{[R]_0}{[R]} = \frac{2.303}{\left(\frac{0.693}{5730}\right)}\log\frac{100}{80}$

$= \frac{2.303\times 5730}{0.693}\times 0.0969 = 1845$ years

50. **(d)** Hybridisation

$\underset{d^2sp^3}{[Fe(CN)_6]^{4-}}, \underset{d^2sp^3}{[Mn(CN)_6]^{4-}},$

$\underset{d^2sp^3}{[Co(NH_3]^{3+}}, \underset{sp^3d^2}{[Ni(NH_3)_6]^{2+}}$

Hence $[Ni(NH_3)_6]^{2+}$ is outer orbital complex.

51. (409.5) According to combined gas equation,

$\frac{PV}{T} = \frac{P_1V_1}{T_1}$

$P = 1$ atm, $P_1 = \frac{3}{4}$ atm (on reducing by 25%)

$V = v, V_1 = 2v, T = 273K, T_1 = ?$

$\frac{1\times v}{273} = \frac{3\times 2v}{4\times T_1}$

$T_1 = \frac{3\times 2\times 273}{4} = 409.5\,K$

52. **(4)** C_7H_7Cl has 4 isomers

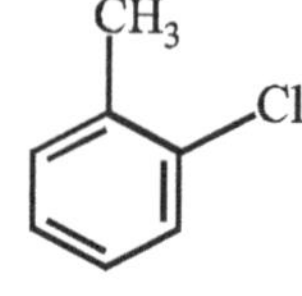

o-Chlorotoluene | m-Chlorotoluene | p-Chlorotoluene | benzyl chloride

53. **(8.4)** Normality of $H_2O_2 = \dfrac{\text{vol. strength}}{5.6}$

Volume of (1N) H_2O_2 solution = 5.6 volumes.

$\therefore$ Volume strength of 1.5 N H_2O_2

$= 1.5 \times 5.6 = 8.4$ volumes.

54. **(26)** ABAB.... is hexagonal close packing (*hcp*) in which space occupied = 74 % and, empty space = 26%.

55. **(3)** $M_2O_x \xrightarrow{\text{Reduction}} M$

Eq. of M_2O_x = eq. of Metal

$$\frac{\text{Wt. of } M_2O_x}{\text{Eq. wt. of } M_2O_x} = \frac{\text{Wt.of Metal}}{\text{Eq. wt. of Metal}}$$

$$\frac{4}{\dfrac{2\times 56 + x\times 16}{2x}} = \frac{2.8}{\dfrac{56}{x}}$$

On solving we get,

$$\Rightarrow \frac{4}{56+8x} = \frac{2.8}{56} \Rightarrow \frac{1}{14+2x} = \frac{1}{20} \Rightarrow 2x = 6 \Rightarrow x = 3$$

Hence, the oxide is M_2O_3.

56. **(4)**

$NH_2–CH_3–C(=O)–NH–CH(CH_2–CH_2–C(=O)–OH)–C(=O)–NH–CH(CH_2–COOH)–C(=O)–NH–CH(COOH)–CH_2–C_6H_4–OH$

$\downarrow$ pH = 12

$NH_2–CH_2–C(=O)–NH–CH(CH_2–CH_2–C(=O)–O^{\ominus})–C(=O)–NH–CH(CH_2–C(=O)–O^{\ominus})–C(=O)–NH–CH(COO^{\ominus})–CH_2–C_6H_4–O^{\ominus}$

So, total number of negative charge produced = 4

57. **(4)** Rate $= \frac{d[B]}{dt} = \frac{0.2}{0.5} = 0.4$

$= 4 \times 10^{-1}$

58. **(4)** Concentration of glucose in blood = 0.72g/L

$= \frac{0.72}{180} = 4 \times 10^{-3}$M

59. **(7.0)** Since, $(NH_4)_3PO_4$ is salt of weak acid (H_3PO_4) and weak base (NH_4OH).

$pH = 7 + \frac{1}{2}(pK_a - pK_b)$

$= 7 + \frac{1}{2}(5.23 - 4.75)$

$= 7.24 \approx 7.0$

60. **(10)** Staggered form is produced when the rearrangement of atoms or group takes place by an angle of 60°. 1, 1, 1 trichloroethane ($CCl_3 - CH_3$) in eclipsed form on rotation by 60° gives staggered form.

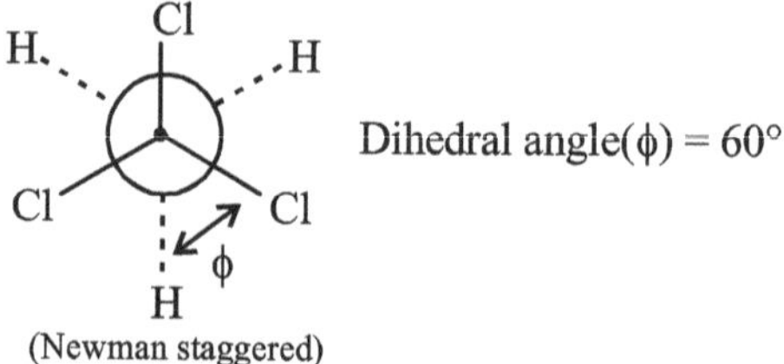

(Newman staggered)

MATHEMATICS

61. **(d)** $T_4 = {}^nC_3\, x^{n-3}\left(\frac{\alpha}{2x}\right)^3 \Rightarrow {}^nC_3\, x^{n-6}\left(\frac{\alpha}{2}\right)^3 = 20$

If $n = 6$, then ${}^6C_3\left(\frac{\alpha}{2}\right)^3 = 20 \Rightarrow \alpha = 2$

62. **(b)** Given equation is $x^2 + px + q = 0$
Sum of roots = tan30° + tan15° = –p
Product of roots = tan30° . tan15° = q

$$\tan 45° = \frac{\tan 30° + \tan 15°}{1 - \tan 30°.\tan 15°} = \frac{-p}{1-q} = 1$$

$\Rightarrow\ -p = 1 - q \Rightarrow q - p = 1$

$\therefore\ 2 + q - p = 3$

63. (a) $\because a^2, b^2, c^2$ are in A.P.

$\therefore a^2 + ab + bc + ca, b^2 + bc + ca + ab, c^2 + ca + ab + bc$ ..... are also in A.P. [adding $ab + bc + ca$]

or $(a+c)(a+b), (b+c)(a+b), (c+a)(b+c)$ .. are also in

A.P. $\Rightarrow \frac{1}{b+c}, \frac{1}{c+a}, \frac{1}{a+b}$ are in A.P.

[dividing by $(a+b)(b+c)(c+a)$]

64. (d) Let M(h, k) be the mid-point of chord AB where

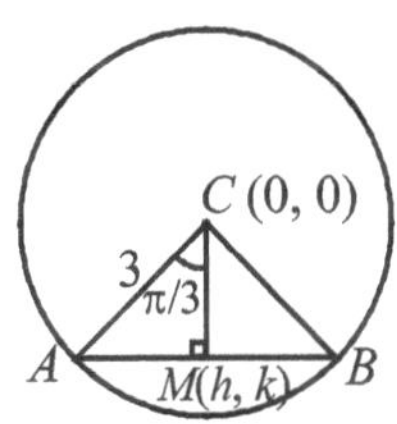

$\angle ACB = \frac{2\pi}{3}$

$\therefore\ \angle ACM = \frac{\pi}{3}$

Also $CM = 3\cos\frac{\pi}{3} = \frac{3}{2}$

$\Rightarrow \sqrt{h^2 + k^2} = \frac{3}{2} \Rightarrow h^2 + k^2 = \frac{9}{4}$

$\therefore$ Locus of (h, k) is $x^2 + y^2 = \frac{9}{4}$

65. (c) $y = \tan^{-1}\left(\frac{\log_e(e/x^2)}{\log_e(ex^2)}\right) + \tan^{-1}\left(\frac{3 + 2\log_e x}{1 - 6\log_e x}\right)$

$= \tan^{-1}\left(\frac{1 - 2\log_e x}{1 + 2\log_e x}\right) + \tan^{-1}\left(\frac{3 + 2\log_e x}{1 - 3.2\log_e x}\right)$

$= \tan^{-1}(\text{a}) - \tan^{-1}(2\log_e x)$

$+ \tan^{-1}(\text{c}) + \tan^{-1}(2\log_e x)$

$= \tan^{-1}(\text{a}) + \tan^{-1}(\text{c})$

$\therefore\ \frac{dy}{dx} = 0$

66. (d) $\{x^2\} - 2\{x\} \geq 0$

$\Rightarrow \{x\}(\{x\} - 2\} \geq 0$

$\Rightarrow \{x\} \le 0$ or $\{x\} \ge 2$
Second case is not possible.
Hence $\{x\} = 0$, as $\{x\} \le [0, 1)$
Hence range of $f(x)$ contains only one element 0.

67. **(d)** Here $p = 7$ and $\alpha = 30°$
$\therefore$ Equation of the required line is
$x \cos 30° + y \sin 30° = 7$

or $x\frac{\sqrt{3}}{2} + y \times \frac{1}{2} = 7$

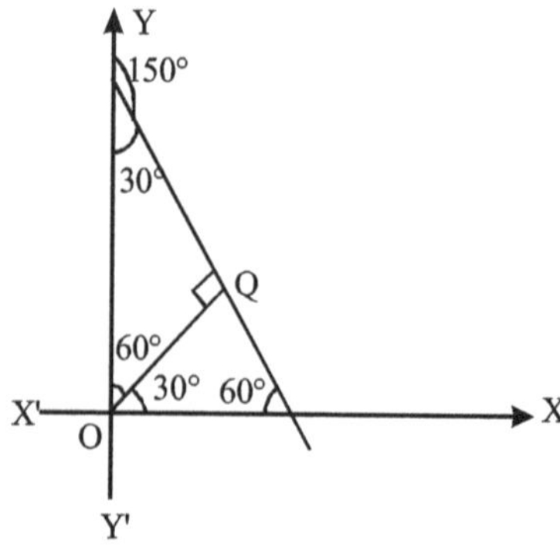

or $\sqrt{3}\,x + y = 14$

68. **(c)** $I = \int \frac{dx}{\cos x + \sqrt{3} \sin x}$

$$I = \int \frac{dx}{2\left[\frac{1}{2}\cos x + \frac{\sqrt{3}}{2}\sin x\right]}$$

$$= \frac{1}{2}\int \frac{dx}{\left[\sin\frac{\pi}{6}\cos x + \cos\frac{\pi}{6}\sin x\right]} = \frac{1}{2}\int \frac{dx}{\sin\left(x + \frac{\pi}{6}\right)}$$

$$\Rightarrow I = \frac{1}{2}\int \operatorname{cosec}\left(x + \frac{\pi}{6}\right)dx$$

$$\because \int \operatorname{cosec} x\, dx = \log|(\tan x/2)| + C$$

$$\therefore I = \frac{1}{2}\log\tan\left(\frac{x}{2} + \frac{\pi}{12}\right) + C$$

69. **(c)** Given $\dfrac{\tan 3\theta - 1}{\tan 3\theta + 1} = \sqrt{3}$

$\Rightarrow \sqrt{3}(\tan 3\theta + 1) = \tan 3\theta - 1$

$\Rightarrow \sqrt{3}\tan 3\theta + \sqrt{3} = \tan 3\theta - 1$

$\Rightarrow \sqrt{3}\tan 3\theta - \tan 3\theta + 1 + \sqrt{3} = 0$

$\Rightarrow \tan 3\theta(\sqrt{3} - 1) + (1 + \sqrt{3}) = 0$

$\Rightarrow \tan 3\theta(\sqrt{3} - 1) = -(1 + \sqrt{3})$

$\Rightarrow \tan 3\theta = \dfrac{-(\sqrt{3}+1)}{(\sqrt{3}-1)} = \dfrac{-(1+\sqrt{3})}{-(1-\sqrt{3})} = \dfrac{1+\sqrt{3}}{1-\sqrt{3}}$

$\Rightarrow \tan 3\theta = \tan 105° = \tan \dfrac{7\pi}{12}$

[**Note :** $\tan\theta = \tan\alpha \Rightarrow \theta = n\pi + \alpha$]

$\therefore\ 3\theta = n\pi + \dfrac{7\pi}{12} \Rightarrow \theta = \dfrac{n\pi}{3} + \dfrac{7\pi}{36}$

70. **(c)** Equation of normal in slope form on $y^2 = 4Ax$ is

$y = mx - 2Am - Am^3$ ...(i)

$= mx - 2\left(\dfrac{1}{4}\right)m - \left(\dfrac{1}{4}\right)m^3$ $\left[\begin{array}{l} \because y^2 = x \\ \therefore A = \dfrac{1}{4} \end{array}\right]$

$\Rightarrow 4mx - 4y - m^3 - 2m = 0$

$\because$ $(a, 0)$ lies on the normal. Then, $4m \times a - 4 \times 0 - m^3 - 2m = 0$

$\Rightarrow m(m^2 + 2 - 4a) = 0$

$\Rightarrow m = 0$ or $m^2 + 2 - 4a = 0$

If $m = 0$, then from (i),

$y = 0$ i.e., x-axis is one normal.

If $m^2 + 2 - 4a = 0 \Rightarrow m^2 = 4a - 2$ $[\because m^2 > 0]$

$\Rightarrow 4a - 2 > 0 \Rightarrow a > \dfrac{1}{2}$.

71. **(d)** By the diagram only 2 rectangles are formed *ADEH*, *GFCB*.

$\therefore$ number of favourable cases = 2

Total number of cases = ${}^8C_4$

$\therefore$ required probability $= \dfrac{2}{{}^8C_4} = \dfrac{1}{35}$

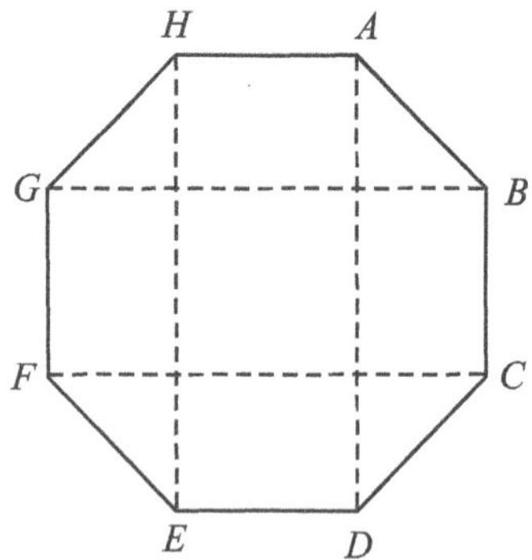

72. **(a)** $f(x)=x^3-3x^2-24x+5$

For increasing, $f'(x)>0, 3x^2-6x-24>0$

$\Rightarrow x^2-2x-8>0 \Rightarrow x^2-4x+2x-8>0$

$\Rightarrow (x+2)(x-4)>0$.

Now, by the sign scheme for $3x^2-6x-24$,

$\Rightarrow x \in (-\infty, -2) \cup (4, \infty)$

73. **(c)** Given that $y=y(x)$ and $x\cos y + y\cos x = \pi$ ...(i)

For $x=0$ in (i) we get $y=\pi$

Differentiating (i) with respect to x, we get,

$-x\sin y.y' + \cos y + y'\cos x - y\sin x = 0$

$$\Rightarrow y' = \frac{y\sin x - \cos y}{\cos x - x\sin y} \quad ....(ii)$$

$\Rightarrow y'(0)=1$ (Using $y(0)=\pi$)

Differentiating (ii) with respect to x, we get,

$$y'' = \frac{(y'\sin x + y\cos x + \sin y.y')(\cos x - x\sin y) - (-\sin x - \sin y - x\cos y.y')(y\sin x - \cos y)}{(\cos x - x\sin y)^2}$$

$$\Rightarrow y''(0) = \frac{\pi(1)-0}{1} = \pi.$$

74. **(b)** DP is a clock tower standing at the middle point D of BC.

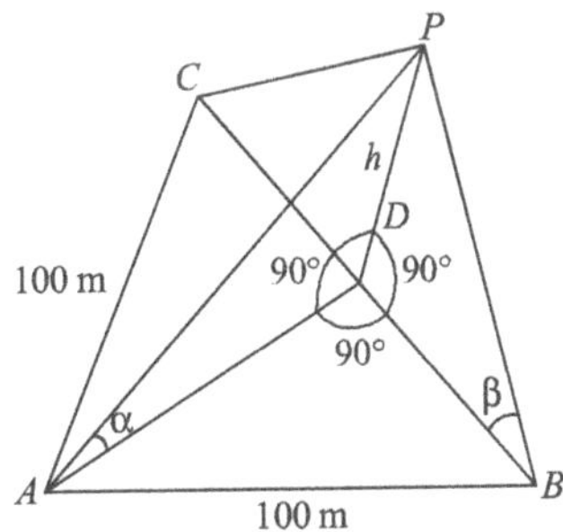

$\angle PAD = \alpha = \cot^{-1} 3.2 \Rightarrow \cot \alpha = 3.2$
and $\angle PBD = \beta = \text{cosec}^{-1} 2.6 \Rightarrow \text{cosec}\, \beta = 2.4$

$\therefore \cot \beta = \sqrt{(\text{cosec}^2 \beta - 1)} = \sqrt{(5.76)} = 2.4$

In the triangles PAD and PBD,
$AD = h \cot \alpha = 3.2\, h$ and $BD = h \cot \beta = 2.4\, h$
In the right angled ΔABD, $AB^2 = AD^2 + BD^2$
$\Rightarrow 100^2 = [(3.2)^2 + (2.4)^2]\, h^2 = 16\, h^2 \Rightarrow h = 25$ m.

75. (b)

A
$-3\hat{i} + 4\hat{k}$
$5\hat{i} - 2\hat{j} + 4\hat{k}$
B D C

$$\overrightarrow{AD} = \frac{(-3+5)\hat{i} + (0-2)\hat{j} + (4+4)\hat{k}}{2}$$

$$= \frac{2\hat{i} - 2\hat{j} + 8\hat{k}}{2} = \hat{i} - \hat{j} + 4\hat{k}$$

$\therefore$ length of median

$$= |\overrightarrow{AD}| = \sqrt{(1)^2 + (-1)^2 + (4)^2} = \sqrt{18}$$

76. (a) $\sim [p \vee (\sim p \vee q)] \equiv \sim p \wedge \sim (\sim p \vee q)$

$\equiv \sim p \wedge (\sim (\sim p) \wedge \sim q)$

$\equiv \sim p \wedge (p \wedge \sim q)$.

77. (a) $f(x) = x^p \sin \dfrac{1}{x}, x \neq 0$ and $f(x) = 0, x = 0$

Since at x = 0, f(x) is a continuous function

$\therefore \lim_{x\to 0} f(x) = f(0) = 0$

$\Rightarrow \lim_{x\to 0} x^p \sin\frac{1}{x} = 0 \Rightarrow p > 0$

f(x) is differentiable at x = 0, if $\lim_{x\to 0} \frac{f(x)-f(0)}{x-0}$ exists

$\Rightarrow \lim_{x\to 0} \frac{x^p \sin\frac{1}{x} - 0}{x-0}$ exists

$\Rightarrow \lim_{x\to 0} x^{p-1} \sin\frac{1}{x}$ exists

$\Rightarrow p-1>0$ or $p>1$

$\therefore$ for $0 < p \le 1$, f(x) is a continuous function at x = 0 but not differentiable.

78. **(d)** Let *M* be the foot of perpendicular from (7, 14, 5) to the given plane, then *PM* is normal to the plane. So, its d.r.'s are 2, 4, – 1. Since *PM* passes through *P*(7, 14, 5) and has d.r.'s 2, 4, – 1.

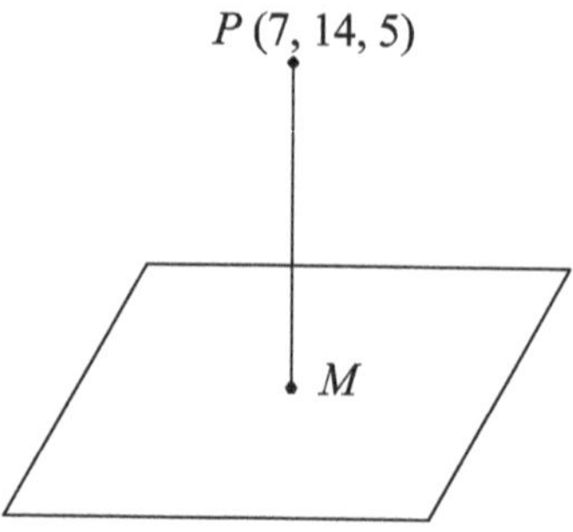

Therefore, its equation is $\frac{x-7}{2} = \frac{y-14}{4} = \frac{z-5}{-1} = r,$

$\Rightarrow x = 2r+7,\ y = 4r+14,\ z = -r+5$

Co-ordinates of *M* be $(2r+7, 4r+14, -r+5)$

Since M lies on the plane $2x+4y-z=2,$ therefore

$2(2r+7)+4(4r+14)-(-r+5) = 2 \Rightarrow r = -3$

Co-ordinates of foot of perpendicular are $M(1, 2, 8)$.

PM = Length of perpendicular from *P*

$$= \sqrt{(1-7)^2 + (2-14)^2 + (8-5)^2} = 3\sqrt{21}.$$

79. **(c)** $\Delta(x) = \begin{vmatrix} e^x & \sin x \\ \cos x & \ln(1+x^2) \end{vmatrix}$

$$= e^x \ln(1+x^2) - \sin x \cos x$$

So, $\lim_{x\to 0} \frac{\Delta(x)}{x} = \lim_{x\to 0} \frac{e^x \ln(1+x^2) - \sin x \cos x}{x}$

$$= \lim_{x\to 0} xe^x \left\{\frac{\ln(1+x^2)}{x^2}\right\} - \lim_{x\to 0}\left(\frac{\sin x}{x}\right)\cos x$$

$$= 0 \times 1 \times 1 - 1 \times 1 = -1$$

80. **(a)** $\tan^{-1} x + \tan^{-1}\frac{1}{y} = \tan^{-1} 3$

$$\Rightarrow \tan^{-1}\frac{x+\frac{1}{y}}{1-\frac{x}{y}} = \tan^{-1} 3 \Rightarrow \frac{xy+1}{y-x} = 3$$

$\Rightarrow y = \frac{1+3x}{3-x} > 0$ [$\because$ x and y are positive]

$\Rightarrow x - 3 < 0 \Rightarrow x < 3$ or $x = 1, 2$

$\therefore y = 2, 7$

solution set is $(x, y) \in \{(1, 2), (2, 7)\}$

81. **(64)** A selection of 3 balls so as to include at least one black ball, can be made in the following 3 mutually exclusive ways

(i) 1 black ball and 2 others $= {}^3C_1 \times {}^6C_2 = 3 \times 15 = 45$

(ii) 2 black balls and one other $= {}^3C_2 \times {}^6C_1 = 3 \times 6 = 18$

(iii) 3 black balls and no other $= {}^3C_3 \times {}^6C_0 = 1$

$\therefore$ Total number of ways $= 45 + 18 + 1 = 64$.

82. (19.5)

Class	Frequency	Cumulative Frequency
5 – 10	5	5
10 – 15	6	11
15 – 20	15	26
20 – 25	10	36
25 – 30	5	41

30 – 35	4	45
35 – 40	2	47
40 – 45	2	49
		N = 49

Here N = 49. $\therefore \frac{N}{2} = \frac{49}{2} = 24.5$

The cumulative frequency just greater than N/2 is 26 and corresponding class is 15–20. Thus 15– 20 is the median class such that $\ell = 15, f = 15$, F = 11, $h = 5$

$$\therefore \text{ median} = \ell + \frac{N/2 - F}{f} \times h$$

$$= 15 + \frac{24.5 - 11}{15} \times 5 = 15 + \frac{13.5}{3} = 19.5$$

83. (3.75) α, β are roots of the equation $2x^2 + 3x + 5 = 0$

Therefore sum of roots $(\alpha + \beta) = -\frac{3}{2}$

And product of roots $(\alpha.\beta) = \frac{5}{2}$.

$$\text{Now, } \begin{vmatrix} 0 & \beta & \beta \\ \alpha & 0 & \alpha \\ \beta & \alpha & 0 \end{vmatrix}$$

$= 0\,|\,0 - \alpha^2\,| - \beta\,|\,0 - \alpha\beta\,| + \beta\,|\,\alpha^2 - 0\,|$

$= \alpha\beta^2 + \beta\alpha^2 = \alpha\beta(\alpha + \beta)$

$$= \frac{5}{2}\left(\frac{-3}{2}\right) = \frac{-15}{4} = -3.75$$

84. (21.5) Let $I = \int_{-3}^{2} \{|x+1| + |x+2| + |x-1|\}\, dx$

Breaking points are

$x + 1 = 0 \Rightarrow x = -1$

$x + 2 = 0 \Rightarrow x = -2$

$x - 1 = 0 \Rightarrow x = 1$

$$\therefore I = \int_{-3}^{-2} f(x)dx + \int_{-2}^{-1} f(x)dx + \int_{-1}^{1} f(x)dx + \int_{1}^{2} f(x)dx$$

where $f(x) = |x+1| + |x+2| + |x-1|$

Now, $I_1 = \int_{-3}^{-2} [-(x+1)-(x+2)-(x-1)]dx$

$$= -\left[\frac{x^2}{2}+x+\frac{x^2}{2}+2x+\frac{x^2}{2}+x\right]_{-3}^{-2} = \frac{7}{2}$$

$$I_2 = \int_{-2}^{-1} [-(x+1)+(x+2)-(x-1)]dx$$

$$= \frac{-x^2}{2} - x + \frac{x^2}{2} + 2x - \frac{x^2}{2} + x\Big|_{-2}^{-1}$$

$$= \frac{-x^2}{2} + 2x\Big|_{-2}^{-1} = \left(\frac{-1}{2}-2\right) - (-2-4)$$

$$= -\frac{5}{2} + 6 = \frac{7}{2}$$

$$I_3 = \int_{-1}^{1} [(x+1)+(x+2)-(x-1)]dx$$

$$= \int_{-1}^{1} (x+4)dx = \frac{x^2}{2} + 4x\Big|_{-1}^{1} = 8$$

$$I_4 = \int_{1}^{2} [(x+1)+(x+2)+(x-1)dx]$$

$$= \int_{1}^{2} (3x+2)dx = \frac{3x^2}{2} + 2x\Big|_{1}^{2} = \frac{13}{2}$$

$\therefore\ I = I_1 + I_2 + I_3 + I_4$

$$= \frac{7}{2} + \frac{7}{2} + 8 + \frac{13}{2} = \frac{43}{2}$$

$$= \frac{27+16}{2} = \frac{43}{2} = 21.5$$

85. (4.5) Given curves are, $y = 2x - x^2$ .....(i)

and $y = -x$ .....(ii)

Putting the value of y in (i),

$-x = 2x - x^2$

$\Rightarrow x(x-3)=0 \Rightarrow x=0,3$

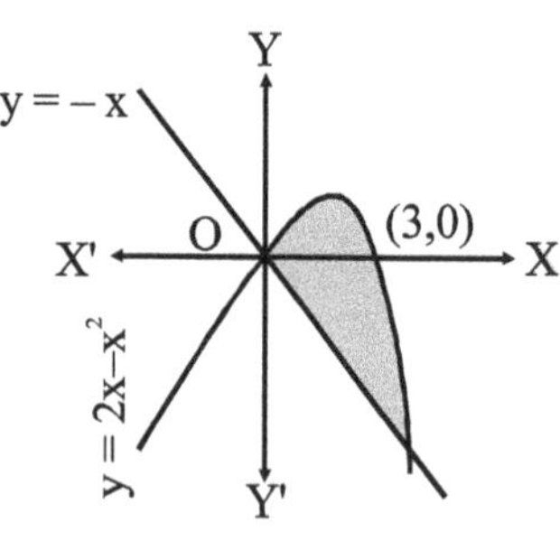

$\therefore$ area under the curve

$= \int_0^3 [(2x-x^2)-(-x)]\,dx$

$= \int_0^3 (3x-x^2)\,dx = \left[\frac{3x^2}{2}-\frac{x^3}{3}\right]_0^3$

$= \frac{27}{2}-\frac{27}{3}=\frac{9}{2}.$

86. (144) Since, origin is circumcentre, then let
$A(r\cos\alpha,\ r\sin\alpha)$, $B(r\cos\beta,\ r\sin\beta)$ and
$C(r\cos\gamma,\ r\sin\gamma)$
Since orthocentre and circumcentre both lies on y-axis, then centroid also lies on y-axis.

$\Rightarrow \cos\alpha+\cos\beta+\cos\gamma=0$

$\Rightarrow \cos^3\alpha+\cos^3\beta+\cos^3\gamma=3\cos\alpha\cdot\cos\beta\cdot\cos\gamma$

Now, $\cos3\alpha+\cos3\beta+\cos3\gamma$

$=4(\cos^3\alpha+\cos^3\beta+\cos^3\gamma)$ $\quad [\because \cos3\theta=4\cos^3\theta-3\cos\theta]$

$\therefore \left(\frac{\cos3\alpha+\cos3\beta+\cos3\gamma}{\cos\alpha\cos\beta\cos\gamma}\right)^2=(12)^2=144.$

87. (28) E_1 = first unit is functioning
E_2 = second unit is functioning
$P(E_1)=0.9, P(E_2)=0.8$

$P(\overline{E}_1)=0.1, P(\overline{E}_2)=0.2$

$P=\frac{0.8\times0.1}{0.1\times0.2+0.9\times0.2+0.1\times0.8}=\frac{8}{28}$

$98P=\frac{8}{28}\times98=28$

88. (11) $3\sin x+4\cos x=k+1$ has a solution, then

$=5\left(\frac{3}{5}\sin x+\frac{4}{5}\cos x\right)=k+1$

$\Rightarrow 5 \sin(x + \alpha) = k + 1$ where $\alpha = \sin^{-1}\dfrac{4}{5}$

$\because \quad -1 \le \sin(x+\alpha) \le 1$

$\Rightarrow \quad -5 \le k + 1 \le 5$

$\Rightarrow \quad -6 \le k \le 4$

$\therefore$ Number of possible integral values of $k = 11$

89. **(5)** Let $z = x + iy$

$|z - 2 - 2i| \le 1$

$|x + iy - 2 - 2i| \le 1$

$|(x-2) + i(y-2)| \le 1$

$(x-2)^2 + (y-2)^2 \le 1$

Now, $|3iz + 6|_{max}$

$= |3i|\left|z + \dfrac{6}{3i}\right| = 3|z - 2i|$

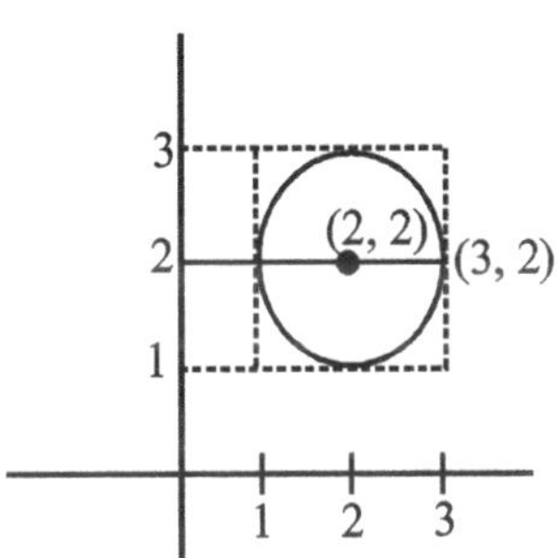

From figure $|3iz + 6|$ is maximum at $3 + 2i$.

$\therefore a + ib = 3 + 2i \Rightarrow a + b = 3 + 2 = 5$

90. **(04)** $f(x) = \displaystyle\int \frac{5x^8 + 7x^6}{x^{14}\left(\frac{1}{x^5} + \frac{1}{x^7} + 2\right)}dx$

$= \displaystyle\int \frac{5x^{-6} + 7x^{-8}}{\left(2 + \frac{1}{x^5} + \frac{1}{x^7}\right)^2}dx$

Put $2 + \dfrac{1}{x^5} + \dfrac{1}{x^7} = t$

$(-5x^{-6} - 7x^{-8})dx = dt$

$\Rightarrow \quad f(t) = \displaystyle\int \frac{-dt}{t^2} = \frac{1}{t} + c$

$\therefore \quad f(x) = \dfrac{x^7}{2x^7 + x^2 + 1} + c \quad \left[\because \; t = 2 + \dfrac{1}{x^5} + \dfrac{1}{x^7}\right]$

$\because \quad f(0) = 0 \Rightarrow c = 0$

$\therefore \quad f(x) = \dfrac{x^7}{2x^7 + x^2 + 1}$

$\Rightarrow \quad f(1) = \dfrac{1}{4} \Rightarrow k = 4$

MOCK TEST-2

PHYSICS

1. (d) Let the scooterist velocity be v. Then
$1000+(10\times 100)=v\times 100$
$$\Rightarrow 100\,v=2000 \Rightarrow v=\frac{2000}{100}=20\text{m/s}$$

2. (b) We have, $F=kx$
where, F, x and k are force, length and constant respectively.
$\therefore\quad 5=kx$ ......(1)
and $7=ky$ ......(2)
Multiplying eq. (2) by 2
$14=2ky$ ......(3)
Subtracting eq. (1) from (3),
$14-5=2ky-kx$ or $9=k(2y-x)$
Hence, required length $=2y-x$

3. (b) In the given equation $[\rho]=[b][x]$;
$\therefore [b]=[\rho]/[x]$. But ρ is mass per unit length and x is distance, therefore $[b]=ML^{-1}/L=ML^{-2}T^0$

4. (d) Point A is at rest w.r.t. motion, hence, v at A = 0. At point B there are two horizontal velocities. Hence, $v_B=2v$.

5. (d) $mg=2TL \Rightarrow \pi r^2 Ldg=2TL \Rightarrow \pi r^2 dg=2T$.
This relation is independent of L.

6. (d) $\omega_{rod}=\omega_{point}=\left(\frac{v_{rel}}{r}\right)$,
v_{rel} represents the velocity of one point w.r.t. other.
$=\frac{3v-v}{r}$ and 'r' being the distance between them.
$=\frac{2v}{r}$

7. (d) Both are diatomic gases and $C_P-C_V=R$ for all gases.

8. (b) More the initial temperature more is the rate of cooling.
Hence, $T_3>T_2>T_1$

or

The rate of cooling decreases with decrease in temperature difference between body and surrounding.

9. (c) $$\frac{1}{C_\infty}=\frac{1}{C_\infty+C}+\frac{2}{C}=\frac{3C+2C_\alpha}{C_\alpha(C_\alpha+C)}$$
$$2C_\infty^2+2CC_\infty-C^2=0\rightarrow C_\infty=C\left(\frac{-1+\sqrt{3}}{2}\right)$$

10. **(b)** R increases with increasing temp:
$V = IR$

Slope of graph $= \frac{I}{V} = \frac{1}{R}$; Slope of T_1 is more i.e $\frac{1}{R_1}$ is more, hence R_1 is less. This concludes that T_1 will be less than T_2 as R_1 is less than R_2.

11. **(c)** $R_{eq} = \frac{R_1 R_2}{R_1 + R_2}$ (Parallel) $= \frac{4 \times 2}{4+2} = \frac{8}{6} = \frac{4}{3}\Omega$

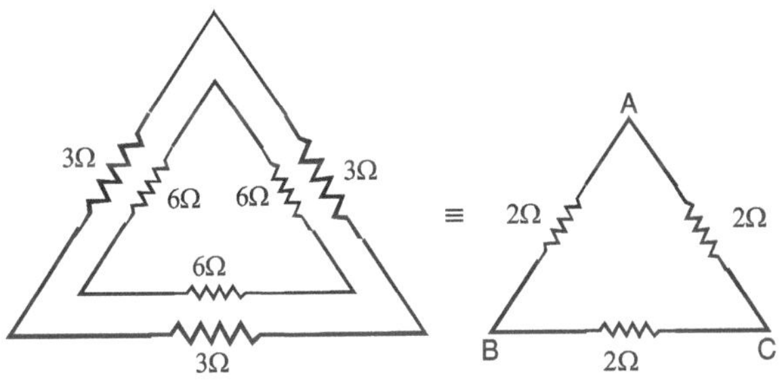

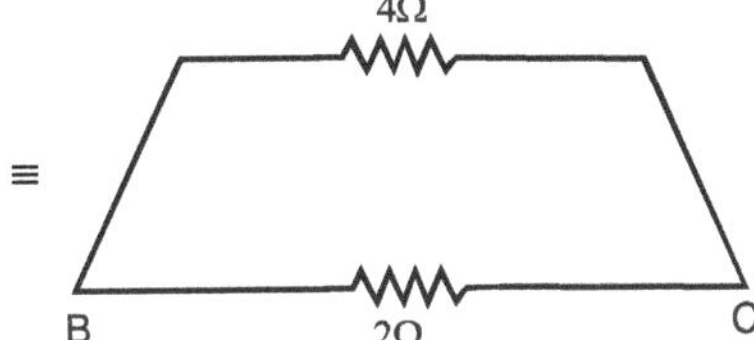

12. **(d)** $i_R = \frac{V_0}{R} = \frac{100}{20} = 5$, $i_L = \frac{V_0}{X_L} = \frac{100}{10} = 10$ and $i_C = \frac{V_0}{X_C} = \frac{100}{20} = 5$

Current, $i = \sqrt{i_R^2 + (i_C - i_L)^2} = \sqrt{5^2 + 5^2} = 5\sqrt{2}$ amp.

13. **(a)** $f_{max} = \mu mg$, $a_{max} = \mu g$.

If A is the amplitude $a_{max} = A\omega^2 = 4\pi^2 AV^2 = \mu g$.

Therefore, $A = \frac{\mu g}{4\pi^2 V^2}$.

14. **(c)** Total time taken to travel distance d is :

$$\frac{d}{2n_1} + \frac{d}{2n_2} = d\left(\frac{n_1 + n_2}{2n_1 n_2}\right) = \frac{d}{n_{eff}}; \quad n_2 = 3n_1 \Rightarrow n_{eff} = \frac{3}{2}n_1$$

15. **(b)** On the screen, we have four amplitudes pair wise coherent.
$(A_1 + A_2) + (A_3 + A_4) \equiv A_{12} + A_{34}$

However, if A_{12} and A_{34} have equal magnitude because of random phase of A_{12} and A_{34}, no fringes will be seen.

16. (a) $mvr = \frac{nh}{2\pi}, \lambda = \frac{h}{mv};$

Using the two concept we get, $mvr = \frac{nh}{2\pi}$ (where n = 1)

$$2\pi r = \frac{1 \times h}{mv} \quad ....(1)$$

$$\lambda = \frac{h}{mv} \quad ....(2)$$

Divide (2) by (1), $\frac{2\pi r}{\lambda} = \frac{h \times mv}{mv \times h} = \frac{1}{1} = 1:1$

17. (d) 1. $\lambda = \frac{0.693}{t^{1/2}}$ 2. $R = \lambda N_t$

Radioactivity at T_1 is $R_1 = \lambda N_1$,
Radioactivity at T_2 is $R_2 = \lambda N_2$
$\therefore$ Number of atoms decayed in time
$(T_1 - T_2) = (N_1 - N_2)$ or $\frac{R_1 - R_2}{\lambda} = \frac{(R_1 - R_2)T}{0.693}$
i.e., $\alpha (R_1 - R_2)T$

18. (d) In the graph given, slope of curve 2 is greater than the slope of curve 1.

$$\left(\frac{\gamma P}{V}\right)_2 > \left(\frac{\gamma P}{V}\right)_1 \Rightarrow \gamma_2 > \gamma_1$$

$$\gamma_{He} > \gamma_{O_2}$$

Since, $\gamma_{monoatomic} > \gamma_{diatomic}$
Hence, curve 2 corresponds to helium and curve 1 corresponds to oxygen.

19. (b) $V_A = \frac{1}{4\pi \epsilon_0}\left[\frac{Q_1}{R} + \frac{Q_2}{\sqrt{2}R}\right];$ $V_B = \frac{1}{4\pi \epsilon_0}\left[\frac{Q_2}{R} + \frac{Q_1}{\sqrt{2}R}\right]$

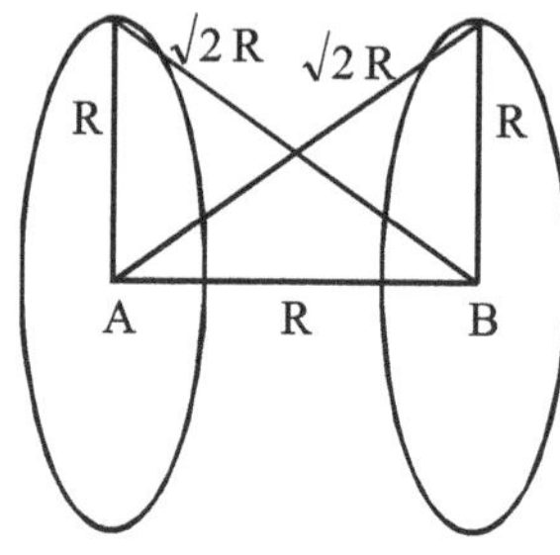

$$V_A - V_B = \frac{1}{4\pi \in_0 R}\left[Q_1 + \frac{Q_2}{\sqrt{2}} - Q_2 - \frac{Q_1}{\sqrt{2}}\right]$$

Work done $= Q \times V = q \times (V_A - V_B)$

$$= \frac{q}{4\pi \in_0 R}\left[Q_1 + \frac{Q_2}{\sqrt{2}} - Q_2 - \frac{Q_1}{\sqrt{2}}\right]$$

$$= \frac{q}{4\pi \in_0 R} \times \frac{1}{\sqrt{2}}\left[\sqrt{2}Q_1 + Q_2 - \sqrt{2}Q_2 - Q_1\right]$$

$$= \frac{q(Q_1 - Q_2)(\sqrt{2} - 1)}{(\sqrt{2}\ 4\pi \in_0 R)}$$

20. **(b)** When there is no change in liquid level in vessel then $\gamma'_{real} = \gamma'_{vessel}$
Change in volume in liquid relative to vessel

$$\Delta V_{app} = V\gamma'_{app}\,\Delta\theta = V(\gamma'_{real} - \gamma'_{vessel})$$

21. **(10)** Here, $m_A = 0.5kg$; $m_B = 1kg$

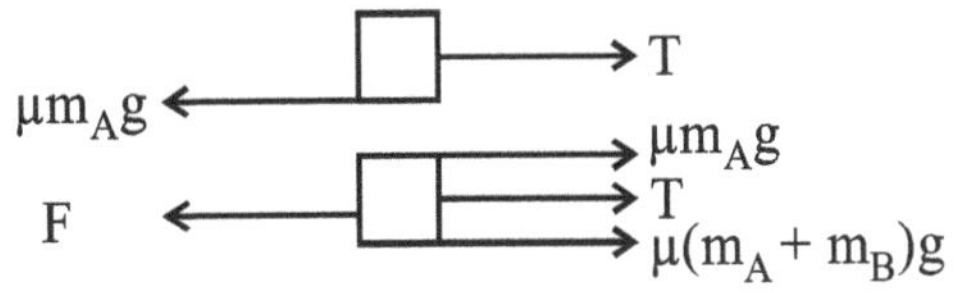

$\mu m_A g \leftarrow$ [A] $\rightarrow T$

$F \leftarrow$ [B] $\rightarrow \mu m_A g$, $\rightarrow T$, $\rightarrow \mu(m_A + m_B)g$

Force on block A

$T = \mu m_A g$ ......(1)

Force acting on block B

$F = T + \mu m_A g + \mu(m_A + m_B)g$ ......(2)

From (1) & (2),

$F = \mu m_A g + \mu m_A g + \mu m_A g + \mu m_B g$

$F = 3\mu m_A g + \mu m_B g = \mu g(3m_A + m_B)$

$= 0.4 \times 10 \times (3 \times 0.5 + 1) = 10N$

22. **(10.6)**

Work done in going from a distance r_1 to a distance r_2 away from centre of the earth, by a body of mass m, is,

$W = GMm\,(1/r_1 - 1/r_2)$,

For our case wc should have

$1/2\,mv^2 = GMm\,[(1/R_e) - (1/10R_e)]$

$= (GMm/R_e) \times (9/10)$

$v = \sqrt{[(2GM/R_e) \times (9/10)]} = \sqrt{(9/10)} \times$ escape velocity

$= \sqrt{(9/10)} \times 11.1$ km/s $= 10.6$ km/s

23. (300)

Here the number of molecules is same. Hence,

$$T_{final} = \frac{T_1 + T_2}{2} = \frac{200+400}{2} = 300\,K$$

24. (83.3) Power of source = EI = 240 × 0.7 = 166

$$\Rightarrow \text{Efficiency} = \frac{140}{166} \Rightarrow \eta = 83.3\%$$

25. (0.5) Magnetic induction at O due to coil Y is given by,

$$B_Y = \frac{\mu_0}{4\pi} \times \frac{2\pi I(2r)^2}{\left[(2r)^2 + d^2\right]^{3/2}} \quad \text{......(1)}$$

Similarly, the magnetic induction at O due to coil X is given by

$$B_X = \frac{\mu_0}{4\pi} \times \frac{2\pi Ir^2}{\left[r^2 + (d/2)^2\right]^{3/2}} \quad \text{......(2)}$$

From eq. (1) & (2) $\frac{B_Y}{B_X} = \frac{1}{2}$

26. (20)

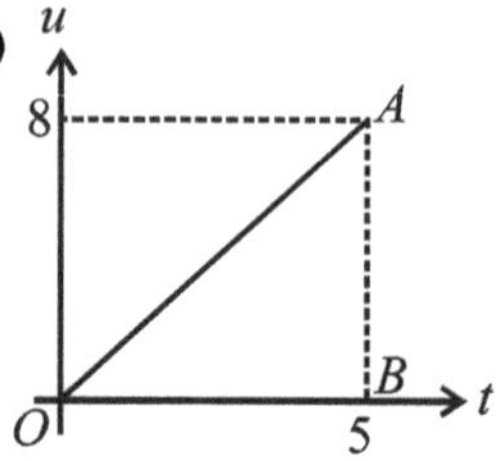

Distance travelled = Area of speed-time graph

$$= \frac{1}{2} \times 5 \times 8 = 20 \text{ m}$$

27. (10) Activity is given by

$A = A_0 e^{-\lambda t}$

Here,

A_0 = initial activity

λ = disintegration constant

According to question,

$$\frac{A_0}{8} = A_0 e^{-\lambda t} \Rightarrow \lambda t = \text{In}8 \Rightarrow \lambda t = 3\text{In}2$$

$$\Rightarrow \text{Half Life} = \frac{\text{In}2}{\lambda} = \frac{t}{3} = \frac{30}{3} = 10 \text{ years}$$

28. **(25)** From law of conservation of linear momentum

$P_i = P_f \Rightarrow m_1 u_1 + m_2 u_2 = m_1 v_1 + m_2 v_2$ ...(i)

$2 \times 4 + 0 = 2 \times 1 + m_2 v_2$

In elastic collision coefficient of restitution, e = 1 and

$$e = \frac{v_2 - v_1}{u_1 - u_2}$$

$\Rightarrow v_2 - v_1 = e(u_1 - u_2)$

$\Rightarrow v_2 - 1 = 1(4 - 0)$ or, $v_2 = 5$

Now from eq. (i)

$8 = 2 + m_2 \times 5$

$$\Rightarrow m_2 = \frac{6}{5}$$

Velocity of centre of mass

$$V_{cm} = \frac{m_1 v_1 + m_2 v_2}{m_1 + v_2} = \frac{2 \times 4 + 0}{2 + \frac{6}{5}} = \frac{25}{10} \text{m/s}$$

29. **(543)** Given,

Accelerating potential, V = 12 kV

Let number of revolution = n

$$= \frac{1}{2} m_p \times \left(\frac{C}{6}\right)^2$$

$$n[2 \times e \times V] = \frac{1}{2} m_P \times v_P^2$$

$$\Rightarrow n\left[2 \times 1.6 \times 10^{-19} \times 12 \times 10^3\right]$$

$$= \frac{1}{2} \times 1.67 \times 10^{-27} \times \left[\frac{3 \times 10^8}{6}\right]^2$$

$$\Rightarrow n\left(38.4\times10^{-16}\right)=0.2207\times10^{-11}$$

$$\Rightarrow n=543.6197$$

30. **(100)** From first law of thermodynamics

$\Delta Q=\Delta U+W$ or, $\Delta Q=W$

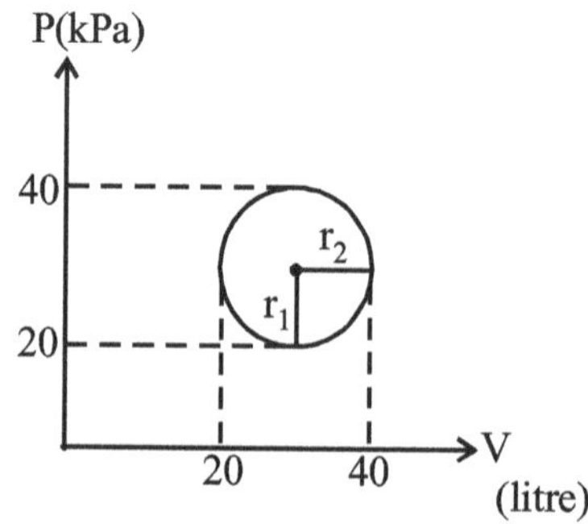

[$\because$ $\Delta U=0$ in cyclic process]

$\Delta Q=W=$ area covered by P – V graph $=\pi r_1 r_2$

or, $\Delta Q=\pi(10\times10^3)\times(10\times10^{-3})=100\pi J$

CHEMISTRY

31. **(b)** The molecule 2,3 - pentadiene does not have any chiral C but at the same time it does not have any mirror plane which makes the molecule chiral.

32. **(a)** In such a case there is no change in velocity

$$u=\sqrt{(3RT/M)}=\sqrt{(3PV/M)}$$

The increase in temperature = 4 times &

also the increase in pressure = 4 times. Both of these reinforce each other

33. **(b)** (cyclohexenone, O) $+(CH_3)_2CHOH \xrightarrow[{[(CH_3)_2CHO]_3Al}]{}$

(cyclohexenol, HO) $+(CH_3)_2C=O$

34. **(d)** In N_2^+, there is one unpaired electron hence it is paramagnetic.

35. **(d)** In Ag_2O (O.N. of Ag +1) in Ag the O.N. is O. There is gain of electrons, hence H_2O_2 is acting as reducing agent.

36. **(c)** We know that

$$H_2C\underset{O}{-}CH_2 + RMgX \longrightarrow \underset{OMgX}{CH_2} - \underset{R}{CH_2} \xrightarrow[-Mg(OH)X]{H_2O} \underset{OH}{CH_2} - \underset{R}{CH_2}$$

37. (c) (I) $C_6H_6 \xrightarrow[AlCl_3]{CO,\ HCl} C_6H_5CHO$ (Gatterman Koch Reaction)

(II) $C_6H_5C \equiv N \xrightarrow[HCl]{SnCl_2 + H_3O^+} C_6H_5CHO$ (Stephen's Reduction)

(III) $C_6H_5COCl \xrightarrow[Quinoline,\ S]{H_2,\ Pd\text{-}BaSO_4} C_6H_5CHO$ (Rosenmund Reduction)

38. (c) Sucrose is an example of disaccharide & non reducing sugar because it doesnot contain free hemiacetal linkage.
It involves glycoside linkage between C_1 of α-D-glucose C_2 of β-D-fructose.

39. (d) Tertiary halides on treatment with base, such as sodium methoxide, readily undergo elimination resulting in the formation of alkenes. (Williamson's Synthesis)

$$CH_3 - \underset{CH_3}{\overset{CH_3}{C}} - Cl + N\overset{+}{a}\overset{-}{O}\,CH_2CH_3 \xrightarrow{E2} CH_3 - \underset{CH_3}{C} = CH_2$$

40. (b) $s_0 = \sqrt{K_{sp}}; s_1 = K_{sp}/0.02\ M;\ s_2 = K_{sp}/0.01\ M;\ s_3 = K_{sp}/0.05\ M$

Obviously $s_0 > s_2 > s_1 > s_3$

41. (b) $C_6H_5NH_2 + NaNO_2 + HCl \xrightarrow{0°C} C_6H_5N = NCl$

$$C_6H_5N_2Cl + \text{(2-naphthol, OH)} \longrightarrow$$

OH

N=N

Red dye

42. (c) Multiple bonds formation tendency with carbon and nitrogen decreases from sulphur to tellurium.
CS_2 (S = C = S) is moderately stable,
CSe_2 (Se = C = Se) decomposes readily whereas,
CTe_2 (Te = C = Te) does not exist

43. (d) Liquation is the principle based on difference in melting points.

44. (c) In NO_2^+ odd (unpaired) electron is removed. In peroxides (O_2^{2-}) no unpaired electrons are persent as the antibonding pi M.O.'s acquired one more electron each for pairing. AlO_2^- containing Al^{3+} ($2s^2p^6$) configuration and 2 oxides (O^{2-}) ions each of which does not contain unpaired electron. Superoxide O_2^- has one unpaired electron in pi antibonding M.O.

45. (a) The two solutions are isotonic hence there will be no movement of H_2O.

46. (b) Hydrated $CoCl_2 . 6H_2O$ is pink coloured and contains octahedral $[Co(H_2O)_6]^{2+}$ ions. If this is partially dehydrated by heating, then blue coloured tetrahedral ions $[Co(H_2O)_4]^{2+}$ are formed.

$$\underset{\text{pink}}{[Co(H_2O)_6]^{2+}} \rightleftharpoons \underset{\text{blue}}{[Co(H_2O)_4]^{2+}} + 2H_2O$$

47. (c) In $(NH_4)_2 [(TiCl_6)]$, Ti^{4+} ($3d^0 4s^0$) has no unpaired electrons.
In $K_2Cr_2O_7$, Cr^{6+} ($3p^6 d^0$) has no unpaired electrons.
In $CoSO_4$, Co^{2+} (d^7) has unpaired electrons in *d*-orbitals, so it is both paramagnetic and coloured.
In $K_3[Cu(CN)_4]$, Cu^+ ($3d^{10}$), has no unpaired electron.

48. (b) $\log K = \log A - \frac{E_a}{2.303R}\frac{1}{T}$ (Arrhenius equation)

Plot of log K Vs 1/T gives a straight line with slope $-E_a/2.303R$

49. (b)
- Li does not form peroxide or superoxide due to it small size.
- Solubility of carbonates and biocarbonates increases on moving down the group.
- The increasing order of size of hydrated ions of alkali metals is $Li^+ > Na^+ > K^+ > Rb^+ > Cs^+$
- Cesium used in photoelectric cells due to its low I.E. Hence statements (b) is the only correct choice.

50. **(d)** Cell reaction $Zn + Cu^{++} \longrightarrow Zn^{++} + Cu$

$E_1 = E^\circ_{cell} - \frac{0.059}{2}\log\frac{0.01}{1.0}$ $\therefore E_1 = (E^\circ_{cell} + 0.059)\,V$

$E_2 = E^\circ_{cell} - \frac{0.059}{2}\log\frac{1.0}{0.01}$

$\therefore E_2 = (E^\circ_{cell} - 0.059)\,V$. Thus, $E_1 > E_2$.

51. **(69.60)** $\frac{P^\circ - P_S}{P^\circ} = \frac{w/m}{W/M}$; (640–600)/640 = wM/mW

$40/640 = 2.175 \times 78/m \times 39.08$

$m = 2.175 \times 78 \times 640 / 39.08 \times 40 = 69.458 \cong 69.60$

52. **(0.17)** $\Delta x = (h/4\pi) \times m \times \Delta v$

$$= \frac{6.6 \times 10^{-27} \times 100}{4 \times 3.14 \times 9.1 \times 10^{-28} \times 3 \times 10^4 \times 0.011} = 0.175\text{ cm}$$

53. **(3.8)** $K = \frac{[H_3O^+][HCO_3^-]}{[CO_2][H_2O]^2}$ As pH = 6.0 $[H_3O]^+ = 10^{-6}$

$K = \frac{[H_3O^+][HCO_3^-]}{[CO_2][H_2O]^2}$ (H_2O is in excess, therefore its conc. remains constant)

$$\frac{[HCO_3^-]}{[CO_2]} = \frac{K}{[H_3O^+]} = \frac{3.8 \times 10^{-6}}{10^{-6}} = 3.8$$

54. **(136800)** ν for hydrogen like species

$= \nu_H \times Z^2 = 15200 \times 3^2 = 15200 \times 9 = 136800\text{ cm}^{-1}$

55. **(32.06)** Calorific value of butane $= \frac{\Delta H_c}{\text{mol. wt.}} = \frac{2658}{58} = 45.8$ kJ/g

Cylinder consist 14 Kg of butane means 14000 g of butane

$\therefore$ 1g gives = 45.8 kJ/g

$\therefore$ 14000 g gives = $14000 \times 45.8 = 641200$ kJ

Family need 20,000 kJ/day

So gas full fill the requirement for $\frac{641200}{20,000} = 32.06$ days

56. **(271)** molality $= \frac{\left(\frac{40}{180}\right)\text{mol}}{0.2\text{Kg}} = \left(\frac{10}{9}\right)$ molal

$$\Rightarrow \Delta T_f = T_f - T_f' = 1.86 \times \frac{10}{9}$$

$$\Rightarrow T_f' = 273.15 - 1.86 \times \frac{10}{9}$$

$= 271.08\text{ K} \simeq 271\text{K}$ (nearest-integer)

57. **(3)**

$H_2N{-}C(=O){-}NH{-}N{=}C(CH_3)_2$

Semicarbazone molecule of acetone

58. **(40)** Mass of organic compound $= 0.2\text{g}$
Mass of AgBr $= 0.188\text{g}$
Molar mass of AgBr $= 108 + 80 = 188$

Mass of Br $= \frac{80}{188} \times 0.188 = 0.08\text{g}$

$$\text{Br}\% = \frac{0.188}{0.2} \times 100 = 40$$

59. **(5)** $C_6H_5NO_2 \longrightarrow C_6H_5NH_2$ Reagents used can be

(i) $Sn + HCl$ (ii) $Fe + HCl$
(iii) $Zn + HCl$ (iv) $H_2 - Pd$
(v) H_2 (Raney Ni)

60. **(6)** Anode mud contains Sb, Se, Te, Ag, Au and Pt.

MATHEMATICS

61. **(b)** $(a^2+b^2+c^2)p^2-2(ab+bc+cd)p$
$+b^2+c^2+d^2\le 0$

$\Rightarrow(a^2p^2-2abp+b^2)+(b^2p^2-2bcp+c^2)$
$+(c^2p^2-2cdp+d^2)\le 0$

$\Rightarrow(ap-b)^2+(bp-c)^2+(cp-d)^2\le 0$

$\Rightarrow ap-b=0,\ bp-c=0\ \&\ cp-d=0$

$\Rightarrow\frac{b}{a}=\frac{c}{b}=\frac{d}{c}\Rightarrow$ a, b, c and d are in G.P

Also ad = bc

62. **(c)**

(a) $\log(a+2b)=\frac{1}{2}\log(a+2b)^2$

$=\frac{1}{2}\log(a^2+4b^2+4ab)$

$=\frac{1}{2}\log(12ab+4ab)$

$=\frac{1}{2}\log(2^4.ab)$

$=\frac{1}{2}(4\log 2+\log a+\log b)$

(b) Let $\frac{\log x}{b-c}=\frac{\log y}{c-a}=\frac{\log z}{a-b}=k$

$\Rightarrow\log x=k(b-c),\ \log y=k(c-a),$
$\log z=k(a-b)$

$\therefore x^a.y^b.z^c=p^{k[a(b-c))+b(c-a)+c(a-b)]}$

$=p^{k(0)}=1$

where p is any arbitrary base of the log.

(c) Given expression

$=\log_{xyz}xy+\log_{xyz}yz+\log_{xyz}zx$

$=\log_{xyz}(xy.yz.zx)\ =\log_{xyz}(x^2.y^2.z^2)$

$=2\log_{xyz}(xyz)=2\times 1=2$

63. **(b)** $\alpha+\beta+\gamma=\frac{\pi}{2} \Rightarrow \alpha+\gamma=\frac{\pi}{2}-\beta.$

so that $\cot(\alpha+\gamma)= \cot\left(\frac{\pi}{2}-\beta\right)$

$$\Rightarrow \frac{\cot\alpha\cot\gamma-1}{\cot\alpha+\cot\gamma}=\frac{1}{\cot\beta}$$

$\Rightarrow \cot\alpha\cot\gamma-1=2 \Rightarrow \cot\alpha\cot\gamma=3.$

(since $\cot\alpha+\cot\gamma=2\cot\beta$)

64. **(c)** We know, $1+\omega+\omega^2+...+\omega^{n-1}=\frac{1-\omega^n}{1-\omega}$

But $\omega^n=\cos\left(\frac{n\pi}{n}\right)+i\sin\left(\frac{n\pi}{n}\right)$

$$=\cos\pi+i\sin\pi=-1$$

and $1-\omega=2\sin^2\frac{\pi}{2n}-2i\sin\frac{\pi}{2n}\cos\frac{\pi}{2n}$

$$=-2i\sin\left(\frac{\pi}{2n}\right)\left[\cos\frac{\pi}{2n}+i\sin\frac{\pi}{2n}\right]$$

Thus, $1+\omega+\omega^2+...+\omega^{n-1}$

$$=\frac{2}{-2i\sin\left(\frac{\pi}{2n}\right)\left[\cos\frac{\pi}{2n}+i\sin\frac{\pi}{2n}\right]}=\frac{i\left(\frac{\cos\pi}{2n}-i\sin\frac{\pi}{2n}\right)}{\sin\frac{\pi}{2n}}$$

$$=\frac{i\cos\frac{\pi}{2n}}{\sin\frac{\pi}{2n}}-i^2\frac{\sin\frac{\pi}{2n}}{\sin\frac{\pi}{2n}}=1+i\cot(\pi/2n)$$

65. **(a)** $C_1(1,0); C_2(0,-2)$

$r_1=\sqrt{1+15}=4,\ \ r_2=\sqrt{4-3}=1$

$C_1C_2=\sqrt{1+4}=\sqrt{5}$

$r_1-r_2=3 \Rightarrow C_1C_2<r_1-r_2$

Hence, C_2 lies inside C_1.

66. **(d)**

(a) We have $|AB| = |A||B|$

Also for a square matrix of order 3, $|kA| = k^3|A|$ because each element of the matrix A is multiplied by k and hence in this case we will have k^3 common

$\therefore\ |3AB| = 3^3|A||B| = 27(-1)(3) = -81$

(b) Since A is invertible, therefore A^{-1} exists and

$AA^{-1} = I \Rightarrow \det(AA^{-1}) = \det(I)$

$\Rightarrow \det(A)\det(A^{-1}) = 1$

$\Rightarrow \det(A^{-1}) = \dfrac{1}{\det(A)}$

(c) $(A+B)^2 = (A+B)(A+B)$

$= A^2 + AB + BA + B^2$

$= A^2 + 2AB + B^2$ if $AB = BA$.

67. **(b)** For trivial solution,

$$\begin{vmatrix} 1 & -2 & 1 \\ 2 & -1 & 3 \\ \lambda & 1 & -1 \end{vmatrix} \neq 0 \Rightarrow -5\lambda - 4 \neq 0 \text{ or } \lambda \neq -\frac{4}{5}$$

68. **(d)** $f(x) = |x-1| = \begin{cases} -x+1, & x<1 \\ x-1, & x \geq 1 \end{cases}$

Consider $f(x^2) = (f(x))^2$

If it is true it should be $\forall\ x$

$\therefore$ Put $x = 2$

LHS $= f(2^2) = |4-1| = 3$

RHS $= (f(2))^2 = 1$

$\therefore$ (a) is not correct

Consider $f(x+y) = f(x) + f(y)$

Put $x = 2, y = 5$ we get

$f(7) = 6; f(2) + f(5) = 1 + 4 = 5$

$\therefore$ (b) is not correct

Consider $f(|x|) = |f(x)|$

Put $x = -5$ then $f(|-5|) = f(5) = 4$

$|f(-5)| = |-5-1| = 6$

$\therefore$ (c) is not correct.

Hence (d) is the correct alternative.

69. **(d)** Let $a = \tan\theta$ and $b = \tan\phi$

$$\therefore \sin^{-1}\left[\frac{2a}{1+a^2}\right] = \sin^{-1}\left[\frac{2\tan\theta}{1+\tan^2\theta}\right]$$

$$= \sin^{-1}[\sin 2\theta] = 2\theta = 2\tan^{-1} a$$

and $\sin^{-1}\left[\frac{2b}{1+b^2}\right] = \sin^{-1}\left[\frac{2\tan\phi}{1+\tan^2\phi}\right]$

$$= \sin^{-1}[\sin 2\phi] = 2\phi = 2\tan^{-1} b$$

Thus, $\sin^{-1}\left[\frac{2a}{1+a^2}\right] = 2\tan^{-1} a$ and

$$\sin^{-1}\left[\frac{2b}{1+b^2}\right] = 2\tan^{-1} b$$

$$\therefore \quad 2\tan^{-1}x = \sin^{-1}\left[\frac{2a}{1+a^2}\right] + \sin^{-1}\left[\frac{2b}{1+b^2}\right]$$

$$= 2\tan^{-1} a + 2\tan^{-1} b$$

$$\Rightarrow \quad \tan^{-1} x = \tan^{-1}a + \tan^{-1}b$$

$$\tan^{-1} x = \tan^{-1}\frac{a+b}{1-ab}$$

$$\therefore \quad x = \frac{a+b}{1-ab}$$

70. **(a)** We have,

$$AB = \begin{bmatrix} \cos^2\theta & \cos\theta\sin\theta \\ \cos\theta\sin\theta & \sin^2\theta \end{bmatrix}\begin{bmatrix} \cos^2\phi & \cos\phi\sin\phi \\ \cos\phi\sin\phi & \sin^2\phi \end{bmatrix}$$

$$= \begin{bmatrix} \cos^2\theta\cos^2\phi + \cos\theta\cos\phi\sin\theta\sin\phi & \cos^2\theta\cos\phi\sin\phi + \cos\theta\sin\theta\sin^2\phi \\ \cos\theta\sin\theta\cos^2\phi + \sin^2\theta\cos\phi\sin\phi & \cos\theta\cos\phi\sin\theta\sin\phi + \sin^2\theta\sin^2\phi \end{bmatrix}$$

$$= \cos(\theta - \phi) \begin{bmatrix} \cos\theta\cos\phi & \cos\theta\sin\phi \\ \sin\theta\cos\phi & \sin\theta\sin\phi \end{bmatrix}$$

Since $AB = 0$, $\therefore \cos(\theta - \phi) = 0$

$\therefore (\theta - \phi)$ is an odd multiple of $\dfrac{\pi}{2}$

71. **(c)** Since $|x|$ is not diff. at $x = 0$

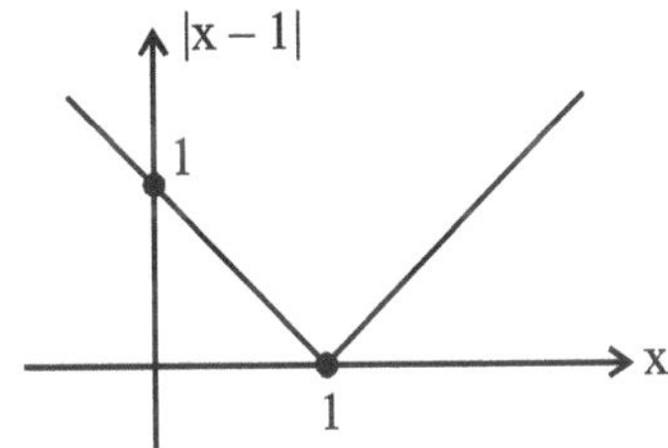

$\Rightarrow |x-1|$ is not diff at $x = 1$.

$x^n |x|$ in n times diff. at $x = 0$

$\Rightarrow (x-1)^2 |x-1|$ is twice diff. at $x = 1$
but not thrice diff. at $x = 1$

72. **(c)** $f(x) = \dfrac{1}{x-1}$ is discontinuous at $x = 1$.

$(gof)(x) = g(f(x)) = -\dfrac{(x-1)^2}{(2x-1)(x-2)}$, which is not defined at $x = 1/2, 2$.

Hence the set of points where (gof) (x) is discontinuous is $\{1/2, 1, 2\}$

73. **(a)** $\sum_{r=0}^{m} {}^{n+r}C_n = \sum_{r=0}^{m} {}^{n+r}C_r \quad (\because {}^{n+r}C_n = {}^{n+r}C_{n+r-n})$
$= {}^nC_0 + {}^{n+1}C_1 + {}^{n+2}C_2 + {}^{n+3}C_3 + ... + {}^{n+m}C_m$
Using, ${}^nC_0 = 1 = {}^{n+1}C_1$
$= ({}^{n+1}C_0 + {}^{n+1}C_1) + {}^{n+2}C_2 + {}^{n+3}C_3 + ... + {}^{n+m}C_m$
Using, ${}^nC_r + {}^nC_{r+1} = {}^{n+1}C_{r+1}$
$= ({}^{n+2}C_1 + {}^{n+2}C_2) + {}^{n+3}C_3 + ... + {}^{n+m}C_m$
Using this again and again, we are left with
$= {}^{n+m}C_{m-1} + {}^{n+m}C_m$
$= {}^{n+m+1}C_m = {}^{n+m+1}C_{n+1}$

74. **(b)** As $x \to \frac{1}{3}$; $\{x+1\} \to \{1+1/3\} \to 1/3$

Similarly $\{x+2\} \to \frac{1}{3}$ as $x \to \frac{1}{3}$

$\Rightarrow \lim_{x \to 1/3} f(x) = \lim_{x \to 1/3} \frac{x-1/3}{x-1/3} = 1$

75. **(b)** Squaring both sides we get highest order as 2.

76. **(d)** $I = \int_{-\pi/4}^{\pi/4} (\underbrace{x|x|}_{\text{odd f}} + \underbrace{\sin^3 x}_{\text{odd f}} + \underbrace{x\tan^2 x}_{\text{odd f}} + 1)\, dx$

$I = \int_{-\pi/4}^{\pi/4} dx = \frac{\pi}{2}$ $\quad\left[\because \int_{-a}^{a} f(x)dx = 0, \text{ as } f(x) \text{ is an odd function}\right]$

77. **(b)** $(1-x-2x^2)^6 = (1+x)^6(1-2x)^6$

$= 1 + a_1x + a_2x^2 + \ldots\ldots\ldots + a_{12}x^{12}$

Putting $x = 1/2$, we have $0 = 1 + a_1/2 + a_2/2^2 + a_3/2^3 + a_4/2^4 + \ldots\ldots\ldots + a_{12}/2^{12}$ .....(1)

Putting $x = -1/2$, we have

$1 = 1 - a_1/2 + a_2/2^2 - a_3/2^3 + a_4/2^4 - \ldots\ldots + a_{12}/2^{12}$....(2)

Adding (1) and (2), we have

$1 = 2(1 + a_2/2^2 + a_4/2^4 + \ldots\ldots + a_{12}/2^{12})$

$\Rightarrow a_2/2^2 + a_4/2^4 + a_6/2^6 \ldots\ldots + a_{12}/2^{12} = -1/2$

78. **(b)** $y^2 = 4x$ & $\frac{x^2}{8} + \frac{y^2}{2} = 1$

Equation of tangent to above curves are respectively.

$y^2 = mx + \frac{1}{m}$ and $y = mx + \sqrt{8m^2+2}$

Comparing $\frac{1}{m} = \sqrt{8m^2+2}$

$\Rightarrow m^2(8m^2+2) = 1$

seeing the options

$m = \pm\frac{1}{2}$ satisfy the equation

$\Rightarrow y = \pm\frac{1}{2}x \pm 2 \Rightarrow 2y = \pm x \pm 4$

i.e. $2y = x + 4$ & $x + 2y + 4 = 0$

79. (b) Let the point be (x_1, y_1).

Therefore $y_1 = (x_1 - 3)^2$ ...(i)

$\therefore$ Now slope of the tangent at (x_1, y_1) is $2(x_1 - 3)$, but it is equal to 1.

Therefore, $2(x_1 - 3) = 1 \Rightarrow x_1 = \frac{7}{2}$

$y_1 = \left(\frac{7}{2} - 3\right)^2 = \frac{1}{4}$.

Hence the point is $\left(\frac{7}{2}, \frac{1}{4}\right)$.

80. (c) $x = \tan A$, $y = \tan B$, $-z = \tan C$. Then $(x + y - z) = -xyz$.

$\Rightarrow \tan A + \tan B + \tan C = \tan A \tan B \tan C$

$\Rightarrow A + B + C = \pi \quad \Rightarrow 2A + 2B = 2\pi - 2C$

$\Rightarrow \tan(2A + 2B) = \tan(2\pi - 2C) = -\tan 2C$

$\Rightarrow \tan 2A + \tan 2B + \tan 2C = \tan 2A . \tan 2B . \tan 2C$

$$\Rightarrow \frac{2\tan A}{1-\tan^2 A} + \frac{2\tan B}{1-\tan^2 B} + \frac{2\tan C}{1-\tan^2 C}$$

$$= \frac{2\tan A}{1-\tan^2 A} . \frac{2\tan B}{1-\tan^2 B} . \frac{2\tan C}{1-\tan^2 C}$$

Put the value of $\tan A$, $\tan B$, $\tan C$, we get

$$\Rightarrow \frac{2x}{1-x^2} + \frac{2y}{1-y^2} - \frac{2z}{1-z^2}$$

$$= -\frac{8xyz}{(1-x^2)(1-y^2)(1-z^2)}$$

81. (12.25) $4^2 + 4p + 12 = 0 \Rightarrow p = -7$

The equation $x^2 + px + q = 0$ has equal roots then $D = 0$.

or $\quad p^2 = 4q \Rightarrow q = \frac{49}{4}$

82. (0.125)

$\cos 36°\cos 42°\cos 78°$

$= \cos 36°\cos(60° - 18°)\cos(60° + 18°)$

$$= \frac{\sqrt{5}+1}{4}\left(\cos^2 60° - \sin^2 18°\right)$$

$$= \left(\frac{\sqrt{5}+1}{4}\right)\left[\frac{1}{4} - \left(\frac{\sqrt{5}-1}{4}\right)^2\right]$$

$$= \left(\frac{\sqrt{5}+1}{4}\right)\frac{1}{4} - \left(\frac{\sqrt{5}+1}{4}\right)\left(\frac{5+1-2\sqrt{5}}{16}\right)$$

$$= \left(\frac{\sqrt{5}+1}{16}\right) - \frac{(\sqrt{5}+1)(\sqrt{5}-1)^2}{64} = \frac{\sqrt{5}+1}{16}\left[1 - \frac{(\sqrt{5}-1)^2}{4}\right]$$

$$= \frac{\sqrt{5}+1}{16}\left[\frac{4-6+2\sqrt{5}}{4}\right] = \frac{1}{8}$$

83. (0.2) The given expression is equal to

$\cos(\cos^{-1}x + \sin^{-1}x + \sin^{-1}x)$

$$= \cos\left(\frac{\pi}{2} + \sin^{-1}x\right) = -\sin(\sin^{-1}x) = -x = -\frac{1}{5}$$

[Using $\cos^{-1}x + \sin^{-1}x = \frac{\pi}{2}$]

84. (4) Let $\tan\theta_1, \tan\theta_2$ be the roots of the equation $2\tan^2\theta - 4\tan\theta + 1 = 0$. Thus $\tan\theta_1 + \tan\theta_2 = 4/2 = 2$; $\tan\theta_1\tan\theta_2 = 1/2$.
Now $\tan(\theta_1 + \theta_2) = [(\tan\theta_1 + \tan\theta_2)/(1 - \tan\theta_1\tan\theta_2)]$
$= 2/[1 - (1/2)] = 4$.

85. (2.25) Given, in ΔABC $\begin{vmatrix} 1 & a & b \\ 1 & c & a \\ 1 & b & c \end{vmatrix} = 0$

$\Rightarrow\ 1(c^2 - ab) - a(c - a) + b(b - c) = 0$
$\Rightarrow\ a^2 + b^2 + c^2 - ab - bc - ca = 0$
$\Rightarrow\ 2a^2 + 2b^2 + 2c^2 - 2ab - 2bc - 2ca = 0$
$\Rightarrow\ (a^2 + b^2 - 2ab) + (b^2 + c^2 - 2bc) + (c^2 + a^2 - 2ca) = 0$

$\Rightarrow \quad (a-b)^2+(b-c)^2+(c-a)^2=0$

Here, sum of squares of three members can be zero if and only if a = b = c

$\Rightarrow \quad \Delta ABC$ is equilateral.

$\Rightarrow \angle A = \angle B = \angle C = 60°$

$\therefore \ \sin^2 A + \sin^2 B + \sin^2 C$

$= (\sin^2 60° + \sin^2 60° + \sin^2 60°)$

$= 3 \times \left(\frac{\sqrt{3}}{2}\right)^2 = \frac{9}{4}$

86. **(6)** $\frac{(2i)^n}{(1-i)^{n-2}} = \frac{(2i)^n}{(-2i)^{\frac{n-2}{2}}} = \frac{(2i)^{\frac{n+2}{2}}}{(-i)^{\frac{n-2}{2}}} = \frac{2^{\frac{n+2}{2}} \cdot i^{\frac{n+2}{2}}}{(-i)^{\frac{n-2}{2}}}$

in positive integer, when n = 2, 4, 6 .....

(Here n = 2, 4 be rejected)

So, least positive integer n = 6.

87. **(136)** ${}^1P_1 + 2.\,{}^2P_2 + 3.\,{}^3P_3 + ... + 15\,.\,{}^{15}P_{15}$

$= 1! + 2.2! + 3.3! + ... 15 \times 15!$

$= 1! + (3!\,.\,2!) + ... + (16!\ 15!)$

$\sum_{r=1}^{15}(r+1)! - (r)! = 16! - 1 = {}^{16}P_{16} - 1 \Rightarrow q = r = 16, s = 1$

${}^{q+8}C_{???} = {}^{17}C_{13} = \frac{17 \times 16}{2} = 136$

88. **(6)** $I = \int \frac{x^2-1}{(x^4+3x^2+1)\tan^{-1}\left(\frac{x^2+1}{x}\right)}dx + \int \frac{1}{x^4+3x^2+1}dx$

$I = I_1 + I_2$ ...(i)

For I_1, let $\tan^{-1}\frac{x^2+1}{x} = t$, and $\frac{x^2-1}{x^4+3x^2+1}dx = dt$

$I_1 = \int \frac{1}{t}dt = \log t = \log\left|\tan^{-1}\left(\frac{x^2+1}{x}\right)\right| + C_1$ ...(ii)

$I_2 = \frac{1}{2}\int \frac{(x^2+1)-(x^2-1)}{x^4+3x^2+1}$

$$=\frac{1}{2}\int\frac{x^2+1}{x^4+3x^2+1}-\frac{1}{2}\int\frac{x^2-1}{x^4+3x^2+1}$$

Divide Nr and Dr by x^2, we get

$$=\frac{1}{2}\int\frac{1+\frac{1}{x^2}}{\left(x-\frac{1}{x}\right)^2+5}-\frac{1}{2}\int\frac{1-\frac{1}{x^2}}{\left(x+\frac{1}{x}\right)^2+1}$$

$$=\frac{1}{2\sqrt{5}}\tan^{-1}\left(\frac{x^2-1}{\sqrt{5}x}\right)-\frac{1}{2}\tan^{-1}\left(\frac{x^2+1}{x}\right) \quad ...(iii)$$

$$\alpha=1,\ \beta=\frac{1}{2\sqrt{5}},\ \gamma=\frac{1}{\sqrt{5}},\ \delta=\frac{-1}{2}$$

So, $10(\alpha+\beta\gamma+\delta)=10\left(1+\frac{1}{10}-\frac{1}{2}\right)=6$

89. **(90)** Since, $\vec{a}$ is perpendicular to $\vec{b}$

$\Rightarrow \vec{a}.\vec{b}=0$

$\Rightarrow 1+15+\alpha\beta=0 \Rightarrow \alpha\beta=-16 \quad ...(i)$

Also,

$\left|\vec{b}\times\vec{c}\right|^2=75 \Rightarrow \left(10+\beta^2\right)14-(5-3\beta)^2=75$

$\Rightarrow 5\beta^2+30\beta+40=0$

$\Rightarrow \beta=-4,-2$

Then, from (i)

$\alpha=4,8$

$\Rightarrow |\vec{a}|^2_{max}=\left(26+\alpha^2\right)_{max}=90$

90. **(11)** $3\sin x+4\cos x=k+1$ has a solution, then

$$=5\left(\frac{3}{5}\sin x+\frac{4}{5}\cos x\right)=k+1$$

$\Rightarrow 5\sin(x+\alpha)=k+1$ where $\alpha=\sin^{-1}\frac{4}{5}$

$\because \quad -1\le\sin(x+\alpha)\le 1$

$\Rightarrow \quad -5\le k+1\le 5$

$\Rightarrow \quad -6\le k\le 4$

$\therefore$ Number of possible integral values of $k=11$

MOCK TEST-3

PHYSICS

1. (c) Resolving power of eye $= \lambda / a$

$$= \frac{500 \times 10^{-9}}{5 \times 10^{-3}} = 10^{-4} \text{ radians}$$

Now, arc = angle × radius

$$= 10^{-4} \times (500 \times 10^{3}) \text{m} = 50 \text{m}$$

2. (b) Frequency does'nt depend on medium

$$\frac{\mu_1}{\mu_2} = \frac{V_2}{V_1} = \frac{\lambda_2 f}{\lambda_1 f}, \quad \text{or} \quad \mu_2 \lambda_2 = \lambda_1 \mu_1$$

$\mu_2 = 3680$ Å

3. (a) Total momentum will be conserved.
Initial momentum = Final momentum

$$M.v = m \times 0 + (M - m)v'$$

$$\therefore v' = \frac{Mv}{M - m}$$

4. (c) Force, $F = \frac{1}{4\pi\varepsilon_0} \frac{q_1 q_2}{r^2}$

$$\Rightarrow \varepsilon_0 = \frac{q_1 . q_2}{4\pi F r^2}$$

So dimension of ε_0

$$= \frac{[AT]^2}{[MLT^{-2}][L^2]} = [M^{-1}L^{-3}T^4A^2]$$

5. (c) Heat radiated by black body

$$E = \sigma A T^4 \Rightarrow E \, \alpha \, T^4$$

$$\text{or } \frac{E_1}{E_2} = \frac{{T_1}^4}{{T_2}^4}$$

$$\text{or } \frac{20}{E_2} = \left(\frac{500}{1000}\right)^4 = \left(\frac{1}{2}\right)^4 = \frac{1}{16}$$

$$\Rightarrow E_2 = 16 \times 20 \text{ cal m}^{-2} \text{s}^{-1}$$
$$= 320 \text{ cal m}^{-2} \text{s}^{-1}$$

6. (c) Velocity of wave $v = n\lambda$

where n = frequency of wave $\Rightarrow n = \frac{v}{\lambda}$

$$n_1 = \frac{v_1}{\lambda_1} = \frac{396}{99 \times 10^{-2}} = 400 \text{ Hz}$$

$$n_2 = \frac{v_2}{\lambda_2} = \frac{396}{100 \times 10^{-2}} = 396\,\text{Hz}$$

no. of beats $= n_1 - n_2 = 4$

7. (a) Terminal velocity attained by falling object

$$V_t = \frac{3r^2(d-\rho)g}{a\eta}$$

thus, $V_t \alpha r^2$

8. (d) Young's modulus, $Y = \frac{\text{Stress}}{\text{Strain}}$

or stress = Y. strain

or strain = Stress / Y

or $\Delta l = \frac{Fl}{YA}$; $\frac{\Delta l_1}{\Delta l_2} = \frac{F_1 l_1}{A_1 Y_1} \cdot \frac{A_2 Y_2}{F_1 l_1}$

$l_1 = l_2$ & $Y_1 = Y_2$, $F_1 = F_2$

$$\Rightarrow \frac{\Delta l_1}{\Delta l_2} = \frac{\pi r_2{}^2}{\pi r_1{}^2} = \frac{4r^2}{r^2} = 4$$

9. (b) $E = mc^2 = (2 \times 1.6 \times 10^{-27}) \times (3 \times 10^8)^2$

$= 28.8 \times 10^{-27} \times 10^{16}\,\text{J} = 28.8 \times 10^{-11}\,\text{J}$

$= 28.8 \times 10^{-10}\,\text{J}$

10. (b) $y = 2\sin\left(\frac{\pi t}{2} + \phi\right)$

velocity of particle $\frac{dy}{dt} = 2 \times \frac{\pi}{2}\cos\left(\frac{\pi t}{2} + \phi\right)$

acceleration $\frac{d^2y}{dt} = -\frac{\pi^2}{2}\sin\left(\frac{\pi t}{2} + \phi\right)$

Thus, $a_{max} = \frac{\pi^2}{2}$

11. (a)

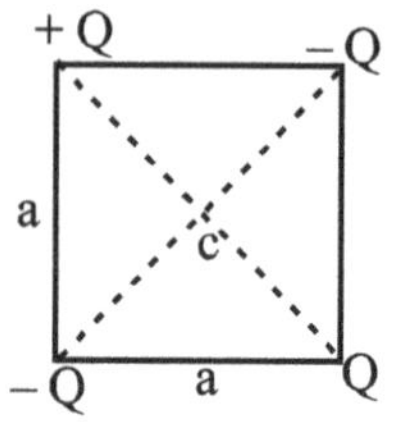

Electric potential at centre

$$= \frac{1}{4\pi\varepsilon_0}\frac{Q}{\sqrt{2}a} + \frac{1}{4\pi\varepsilon_0}\frac{Q}{\sqrt{2}a} - \frac{1}{4\pi\varepsilon_0}\frac{Q}{\sqrt{2}a} - \frac{1}{4\pi\varepsilon_0}\frac{Q}{\sqrt{2}a} = 0$$

12. **(a)** Let the body be depressed by distance x from its equilibrium position. The extra upthrust created is x ρAg which applies to whole body. If a be acceleration created then,

$$x\rho Ag = mga \Rightarrow a = \frac{\rho A}{m}x$$

Since, acceleration α x. So it is equation of S.H.M.

$$\text{So, } \omega^2 = \frac{\rho A}{m} \Rightarrow T = 2\pi\sqrt{\frac{m}{\rho A}}$$

$$T \propto \frac{1}{\sqrt{A}}$$

13. **(b)** The specific resistance (ρ) is determined by the formula

$$\rho = \frac{X\pi D^2}{4L}$$

where symbols have their usual meaning.

14. **(b)** Clearly the co-ordinates of A are (2f, 2f)

$$\therefore f = \frac{40}{2} = 20 \text{ cm.}$$

15. **(a)** Number of electrons falling on the metal plate *A*
$= 10^{16} \times (5 \times 10^{-4})$

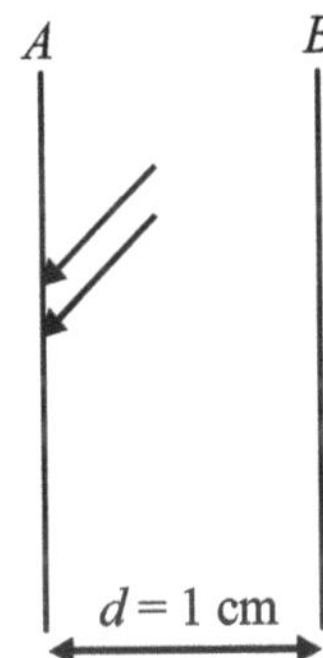

∴ Number of photoelectrons emitted from metal plate *A* upto 10 seconds is

$$n_e = \frac{(5\times10^{-4})\times10^{16}}{10^6}\times10 = 5\times10^7$$

16. **(b)**

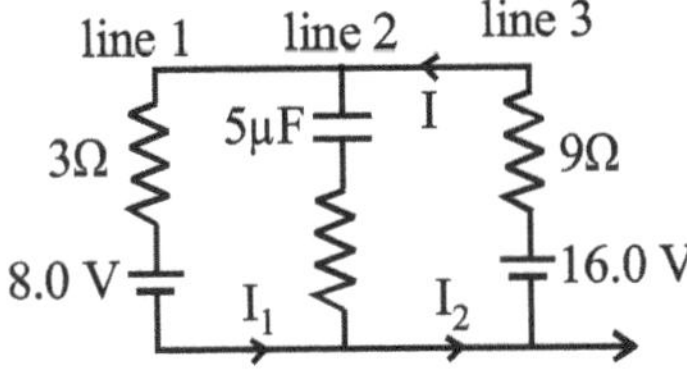

In steady state capacitor is fully charged hence no current will flow through line 2.

By simplyfing the circuit

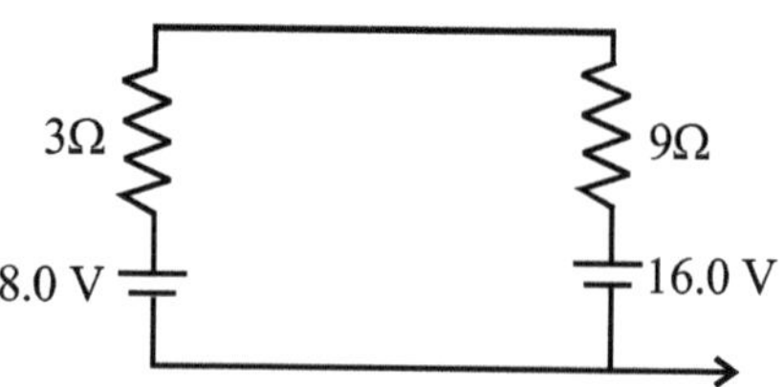

Hence resultant potential difference across resistances will be 8.0 V.

Thus current $I = \frac{V}{R} = \frac{8.0}{3+9} = \frac{8}{12}$

or, $I = \frac{2}{3} = 0.67\,A$

17. (c) Given: Amplitude of electric field,

$E_0 = 4$ v/m

Absolute permitivity,

$\varepsilon_0 = 8.8 \times 10^{-12}\,c^2/N\text{-}m^2$

Average energy density $u_E = ?$

Applying formula,

Average energy density $u_E = \frac{1}{4}\varepsilon_0 E^2$

$\Rightarrow \quad u_E = \frac{1}{4} \times 8.8 \times 10^{-12} \times (4)^2$

$= 35.2 \times 10^{-12}\,J/m^3$

18. (a) When springs are in parallel, then

$T = 2\pi\sqrt{\frac{m}{K_1 + K_2}} \Rightarrow \frac{2\pi}{T} = \omega = \sqrt{\frac{K_1 + K_2}{m}}$

19. (c) Lateral magnitude = v/u;

Mag. along axis $= \left|\frac{dv}{du}\right| = \frac{u^2}{v^2} = 1$ if $v = u$, $\therefore u = 2$

20. (d) In linear S.H.M., the restoring force acting on particle should always be proportional to the displacement of the particle and directed towards the equilibrium position.

i.e., $F \propto x$

or $F = -bx$ where b is a positive constant.

21. **(6)** According to Doppler's effect

$$f = \left(\frac{\nu \pm \nu_0}{\nu \pm \nu_s}\right) f$$

here $\upsilon_0 = 0$ and $\upsilon_s = 0.5\upsilon$

$$\therefore f = \left(\frac{\nu}{\nu - .5\nu}\right) 3 = 6\,\text{kHz}$$

22. **(300)** $\eta = \left(1 - \frac{T_c}{T_H}\right) \times 100$

$$\Rightarrow 70 = \left(1 - \frac{T_c}{1000}\right) \times 100$$

$$0.7 = 1 - \frac{T_c}{1000}$$

$$\therefore \frac{T_c}{1000} = 0.3 \text{ or } T_c = 300\text{K}.$$

23. **(11.2)** Escape velocity $v_e = \sqrt{2gR}$

thus, it doesn't depend on mass.

24. **(0.4)** $r = 5$ cm. $= 5 \times 10^{-2}$m

$B_E = 0.5 \times 10^{-5}$ W/m^2

r=5cm

we know that field due to coil at

centre $B = \frac{\mu_0 I}{2r}$

it annuals the earth's megnetic field

So, $\frac{\mu_0 I}{2r} = 0.5 \times 10^{-5}$

$$I = \frac{2R \times 0.5 \times 10^{-5}}{\mu} = \frac{5}{4\pi} A = 0.4A$$

25. **(1.2×10^{-7})** Pressure of light on totally reflecting surface

$$P = \frac{2I}{C} \qquad (C = \text{velocity of light})$$

$$P = \frac{F}{A} = \frac{2I}{C}$$

$$\Rightarrow F = \frac{2IA}{C} = \frac{2 \times 12 \times 1.5 \times 10^{-4}}{10^{-4} \times 3 \times 10^{8}}$$

$$= \frac{8 \times 15 \times 10^{-8}}{10} = 12 \times 10^{-8} = 1.2 \times 10^{-7}\,\text{N}$$

26. **(2)** Work done by A = Work done by B

F_A dcos 45° = F_B dcos 60°

$$\Rightarrow F_A \times \frac{1}{\sqrt{2}} = F_B \times \frac{1}{2}$$

$$\Rightarrow \frac{F_A}{F_B} = \frac{\sqrt{2}}{2} = \frac{1}{\sqrt{2}}$$

$\Rightarrow x = 2$

27. **(300)** Position of 1st bright fringe is given by

$$y = n\frac{\lambda D}{d}$$

$$\text{For red, } y_1 = \frac{D\lambda_{\text{red}}}{d} = 3.5 \text{ mm}$$

$$\text{For violet, } y_2 = \frac{D}{d}\lambda_{\text{violet}}$$

$y_1 - y_2 = 3.5 - 2 = 1.5$ mm

$$1.5 \text{ mm} = \frac{D}{d}(\lambda_{\text{red}} - \lambda_{\text{violet}})$$

Put $D = 1.5\, m$

$\lambda_{\text{red}} - \lambda_{\text{violet}} = 3 \times 10^{-7} = 300$ mm

28. **(8)** Given,

Young modulus of Steel rod, $Y = 2 \times 10^{11}\ Nm^{-2}$

Change in temperature, $\Delta T = 400°C - 0°C = 400°C$

Area of Cross-section, $A = 10\ cm^2 = 10 \times 10^{-4} m^2$

Thermal force $F = Y\alpha A\Delta T$

$$\Rightarrow F = (10 \times 10^{-4})(2 \times 10^{11})(10^{-5})(400)$$

$$\Rightarrow F = 8 \times 10^5 N = x \times 10^5 N$$

$\Rightarrow x = 8$

29. **(8)** As per question,

$$T_x = \frac{1}{2} \times T_y \Rightarrow 3T_y = 6T_x$$

$$\therefore N_x = \frac{N_1}{2^6} \text{ and } N_y = \frac{N_2}{2^3}$$

$\because N_x = N_y \Rightarrow \frac{N_1}{64} = \frac{N_2}{8} \Rightarrow \frac{N_1}{N_2} = \frac{64}{8} = \frac{8}{1}.$

30. **(40)** Let m be mass that can be placed in the pan. For wire W_1

$$\text{Stress} = \frac{\text{Maximum weight}}{\text{Area}} = \frac{(m+30)g}{8\times10^{-7}}$$

$\Rightarrow m + 30 = 1.25 \times 10^9 \times 8 \times 10^{-7}$

$\Rightarrow m + 30 = 100 \Rightarrow m = 70\ \text{kg}$

For wire W_2

$$\text{Stress} = \frac{(m+10)g}{4\times10^{-7}} = 1.25\times10^9$$

$\Rightarrow m + 10 = 50 \Rightarrow m = 40\ \text{kg}$

Maximum mass that can be placed = 40 kg.

CHEMISTRY

31. **(d)** (a) $\underset{CH_2Cl}{\overset{CH_2Cl}{|}} \xrightarrow[\text{alcohol}]{\text{KOH}} \underset{CH}{\overset{CH}{|||}}$;

$\underset{CH}{\overset{CH_3Cl}{|}} \xrightarrow[\text{alcohol}]{\text{KOH}} \underset{CH}{\overset{CH}{|||}}$; hence true

(b) Both are position isomers

(c) Since, they are isomers, precentage of C, H and Cl in both will be same.

(d) $\underset{CH_2Cl}{\overset{CH_2Cl}{|}} \xrightarrow{\text{hydrolysis}} \underset{CHOH;}{\overset{CH_2OH}{|}}$

$\underset{CHCl_2}{\overset{CH_3}{|}} \xrightarrow{\text{hydrolysis}} \underset{CH(OH)_2}{\overset{CH_3}{|}} \xrightarrow{-H_2O} \underset{CHO}{\overset{CH_3}{|}}$

Hence, statement (d) is wrong.

32. **(d)** Sodium carbonate is the salt of a weak acid (H_2CO_3) with a strong base (NaOH). In solution, it is completely ionised as Na^+ and CO_3^{2-} ions. The CO_3^{2-} ion being the conjugate base of the weak acid H_2CO_3 undergoes hydrolysis in solution according to the equilibrium of hydrolysis:

$CO_3^{2-} + H_2O \rightleftharpoons OH^- + HCO_3^-$

The OH^- ion produced being a strong base makes the solution basic, hence the pH of the solution will be greater than 7.

33. (a) According to the kinetic theory of gases, the average velocity of the molecules in the gas is given by the expression $v=\sqrt{\frac{8RT}{\pi M}}$ where T is the absolute temperature and R is the gas constant. Thus the average velocity can be taken as proportional to the square root of the absolute temperature. Hence the ratio of the average velocity at 200°C to that at 50°C will be equal to $\sqrt{\frac{273+200}{273+50}}$ which is 1.21.

34. (d) No. of atoms of hydrogen in 0.046 g of alcohol

$=\frac{0.046}{46}\times 6\times 10^{23}\times 6$

$=1\times 10^{-3}\times 6\times 10^{23}\times 6=3.6\times 10^{21}$

35. (b) Since the gas B turns $CuSO_4$ solution blue, it can be NH_3.
Since formula of the given compound A is M_3N, A is either lithium or sodium nitride. Of the two, Li_3N is most likely since it is a stable, very high melting compound.

36. (c) (i) $CH_3-\overset{O}{\overset{\|}{C}}-H \xrightarrow[\text{(ii)}H_3O^+]{\text{(i)}CH_3MgBr} CH_3-\underset{CH_3}{\underset{|}{\overset{H}{\overset{|}{C}}}}-OH$ 2-Propanol

(ii) $CH_3-\overset{H}{\overset{|}{C}}=O+C_2H_5OH \xrightarrow{HCl}$

$CH_3-\underset{OH}{\underset{|}{\overset{H}{\overset{|}{C}}}}-OC_2H_5 \xrightarrow[C_2H_5OH]{HCl} CH_3-\overset{H}{\overset{|}{C}}(OC_2H_5)_2$

Hemiacetal — Acetal

37. (b) The temperature of 383 K is equal to 110°C. Although the salts will increase the boiling point of water, it should boil at or below this temperature.

38. (b) Since each of (i), (ii) and (iii) are hexa- coordinated, in the case of (ii), one of the chlorines (chloride ions) is coordinated to the central cobalt ion and in (iii), two such chlorides are coordinately linked. Thus, the ionisable chlorides in (i) is three in (ii) it is two and in (iii) it is only one.
Primary valency means the valency of the complex cation.

39. (b) Polyethylene or Polyethene, $\text{-}[CH_2-CH_2]\text{-}_n$,
is made from a single monomer, it is a homopolymer.

40. (b) Pencillin is bactericidal and bacteriostatic.

41. (c) More the *s* - character, more is the stability of the carbanion. hence the correct order is $sp > sp^2 > sp^3$.

42. (a) The total number of electrons in the molecular species given, respectively

are 17, 16 and 18. Write down the electronic configuration of the molecular species and observe the number of electrons in antibonding orbitals which are respectively 7, 6 and 8.

43. (c) Deviation from ideal gas behaviour is greater, when the pressure is higher and the gas is closed to its liquefaction point or its critical temperature. Thus, the conditions of –100°C and 4 atm pressure among the sets given causes maximum deviation.

44. (b) Heat of neutralisation of strong acid and strong base is always 13.7 kcal.

45. (b) Average atomic weight $= 85\left(\frac{75}{100}\right) + 87\left(\frac{25}{100}\right) = 85.5$.

46. (b) In Kjeldahl's method of estimation of nitrogen, the nitrogen present in most of the organic compounds is quantitatively converted into ammonium sulphate. The $(NH_4)_2SO_4$ so obtained is decomposed with excess of NaOH solution to give NH_3 which is absorbed in an excess of standard HCl or H_2SO_4 and residual mineral acid is then titrated with standard NaOH solution. Thus, option (b) is the correct choice.

47. (c) The secondary amines react with HNO_2 to give the oily nitroso derivative. Amongst the options, (c) is the secondary amine.

48. (a) Addition of a catalyst to a reaction mixture has the effect of lowering the activation energy of the reaction by changing the path or mechanism of the reaction. The reaction rate increases manifold. However, the equilibrium constant and the enthalpy (ΔH) of the reaction are unaffected.

49. (a) Ba ⇒ $[Xe]6s^2$

Ca ⇒ Calcium oxalate is insoluble (sparingly soluble) in water

Li ⇒ LiCl is soluble in organic solvents like pyridine

Na ⇒ NaOH is a very strong monoacidic base

50. (d) Lithium, sodium and potassium are highly electropositive and highly reactive metals. When any of these come in contact with water, the reaction is so swift and intense that the hydrogen evolved catches fire instantaneously. The reaction thus is doubly exothermic, using water to quinch fires caused by these metals makes it explosively dangerous. Likewise CO_2 and nitrogen too are reactive. Small fires can be quinched by asbestos blanket or by covering with dry sand, since these measures prevents contact with oxygen and water vapour and thus become effective.

51. **(0.107)** $N_1V_1 = N_2V_2$

$$N_{NaOH} = M_{NaOH} = 0.164 \Rightarrow 25 \times N = 32.63 \times 0.164$$

$$N = \frac{32.63 \times .164}{25} = 0.214 \text{ N}$$

But $N_{H_2SO_4} = 2 \times M_{H_2SO_4}$

$$\Rightarrow M = \frac{\text{Normality}}{2} = \frac{0.214}{2} = 0.107$$

52. **(50)** Eq. of $KMnO_4$ used $= \frac{50 \times 1}{1000 \times 10} = 0.005$

$\therefore$ Eq of FAS reacted $= 0.005$

$\therefore$ weight of FAS needed $= 0.005 \times 392$

$= 1.96$ g

Thus, percentage purity of FAS is 50%.

53. **(4)** In a '*fcc*' crystal atoms are located at the centre of the 6 faces and at the 8 corners.

On each face their is 1 atom which is shared by 2 cells. Hence, the no. of atoms/ unit cell = 6/2 = 3

Again the corner atom is shared by 8 other cells. Hence no. of atoms = 8/8 = 1

No. of atoms/unit cell = 1 + 3 = 4

54. **(800)** As $AgNO_3$ dissociates completely,

therefore in 0.1 M $AgNO_3$ solution, $[Ag^+] = 0.1$ M

$$\underset{}{AgNO_3} \longrightarrow \underset{0.1}{Ag^+} + \underset{0.1}{NO_3^-}$$

$$Ag_2CO_3 \rightleftharpoons \underset{0.1+2s}{2Ag^+} + \underset{s}{CO_3^-}$$

$$K_{sp} = [Ag^+]^2[CO_3^{2-}]$$

$$= 8 = (0.1 + 2s)^2 \times s$$

$$= 0.01\, s = 8 ; (0.1 + 2s \approx 0.1)$$

$$s = 800$$

55. **(317)** $\underset{x}{CH_4} + \underset{2x}{2O_2} \rightarrow CO_2 + 2H_2O$

$$\underset{(5-x)}{C_3H_8} + \underset{5(5-x)}{5O_2} \rightarrow 3CO_2 + 4H_2O$$

$$2x + 5(5 - x) = 16 \Rightarrow x = 3\text{ L}$$

$$\therefore \text{Heat released} = \frac{3}{22.4} \times 890 + \frac{2}{22.4} \times 2220 = 317.$$

56. **(101)** $\Delta H_{sub} = \Delta H_{fus.} + \Delta H_{vap.} = 2.8 + 98.2 = 101$ kJ/mol

57. **(1)** Anions ccp or fcc $(B^-) = 4\,B^-$ per unit cell

Cations occupy all octahedral voids $(A^+) = 4A^+$ per unit cell

$\therefore$ Cell formula $\Rightarrow A_4B_4$.

Empirical formula $\Rightarrow$ AB

$\Rightarrow x = 1$

58. **(2)** Using ideal gas equation :

$PV = nRT$

$$V = \frac{3.12 \times 0.0821 \times 300}{32 \times 1} = 2.40\,\text{L}$$

$\therefore$ Volume of $O_2(g)$ adsorbed per gram of the adsorbent $= \frac{2.4}{1.2} = 2$

59. **(49)** Fe(Z = 26)

$Fe\,26 \Rightarrow [Ar]\,3d^6 4s^2$

↑↓	↑	↑	↑	↑

Number of unpaired electrons = 4

$\because \mu = \sqrt{n(n+2)}$ BM

$\therefore \mu = \sqrt{4(4+2)} = \sqrt{24}$ BM $= 4.89 \approx 49 \times 10^{-1}$ BM

60. **(2)**

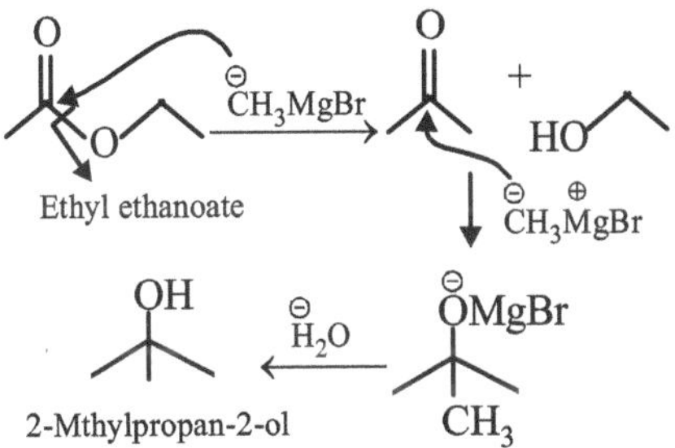

MATHEMATICS

61. **(d)** Given $f(x) = \tan^{-1}(\sin x + \cos x)$

$$f'(x) = \frac{1}{1 + (\sin x + \cos x)^2}.(\cos x - \sin x)$$

$$= \frac{\sqrt{2}.\left(\frac{1}{\sqrt{2}}\cos x - \frac{1}{\sqrt{2}}\sin x\right)}{1 + (\sin x + \cos x)^2}$$

$$\therefore\ f'(x)=\frac{\sqrt{2}\cos\left(x+\frac{\pi}{4}\right)}{1+(\sin x+\cos x)^2}$$

if $f'(x)>0$ then f(x) is increasing function.
Hence f(x) is increasing, if

$$-\frac{\pi}{2}<x+\frac{\pi}{4}<\frac{\pi}{2}\ \Rightarrow\ -\frac{3\pi}{4}<x<\frac{\pi}{4}$$

Hence, f(x) is increasing when $x\in\left(-\frac{\pi}{2},\frac{\pi}{4}\right)$

62. **(a)** $\sqrt{1+x^2}+\sqrt{1+y^2}=\lambda(x\sqrt{1+y^2}-y\sqrt{1+x^2})$

$$\Rightarrow \sqrt{1+x^2}(1+\lambda y)=\sqrt{1+y^2}(\lambda x-1)$$

$$\Rightarrow \frac{\sqrt{1+x^2}}{\sqrt{1+y^2}}=\frac{\lambda x-1}{\lambda y+1}$$

$$\Rightarrow \frac{x^2+1}{y^2+1}=\frac{\lambda^2x^2-2\lambda x+1}{\lambda^2y^2+2\lambda y+1}$$

$$\Rightarrow (y^2+1)(\lambda^2x^2-2\lambda x+1)$$

$$=(x^2+1)(\lambda^2y^2+2\lambda y+1)$$

$$\Rightarrow \lambda^2x^2y^2-2\lambda xy^2+y^2+\lambda^2x^2-2\lambda x+1$$

$$=\lambda^2x^2y^2+2\lambda x^2y+x^2+\lambda^2y^2+2\lambda y+1$$

$$\Rightarrow \lambda^2(x^2-y^2)-2\lambda(xy^2+x^2y+x+y)=0$$

$$\Rightarrow \lambda^2(x+y)(x-y)-2\lambda\ [xy(x+y)+(x+y)]=0$$

$$\Rightarrow \lambda(x+y)[\lambda(x-y)-2xy-2]=0$$

$$\Rightarrow (x+y)[\lambda(x-y)-2xy-2]=0$$

$$\Rightarrow \lambda(x-y)-2xy-2=0$$

$$\Rightarrow \frac{2xy+2}{x-y}=\lambda\ \Rightarrow\ \frac{xy+1}{x-y}=\frac{\lambda}{2}$$

$$\Rightarrow \frac{\left(x\frac{dy}{dx}+y\right)(x-y)-(xy+1)\left(1-\frac{dy}{dx}\right)}{(x-y)^2}=1$$

This is the first order differential equation and clearly degree of $\frac{dy}{dx}$ is 1.

Hence degree of the differential equation is 1.

63. (c) $I=\int_0^2 [x^2]dx$

The function $[x^2]$ varies as follows between x = (0, 2)

$$[x^2]=\begin{cases}0 \text{ if } 0\le x^2<1, \text{ or } 0\le x<1\\ 1 \text{ if } 1\le x^2<2 \text{ or } 1\le x<\sqrt{2}\\ 2 \text{ if } 2\le x^2<3 \text{ or } \sqrt{2}\le x<\sqrt{3}\\ 3 \text{ if } 3\le x^2<4 \text{ or } \sqrt{3}\le x<2\end{cases}$$

$$\Rightarrow I=\int_0^1 0.dx+\int_1^{\sqrt{2}} 1.dx+\int_{\sqrt{2}}^{\sqrt{3}} 2.dx+\int_{\sqrt{3}}^2 3.dx$$

$$=0+(\sqrt{2}-1)+2(\sqrt{3}-\sqrt{2})+3(2-\sqrt{3})$$

$$=\sqrt{2}-1+2\sqrt{3}-2\sqrt{2}+6-3\sqrt{3}=5-\sqrt{2}-\sqrt{3}$$

64. (c) $\alpha+\beta=3;\alpha\beta=a$; $\gamma+\delta=+12\,;\gamma\delta=b$

$\alpha,\beta,\gamma,\delta$ are in increasing G.P.

$\beta=\alpha x,\gamma=\alpha x^2,\delta=\alpha x^3$

$\alpha+\beta=\alpha+\alpha x=3=\alpha(1+x)$ .....(1)

$\gamma+\delta=\alpha x^2+\alpha x^3=12=\alpha x^2(1+x)$ .....(2)

Divding $\frac{3}{12}=\frac{\alpha(1+x)}{\alpha x^2(1+x)}$ or $\frac{1}{4}=\frac{1}{x^2}$ or x = 2

$\Rightarrow \beta=2\alpha$ and $\alpha+2\alpha=3\Rightarrow\alpha=1$ and $\beta=2$

$\therefore a=\alpha\beta=2$

$\gamma = \alpha x^2 = 1\times 2^2 = 4; \delta = \alpha x^3 = 1\times 2^3 = 8$

$\therefore b = \gamma\delta = 4\times 8 = 32$

65. **(a)** Consider the example: Let $A = \{1, 2, 3\}$,
$R = \{(1, 1), (1,2)\}$ and $S = \{(2, 2), (2, 3)\}$
Clearly R and S are transitive relations on A.
$R\cup S = \{(1, 1), (2, 2), (1, 2), (2, 3)\}$
$R\cup S$ is not transitive as $(1,3) \notin R\cup S$.

66. **(d)** $I = \int \log 2x\, dx = \int \log 2x.1.dx$

Using Integration by parts

$$I = \log 2x.\, x - \int \frac{2}{2x}.\int 1.dx$$

$$= x\log 2x - \int \frac{1}{x}.xdx + c = x\log 2x - x + c$$

67. **(a)** For $k = 0$,
it is obvious from the given interval that graph will be increasing from -1 to 1
Similar graphs can be obtained for all values of k.

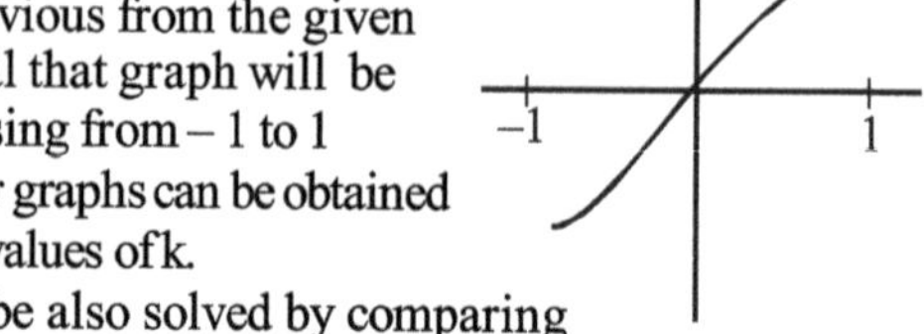

68. **(a)** It can be also solved by comparing with the linear equation $\frac{dy}{dx} + Py = Q$

The integrating factor, I.F. $= e^{\int 1.dx} = e^x$

Therefore, $y\, I.F = \int 2e^{2x}.I.F + C$

$y.e^x = \int 2e^{2x}.e^x + C$

$$y.e^x = 2\int e^{3x} + C = \frac{2}{3}e^{3x} + C \Rightarrow y = \frac{2e^{2x}}{3} + ce^{-x}$$

69. **(c)** $\Delta = \begin{vmatrix} a+x & a-x & a-x \\ a-x & a+x & a-x \\ a-x & a-x & a+x \end{vmatrix} = 0$

$$\Rightarrow \Delta = \begin{vmatrix} 3a-x & a-x & a-x \\ 3a-x & a+x & a-x \\ 3a-x & a-x & a+x \end{vmatrix}, \quad C_1 \to C_1 + C_2 + C_3$$

$$= (3a-x)\begin{vmatrix} 1 & a-x & a-x \\ 1 & a+x & a-x \\ 1 & a-x & a+x \end{vmatrix} = 0$$

Using $R_2 \to R_2 - R_1$ and $R_3 \to R_3 - R_1$

$$\Rightarrow \Delta = (3a-x)\begin{vmatrix} 1 & a-x & a-x \\ 0 & 2x & 0 \\ 0 & 0 & 2x \end{vmatrix} = 0$$

or, $4x^2(3a-x) = 0 \Rightarrow x = 0$ or $3a$

70. **(c)** We know that centroid divides the median in the ratio 2 : 1.

Radius of the circle $= \frac{2}{3} \times$ length of median

$$= \frac{2}{3} \times 3a = 2a$$

Centre of the (given) circle is C(0, 0). Therefore the equation of the circle $(x-0)^2 + (y-0)^2 = (2a)^2 \Rightarrow x^2 + y^2 = 4a^2$

71. **(b)** Its contropositive is 'sum of digits of n is not divisible by 9'
$\Rightarrow$ n is not divisible by 9

72. **(c)** $n = 7$

Prob. of getting any no. out 1, 2, 3, … 9 is $p = 9/15$

$\therefore \quad q = 6/5$

$P(x=7) = {}^7C_7 p^7 q^0$ [Binomial distribution]

$$= \left(\frac{9}{15}\right)^7 = \left(\frac{3}{5}\right)^7$$

73. **(a)** For $x \geq a$, the equation becomes

$$x^2 - 2a(x-a) - 3a^2 = 0 \Rightarrow x = (1+\sqrt{2})a,\ (1-\sqrt{2})a$$

for $x \leq a$, the equation becomes

$$x^2 - 2a[-(x-a)] - 3a^2 = 0 \Rightarrow x^2 + 2ax - 5a^2 = 0$$

$\Rightarrow x = -(1+\sqrt{6})a,\ (-1+\sqrt{6})a$

This shows $(-1+\sqrt{6})a$ is one of the roots.

74. **(c)** $X \cap (X \cup Y)^c = X \cap (X^c \cap Y^c) = (X \cap X^c) \cap Y^c$

$$= \phi \cap Y^c = \phi$$

75. **(a)** $y = \log_2 \{\log_2(x)\} = \log_2\{\log_e x.\log_2 e\}$

$\Rightarrow y = \log_e\{\log_e x.\log_2 e\}.\log_2 e$

$\Rightarrow \frac{dy}{dx} = \log_2 e \frac{d}{dx}[\log_e\{\log_e x.\log_2 e\}]$

$\Rightarrow \frac{dy}{dx} = \log_2 e.\frac{1}{\log_e x.\log_2 e}.\frac{d}{dx}(\log_e x.\log_2 e)$

$\Rightarrow \frac{dy}{dx} = \frac{1}{\log_e x}\log_2 e\frac{1}{x} = \frac{\log_2 e}{x \ln x}$

76. **(c)** The function breaks at x = 0 and multiples of x. Hence the function is differentiable at all other points as the function is continuous at all these pts.

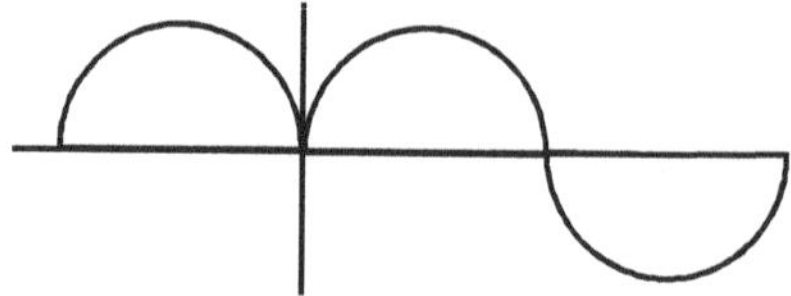

At $x = 0$, for $f(x)$ to be continous

$\lim_{x\to 0} f(0^-) = f(x=0) = \lim_{x\to 0} f(0^+)$

$f(x) = 0$ at $x = 0$

$\text{RHL} = \lim_{x\to 0} \sin(x+h) = \sin\ h > 0$

$\text{L. H. L.} = \lim_{x\to 0} \sin(x-h) = \sin\ (-h) < 0$

Hence, not differentiable at $x = 0$

Similarly, $f(x)$ is not differentiable at all multiples of π, i.e, $n\pi$ where $n = 0$, 1,2..............

77. (d) $\int_0^{\pi/3} \frac{\cos x + \sin x}{\sqrt{1+\sin 2x}} dx$

$$= \int_0^{\pi/3} \frac{\cos x + \sin x}{\sqrt{\sin^2 x + \cos^2 x + 2\sin x \cos x}} dx$$

$$= \int_0^{\pi/3} \frac{\cos x + \sin x}{\sqrt{(\cos x + \sin x)^2}} dx = \int_0^{\pi/3} dx = \frac{\pi}{3}$$

78. (c) The equation of the pair of tangents is given by $SS_1 = T^2$

$(3x^2 + 2y^2 - 5)(3.1^2 + 2.2^2 - 5) = (3x.1 + 2y.2 - 5)^2$

$9x^2 - 4y^2 - 24xy + 40y + 30x - 55 = 0$

further angle, θ between them can be found by using

$$\tan\theta = \frac{2\sqrt{h^2 - ab}}{a+b} = \frac{2\sqrt{(12)^2 - (9)(-4)}}{9 + (-4)}$$

$$= \frac{2\sqrt{180}}{5} = \frac{12\sqrt{5}}{5}, \quad \therefore \theta = \tan^{-1}\frac{12}{\sqrt{5}}$$

79. (d) The roots of the equation $x^2 + x + 1$ are given as ω & ω^2. i.e. say, $\alpha = \omega$ & $\beta = \omega^2$

$\alpha^{19} = \omega^{19} = (\omega^3)^6\omega = \omega; \beta^7 = (\omega^2)^7 = \omega^{14} = (\omega^3)^4\omega^2 = \omega^2$

Hence the equation is $x^2 + x + 1 = 0$

80. (c) $\sin^{-1}(1-x) = \left(\frac{\pi}{2} - \sin^{-1}x\right) - \sin^{-1}x$ $\quad (\because \cos^{-1}x = \frac{\pi}{2} - \sin^{-1}x)$

$$\sin^{-1}(1-x) = \frac{\pi}{2} - 2\sin^{-1}x$$

Taking sum of both sides

$$1 - x = \sin\left(\frac{\pi}{2} - 2\sin^{-1}x\right) = \cos(2\sin^{-1}x)$$

$= \cos 2\theta$, where $\sin^{-1}x = \theta$

$1 - x = 1 - 2\sin^2\theta = 1 - 2x^2$ or $x(1-2x) = 0$ or $x = 0, \frac{1}{2}$

81. **(0.33)**

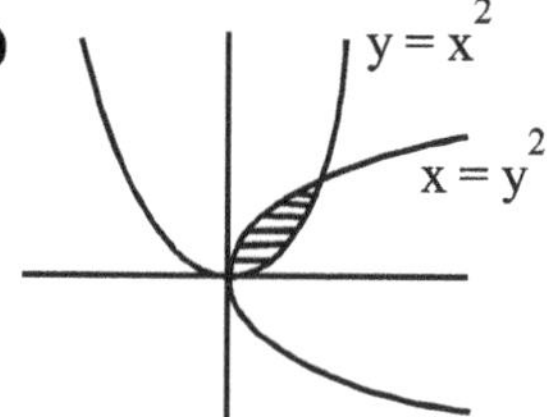

Solving, $y = x^2$ and $x = y^2$

$y = y^4$ or $y(y^3 - 1) = 0 \Rightarrow y = 0$ or $y = 1$

$\therefore$ Point of intersection are (0, 0) & (1, 1)

To find the shaded area, $A = \int_0^1 (\sqrt{x} - x^2)\, dx$

$$= \frac{2}{3}\left[x^{3/2}\right]_0^1 - \left[\frac{x^3}{3}\right]_0^1 = \frac{2}{3} - \frac{1}{3} = \frac{1}{3}$$

82. **(0.63)**

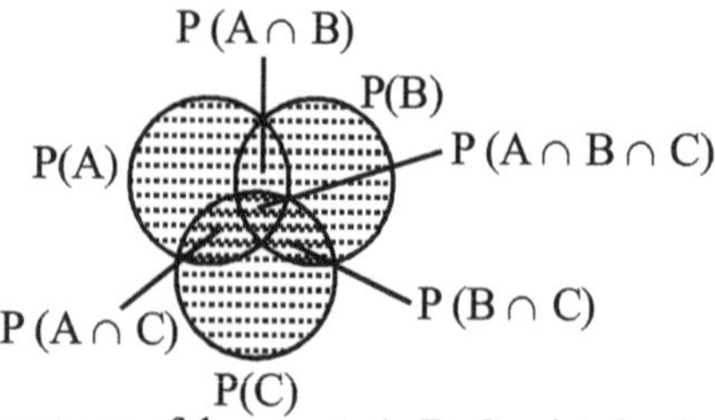

$\therefore$ Probability that atleast one of the events A, B, C exists is given by the shaded region.

Req. prob. $= P(A) + P(B) + P(C) - P(A \cap B)$

$$- P(B \cap C) - P(C \cap A) + P(A \cap B \cap C)$$

$$= \frac{1}{4} + \frac{1}{4} + \frac{1}{4} - 0 - 0 - \frac{1}{8} + 0 = \frac{5}{8}$$

83. **(1)** $T_{r+1} = {}^6C_r x^{6-r}\left(\frac{1}{x^2}\right)^r = {}^6C_r (x)^{6-r-2r}$

For coefficient of x^6, $6 - r - 2r = 6$, or $r = 0$

This means the term is the first term.

$\Rightarrow T_1 = {}^6C_0 x^6 = 1.x^6$

$\Rightarrow$ coefficient of $x^6 = 1$

84. **(3)** For f (x) to be continuous, $\lim_{x \to 0} f(x) = f(0)$

$$f(0) = k \quad \lim_{x\to 0} f(x) = \lim_{x\to 0} = \frac{\sin 3x}{\sin x} = \lim_{x\to 0} \frac{3\cdot\frac{\sin 3x}{3x}}{\frac{\sin x}{x}} = 3$$

$$\left[\because \lim_{x\to 0}\frac{\sin\theta}{\theta} = 1\right]$$

$\Rightarrow k = 3$

85. **(1.33)** Line is $\perp$ to $3x + y = 3$

$\therefore$ Slope of line, $m = \frac{1}{3}$

Equation is, $y = mx + c = \frac{x}{3} + c$

It passes through (2, 2) $\Rightarrow 2 = \frac{2}{3} + c$

$\Rightarrow \quad c = \frac{4}{3}$

$\Rightarrow y - \frac{x}{3} = 4/3 \Rightarrow 3y - x = 4$

$\therefore$ y-intercept $= 4/3$

86. **(9)** Since, diagonal of square $= \sqrt{2} \times \text{side}$

$\Rightarrow \text{side} = \frac{1}{\sqrt{2}}$ diagonal

Given that side of $A_1 = 12$

$\therefore$ Side of $A_2 = \frac{12}{\sqrt{2}}$

Side of $A_3 = \frac{12}{2} = 6$

$\therefore$ Sequence $12, \frac{12}{\sqrt{2}}, 6, \frac{6}{\sqrt{2}}$...... are in G.P.

Since arc of square less than 1

$\therefore (T_n)^2 < 1$

$$\Rightarrow 12\cdot\left(\frac{1}{\sqrt{2}}\right)^{n-1} < 1$$

$\Rightarrow 2^{n-1} > 144 \Rightarrow n-1 \geq 8$

$\Rightarrow n = 9$

87. (238)

Class	10th	11th	12th	
Total students	(5)	6	(8)	
Number of selections	2	2	6	$\Rightarrow {}^5C_2 \times {}^6C_2 \times {}^8C_6$
	3	2	5	$\Rightarrow {}^5C_3 \times {}^6C_2 \times {}^8C_5$
	2	3	5	$\Rightarrow {}^5C_2 \times {}^6C_3 \times {}^8C_5$

$\therefore$ Total number of ways

$= 10 \times 15 \times 28 + 10 \times 15 \times 56 + 10 \times 20 \times 56$

$= 4200 + 11200 + 8400 = 23800 = 100\,K \Rightarrow K = 238$

88. (4) $x\phi(x) = \int_5^x 3t^2 - 2\phi'(t)\,dt$

$\phi(0) = 4, x > -2$

$x\phi(x) = x^3 - 125 - 2[\phi(x) - \phi(5)]$

$x\phi(x) = x^3 - 125 - 2\phi(x) - 2\phi(5)$

$\phi(0) = 4 \Rightarrow \phi(5) = -\frac{133}{2}$

$\phi(x) = \frac{x^3 + 8}{x + 2}$

$\phi(2) = \frac{2^3 + 8}{2 + 2} = \frac{8 + 8}{4} = 4$

89. (4) $y = \begin{cases} x-3; & x \geq 3 \\ -(x-3); & 1 \leq x < 3 \\ x+1; & -1 \leq x < 1 \\ -(x+1); & x < -1 \end{cases}$

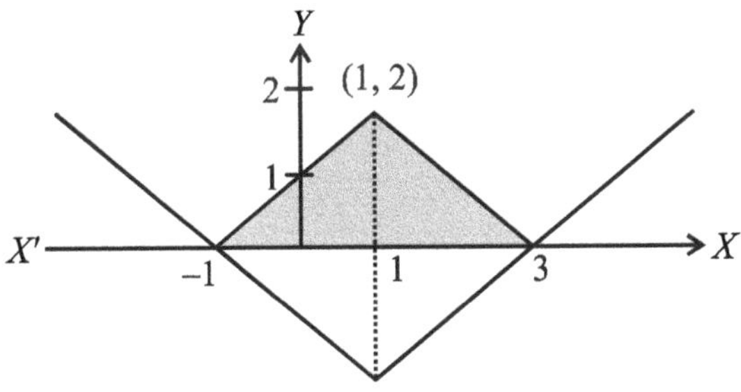

Area of the shaded region $= \frac{1}{2}(4 \times 2) = 4$

90. **(1)** Given that,

$\sqrt{3}\ \cos^2 x = (\sqrt{3} - 1)\cos x + 1$

$\Rightarrow\ \sqrt{3}\ \cos^2 x - \sqrt{3}\ \cos x + \cos x - 1 = 0$

$\Rightarrow\ \sqrt{3}\ \cos x(\cos x - 1) + (\cos x - 1) = 0$

$\Rightarrow\ (\cos x - 1)(\sqrt{3}\ \cos x + 1) = 0$

$\Rightarrow\ \cos x = 1 \text{ or } -\frac{1}{\sqrt{3}}$

So, number of solution in $x \in \left[0, \frac{\pi}{2}\right]$ is 1.

MOCK TEST-4

PHYSICS

1. **(d)** $v=\sqrt{\dfrac{2gh}{1+\dfrac{I}{mr^2}}}=\sqrt{\dfrac{2\times10\times3}{1+\dfrac{mr^2}{2\times mr^2}}}=\sqrt{\dfrac{2\times10\times3}{\dfrac{3}{2}}}=\sqrt{40}$

$$\Rightarrow v=r\omega\Rightarrow r=\frac{v}{\omega}=\frac{\sqrt{40}}{2\sqrt{2}}=\sqrt{\frac{40}{8}}=\sqrt{5}\text{ m.}$$

2. **(a)** By conservation of energy

$$\text{mg}(3\text{h})=\text{mg}(2\text{h})+\frac{1}{2}\text{mv}^2 \quad (\text{v = velocity at B})$$

$$\text{mgh}=\frac{1}{2}\text{mv}^2\ ;\ \text{v}=\sqrt{2\text{gh}}$$

From free body diagram of block at B

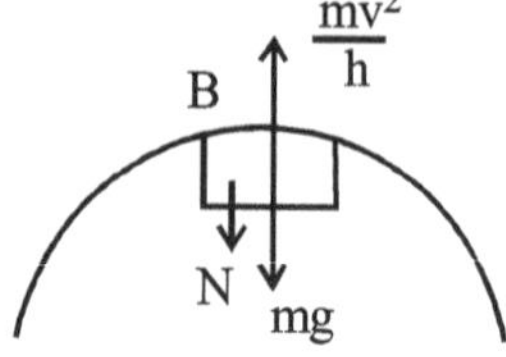

$$\text{N}+\text{mg}=\frac{\text{mv}^2}{\text{h}}=2\text{mg}\ ;\ \text{N}=\text{mg}$$

3. **(b)** Bulk modulus, $B=-V_0\dfrac{\Delta p}{\Delta V}\Rightarrow \Delta V=-V_0\dfrac{\Delta p}{B}$

$$\Rightarrow V=V_0\left[1-\frac{\Delta p}{B}\right]$$

$$\therefore \text{Density, } \rho=\rho_0\left[1-\frac{\Delta p}{B}\right]^{-1}=\rho_0\left[1+\frac{\Delta p}{B}\right]$$

where, $\Delta p=p-p_0=h\rho_0 g$

= pressure difference between depth and surface of ocean

$$\therefore \rho=\rho_0\left[1+\frac{\rho_0 gy}{B}\right] \text{ (As h = y)}$$

4. (b) Here, $\vec{E} = 5\hat{i} - 3\hat{j}\text{kV/m}$

$$V_B - V_A = -\int_{r_A}^{r_B} \vec{E} \cdot \partial r$$

$$= -\int_{(4,0,3)}^{(10,3,0)} (5\hat{i} - 3\hat{j}).(\partial x\hat{i} + \partial y\hat{j} + \partial z\hat{k})$$

$$= -\int_4^{10} 5\partial x - \int_0^3 (-3)\partial y + 0 = -5[x]_4^{10} + 3[y]_0^3$$

$$= -5(10-4) + 3(3-0) = -30 + 9 = -21\text{kV}$$

5. (c) The current upto which bulb of marked 25W -220V, will not fuse

$$I_1 = \frac{W_1}{V_1} = \frac{25}{220} \text{ Amp}$$

Similarly, $I_2 = \frac{W_2}{V_2} = \frac{100}{220}$ Amp

The current flowing through the circuit

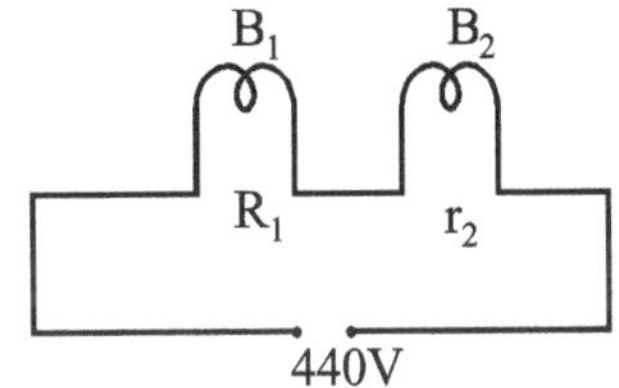

$$I = \frac{440}{R_{eff}}$$

$$R_{eff} = R_1 + R_2$$

$$R_1 = \frac{V_1^2}{P_1} = \frac{(220)^2}{25}; \quad R_2 = \frac{V_2^2}{P} = \frac{(220)^2}{100}$$

$$I = \frac{440}{\frac{(220)^2}{25} + \frac{(220)^2}{100}} = \frac{440}{(220)^2\left[\frac{1}{25} + \frac{1}{100}\right]}$$

$$I = \frac{40}{220} \text{ Amp}$$

$$\because I_1\left(=\frac{25}{220}A\right) < I\left(=\frac{40}{220}A\right) < I_2\left(=\frac{100}{200}A\right)$$

Thus the bulb marked 25W-220 will fuse.

6. (c) When the current flows in both wires in the same direction then magnetic field at half way due to the wire P,

$$\vec{B}_p = \frac{\mu_0 I_1}{2\pi \frac{5}{2}} = \frac{\mu_0 I_1}{\pi \cdot 5} = \frac{\mu_0}{2\pi}$$

(where $I_1 = 5$ amp)

The direction of $\vec{B}_p$ is downward $\odot$

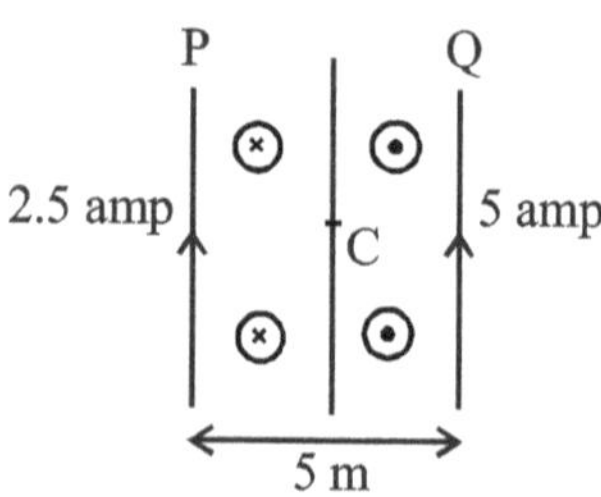

Magnetic field at half way due to wire Q

$$\vec{B}_Q = \frac{\mu_0 I_2}{2\pi \frac{5}{2}} = \frac{\mu_0}{\pi} \qquad \text{[upward } \odot\text{]}$$

[where $I_2 = 5$amp.]

Net magnetic field at half way

$$\vec{B} = \vec{B}_P + \vec{B}_Q = -\frac{\mu_0}{2\pi} + \frac{\mu_0}{\pi} = \frac{\mu_0}{2\pi} \text{ (upward)}$$

Hence, net magnetic field at midpoint $= \frac{\mu_0}{2\pi}$

7. (b)

8. (a) Limiting friction between block and slab

$= \mu_s m_A g = 0.6 \times 10 \times 9.8 = 58.8$ N

But applied force on block A is 100 N. So the block will slip over a slab.

Now kinetic friction works between block and slab

$F_k = \mu_k m_A g = 0.4 \times 10 \times 9.8 = 39.2$ N

This kinetic friction helps to move the slab

$$\therefore \text{Accleration of slab} = \frac{39.2}{m_B} = \frac{39.2}{40} = 0.98 \text{ m/s}^2$$

9. (a) $V_p = \frac{dx_p}{dt} = a + 2bt$

and $V_Q = \frac{dx_Q}{dt} = f - 2t$, Given, $V_p = V_Q$

$\therefore a + 2bt = f - 2t \Rightarrow t = \frac{f-a}{2(b+1)}$

10. (c) Intensity of light

$$I = \frac{\text{Watt}}{\text{Area}} = \frac{\text{nhc}}{A\lambda} \Rightarrow \text{Number of photon} = \frac{IA\lambda}{hc}$$

$\therefore$ Number of photoelectrons emitted $= \frac{1}{100} \times \frac{IA\lambda}{hc}$

$$= \frac{1}{100} \times \frac{1 \times 10^{-4} \times 300 \times 10^{-9}}{6.6 \times 10^{-34} \times 3 \times 10^{8}} = 1.5 \times 10^{12} \text{ per sec}$$

11. (c) The wavelength of spectral line in Balmer series is given

by $\frac{1}{\lambda} = R\left[\frac{1}{2^2} - \frac{1}{n^2}\right]$

For first line of Balmer series, n = 3

$$\Rightarrow \frac{1}{\lambda_1} = R\left[\frac{1}{2^2} - \frac{1}{3^2}\right] = \frac{5R}{36}; \text{ For second line } n = 4.$$

$$\Rightarrow \frac{1}{\lambda_2} = R\left[\frac{1}{2^2} - \frac{1}{4^2}\right] = \frac{3R}{16}$$

$$\therefore \frac{\lambda_2}{\lambda_1} = \frac{20}{27} \Rightarrow \lambda_2 = \frac{20}{27} \times 6561 = 4860 \text{ Å}$$

12. (d) In pure semiconductor electron-hole pair = $7 \times 10^{15}/m^3$

$n_{initial} = n_h + n_e = 14 \times 10^{15}$ after doping donor Impurity

$$N_D = \frac{5 \times 10^{28}}{10^7} = 5 \times 10^{21} \text{ and } n_e = \frac{N_D}{2} = 2.5 \times 10^{21}$$

So, $n_{final} = n_h + n_e$

$\Rightarrow \quad n_{final} \approx n_e \approx 2.5 \times 10^{21}$ ($\because n_e >> n_h$)

$$\text{Factor} = \frac{n_{final} - n_{initial}}{n_{initial}}$$

$$= \frac{2.5 \times 10^{21} - 14 \times 10^{15}}{14 \times 10^{15}} \approx \frac{2.5 \times 10^{21}}{14 \times 10^{15}} = 1.8 \times 10^5$$

13. (a) According to Wien's displacement law

$$\lambda_m \propto \frac{1}{T} \Rightarrow \lambda m_2 < \lambda_{m_1} \; [\because T_1 < T_2]$$

Therefore I-λ graph for T_2 has lesser wavelength (λ_m) and so curve for T_2 will shift towards left side.

14. (b) At resonance, amplitude of oscillation is maximum

$\Rightarrow 2\omega^2 - 36\omega + 9$ is minimum

$\Rightarrow 4\omega - 36 = 0$ (derivative is zero)

$\Rightarrow \omega = 9$

15. (b) Average speed of gas molecules is $\sqrt{\frac{8kT}{\pi m}}$. It depends on temperature and molecules mass. So the average speed of O_2 will be same in (A) and (C).

16. (c) Apparent frequency

$$n' = n\frac{(u + v_W)}{(u + v_W - v_s \cos 60°)} = \frac{510\,(330 + 20)}{330 + 20 - 20\cos 60°}$$

$$= 510 \times \frac{350}{340} = 525 \text{ Hz}$$

17. (c) The area swept by radius OC in one half circle is $\pi r^2/2$. The flux change in time T/2 is thus $(\pi r^2 B/2)$. The induced emf is then $e = \pi r^2 B/T = B\omega r^2/2$

$$\left[\because T = \frac{2\pi}{\omega}\right]$$

The induced current is then $I = e/R = B\omega r^2/2R$

18. (a) The Instantaneous value of voltage is

$E = 100 \sin (100t)$ V

We get

$E_0 = 100$V, $\omega = 100$ rad s^{-1}

The rms value of voltage is

$$E_{rms} = \frac{E_0}{\sqrt{2}} = \frac{100}{\sqrt{2}} \text{V} = 70.7\text{V}$$

The instantaneous value of current is

$$I = 100\sin\left(100t + \frac{\pi}{3}\right) mA$$

Compare it with

$I = I_0 \sin(\omega t + \phi)$

we get

$I_0 = 100$ mA, $\omega = 100$ rad s^{-1}

The rms value of current is

$$I_{rms} = \frac{I_0}{\sqrt{2}} = \frac{100}{\sqrt{2}} mA = 70.7 mA$$

19. **(c)** Incident momentum, $p = \frac{E}{c}$

For perfectly reflecting surface with normal incidence

$$\Delta p = 2p = \frac{2E}{c}$$

$$F = \frac{\Delta p}{\Delta t} = \frac{2E}{ct}$$

$$P = \frac{F}{A} = \frac{2E}{ctA}$$

20. **(a)**

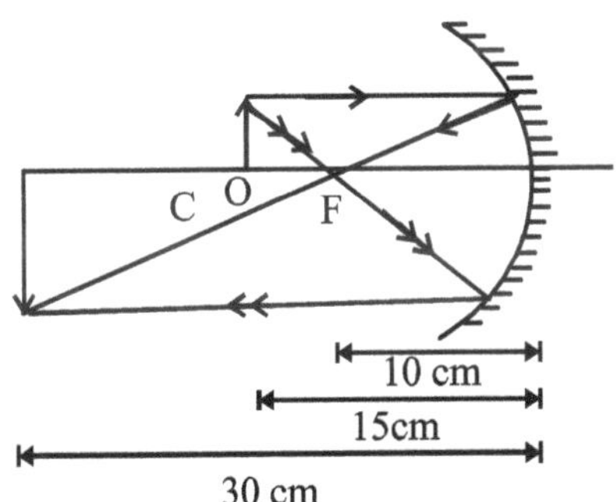

According to New Cartesian sign convention,
Object distance u = – 15 cm
Focal length of a concave lens, f = – 10 cm
Height of the object $h_0 = 2.0$ cm

According to mirror formula, $\frac{1}{v} + \frac{1}{u} = \frac{1}{f}$

$$\frac{1}{v} = \frac{1}{f} - \frac{1}{u} = \frac{1}{-10} - \frac{1}{-15} \Rightarrow v = -30cm.$$

This image is formed 30 cm from the mirror on the same side of the object. It is real image.

Magnification of the mirror, $m = \frac{-v}{u} = \frac{h_1}{h_0}$

$$\Rightarrow \frac{-(-30)}{-15} = \frac{h_1}{2} \Rightarrow h_1 = -4\ cm$$

Negative sign shows that image is inverted.
The image is real, inverted, of size 4 cm at a distance 30 cm in front of the mirror.

21. (1.319)

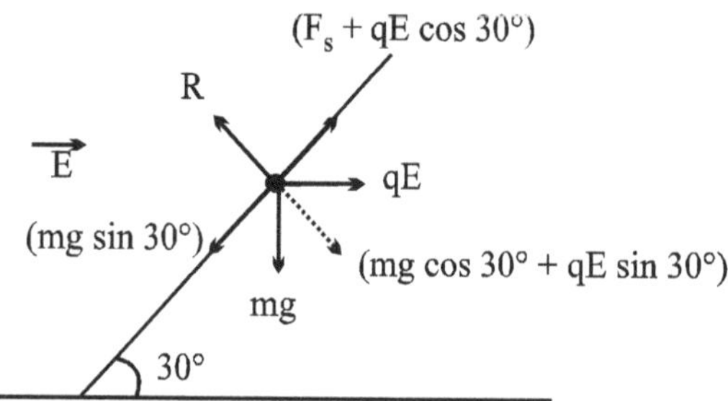

From the figure

$R = mg \cos 30^\circ + qE \sin 30^\circ$

$$= \frac{10\sqrt{3}}{2} + \frac{0.01 \times 100}{2}$$

$= 5\sqrt{3} + 0.5 = 9.16\,N$

Frictional force $F_s = \mu R = 0.2 \times 9.16 = 1.832\,N$

Resultant force along the plane in the downward direction

$F = mg \sin 30^\circ - (F_s + qE \cos 30^\circ)$

$$= 5 - \left(1.832 + 0.01 \times 100 \times \frac{1.732}{2}\right)$$

$= 5 - 2.698 = 2.3N$

$\therefore$ Acceleration along the plane, $f = \frac{F}{m} = 2.3\ m/sec^2$

Distance along the plane $= 1 \times \operatorname{cosec} 30^\circ = 2$ m

$s = ut + (1/2)\,ft^2, u = 0$

$$\therefore\ t = \left(\frac{2s}{f}\right)^{1/2} = \left(\frac{2 \times 2}{2.3}\right)^{1/2}$$

$= 1.319$ sec

22. (3.57×10^7)

Time period of satellite,

$$T = \frac{2\pi(R_E + h)}{\sqrt{\frac{GM_E}{(R_E + h)}}} = \frac{2\pi(R_E + h)^{3/2}}{\sqrt{GM_E}}$$

Squaring both sides, we get

$$T^2 = \frac{4\pi^2 (R_E + h)^3}{GM_E}$$

$$(R_E + h)^3 = \frac{GM_E T^2}{4\pi^2}$$

$$(R_E + h) = \left(\frac{GM_E T^2}{4\pi^2}\right)^{1/3}$$

or $h = \left(\frac{GM_E T^2}{4\pi^2}\right)^{1/3} - R_E$

Here, $M_E = 6 \times 10^{24}$ kg
$R_E = 6400\text{ km} = 6400 \times 10^3\text{ m} = 6.4 \times 10^6\text{m}$
$T = 24\text{ h} = 24 \times 60 \times 60\text{ s} = 86400\text{ s}$
$G = 6.67 \times 10^{-11}\text{ N m}^2\text{ kg}^{-2}$
On substituting the given values, we get

$$h = \left(\frac{6.67 \times 10^{-11} \times 6 \times 10^{24} \times (86400)^2}{4 \times (3.14)^2}\right)^{1/3} - 6.4 \times 10^6$$

$= 4.21 \times 10^7 - 6.4 \times 10^6 = 3.57 \times 10^7\text{ m}$

23. (7) Let initial e.m.f. induced = e.

$\therefore$ Initial current $i = \frac{E - e}{R}$ i.e., $2 = \frac{12 - e}{1}$

This gives $e = 12 - 2 = 10$ volt. As $e \propto \omega$.
when speed is halved, the value of induced e.m.f. becomes

$$\frac{e}{2} = \frac{10}{2} = 5 \text{ volt}$$

$\therefore$ New value of current

$$i' = \frac{E - e}{R} = \frac{12 - 5}{1} = 7\text{ A}$$

24. (40)

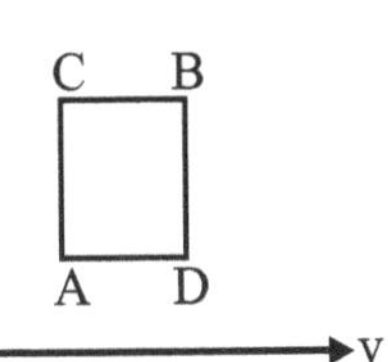

ΔU remains same for both paths ACB and ADB

$\Delta Q_{ACB} = \Delta W_{ACB} + \Delta U_{ACB}$

$\Rightarrow 60\text{ J} = 30\text{ J} + \Delta U_{ACB}$

$\Rightarrow U_{ACB} = 30\text{ J}$

$\therefore \Delta U_{ADB} = \Delta U_{ACB} = 30\text{ J}$

$\Delta Q_{ADB} = \Delta U_{ADB} + \Delta W_{ADB}$

$= 10\text{ J} + 30\text{ J} = 40\text{ J}$

25. **(1.324)**

Energy produced in one day $= 10^6 \times 24 \times 60 \times 60$ joule

$$\eta = 0.8 = \frac{\text{output energy}}{\text{input energy}} = \frac{10^6 \times 24 \times 60 \times 60}{\text{input energy}}$$

$$\text{So input energy} = \frac{10^6 \times 24 \times 60 \times 60}{0.8} = 10.8 \times 10^{10}\text{ J}$$

Energy released in one fission

$= 200 \times 10^6 \times 1.6 \times 10^{-19} = 3.2 \times 10^{-11}\text{ J}$

$$\text{No. of fissions per day} = \frac{10.8 \times 10^{10}}{3.2 \times 10^{-11}} = 3.375 \times 10^{21}$$

Mass of U^{235} consumed per day

= no. of nuclei disintegrating per day × mass of U^{235}

$= 3.375 \times 10^{21} \times 235 \times 1.67 \times 10^{-27} = 1.324\text{ mg}$

26. **(6)** Given,

Height of the water, H = 12 cm

Velocity of water coming out of hole, $v = \sqrt{2gh}$

Range of water, R = vt

$$\Rightarrow R = \sqrt{2gh} \times \sqrt{\frac{2(H-h)}{g}}$$

$$= 2\sqrt{h(H-h)}$$

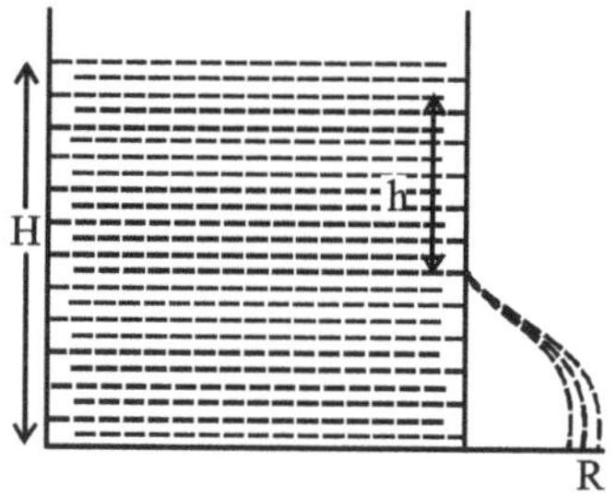

H
h
R

For maximum range $\frac{dR}{dh} = 0$

$\therefore\ h = \frac{H}{2}$

Range is maximum when $h = \frac{12}{2} = 6m$

27. **(600)** Given,

Separation between two slits, $d = 1$ mm

Distance of the screen, $D = 10$ m

Fringe width,

$$\beta = \frac{D\lambda}{d} \Rightarrow 6 \times 10^{-3} = \frac{10\lambda}{10^{-3}}$$

$\therefore\ \lambda = 600$ nm.

28. **(18)** Given, Mass of the body, $m = 2$ kg

Power delivered by engine, $P = 1$ J/s

Time, $t = 9$ seconds

Power, $P = Fv$

$$\Rightarrow P = mav \qquad [\because F = ma]$$

$$\Rightarrow m\frac{dv}{dt}v = P \qquad \left(\because a = \frac{dv}{dt}\right)$$

$$\Rightarrow v\,dv = \frac{P}{m}dt$$

Integrating both sides we get

$$\Rightarrow \int_0^v v\,dv = \frac{P}{m}\int_0^t dt$$

$$\Rightarrow \frac{v^2}{2} = \frac{Pt}{m} \Rightarrow v = \left(\frac{2Pt}{m}\right)^{1/2}$$

$$\Rightarrow \frac{dx}{dt} = \sqrt{\frac{2P}{m}}t^{1/2} \qquad \left(\because v = \frac{dx}{dt}\right)$$

$$\Rightarrow \int_0^x dx = \sqrt{\frac{2P}{m}}\int_0^t t^{1/2}\,dt$$

$$\therefore \text{ Distance, } x = \sqrt{\frac{2P}{m}}\frac{t^{3/2}}{3/2} = \sqrt{\frac{2P}{m}} \times \frac{2}{3}t^{3/2}$$

$$\Rightarrow x = \sqrt{\frac{2 \times 1}{2}} \times \frac{2}{3} \times 9^{3/2} = \frac{2}{3} \times 27 = 18.$$

29. **(40)** Current in the circuit, $I=\frac{12-8}{400}=10^{-2}A$

Power dissipited in each diode, $P=VI$

$\Rightarrow \quad P=4\times10^{-2}=40\,mW$

30. **(2)**

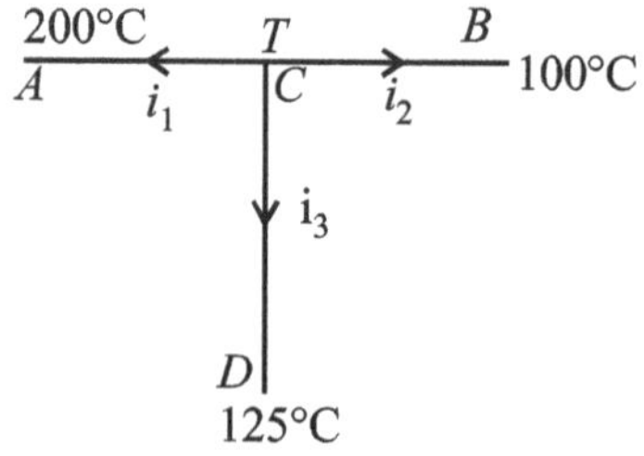

A 200°C, T C, B 100°C, i_1, i_2, i_3, D 125°C

[As AB & CD identical]

$R_{AB}=R_{CD}=10\text{ Kw}^{-1}$

$R_{AC}=R_{CB}=5\text{ kw}^{-1}$

[As AC $=BC$]

$R_{AC}=R_{CB}=5\text{ kw}^{-1}$

at point C

$i_1+i_2+i_3=0$ [Using Kirchoff's current law]

$$\Rightarrow \frac{T-200}{5}+\frac{T-100}{5}+\frac{T-125}{10}=0$$

$\Rightarrow T=145°C$

$$\Rightarrow P=\frac{145-125}{10}w=\frac{20}{10}w$$

$\Rightarrow P=2W$

CHEMISTRY

31. **(b)** When the temperature is increased, energy in form of heat is supplied which increases the kinetic energy of the reacting molecules. This will increase the number of collisions and ultimately the rate of reaction will be enhanced.

32. **(b)** In lanthanides, there is poorer shielding of $5d$ electrons by $4f$ electrons resulting in greater attraction of the nucleus over $5d$ electrons and contraction of the atomic radii.

33. **(b)** $(CH_3)_2CHCH_2MgBr \xrightarrow{C_2H_5OH} (CH_3)_2CHCH_3 + Mg\langle^{OC_2H_5}_{Br}$

34. (c) Using the relation $K_p = K_c.(RT)^{\Delta n}$, we get

$$\frac{K_p}{K_c} = (RT)^{\Delta n}$$

Thus $\frac{K_p}{K_c}$ will be highest for the reaction having highest value of Δn.

The Δn values for various reactions are

(a) $\Delta n = 1 - \left(1 + \frac{1}{2}\right) = -\frac{1}{2}$

(b) $\Delta n = 2 - (1 + 1) = 0$

(c) $\Delta n = (1 + 1) - 1 = 1$

(d) $\Delta n = (2 + 4) - (7 + 2) = -3$

Thus, maximum value of $\Delta n = 1$

35. (d) According to Fajan's rule :

$$\text{Covalent character} \propto \frac{1}{\text{size of cation}}$$

$$\propto \text{size of anion}$$

Among the given species order of size of cations

$N^{3+} < O^{2+} < Pb^{2+} < Ba^{2+}$

Order of size of anions $O^{2-} > Cl^-$.

Hence the order of covalent character is

$NCl_3 > Cl_2O > PbCl_2 > BaCl_2$

$\therefore$ $BaCl_2$ is most ionic in nature.

36. (d) For temporary hardness,

$$Mg(HCO_3)_2 \xrightarrow{\Delta} Mg(OH)_2\downarrow + 2CO_2\downarrow$$

$Mg(OH)_2$ has high solubility product than $MgCO_3$.

37. (c) $CH_3COOH + CaCO_3 \rightarrow (CH_3COO)_2Ca$

$$\xrightarrow{\text{Heat}} \begin{matrix} CH_3 \\ CH_3 \end{matrix}\!\!>CO \xrightarrow{I_2 + NaOH} CHI_3$$

38. (b) $\Delta G = \Delta H - T\Delta S$

At equilibrium, $\Delta G = 0$

$\Rightarrow 0 = (170 \times 10^3\ J) - T(170\ JK^{-1})$

$\Rightarrow T = 1000\ K$

For spontaneity, ΔG is – ve, which is possible only if $T > 1000\ K$.

39. (b) According to gas law

$$PV = nRT,\ n = \frac{PV}{RT}$$

$$\frac{n_A}{n_B}=\frac{\frac{P_1V_1}{RT_1}}{\frac{P_2V_2}{RT_2}};\frac{n_A}{n_B}=\frac{P_1V_1}{T_1}\times\frac{T_2}{P_2V_2}$$

$$\frac{n_A}{n_B}=\frac{2P\times 2V}{2T}\times\frac{T}{PV};\frac{n_A}{n_B}=\frac{2}{1}$$

40. **(a)**

(A)	Calamine	$ZnCO_3$
(B)	Malachite	$CuCO_3.Cu(OH)_2$
(C)	Siderite	$FeCO_3$
(D)	Sphalerite	ZnS

41. **(a)** Carbon atom is connected with four different groups in chiral structure.

42. **(c)** Sr^{90} is harmfull radiological pollutant.

43. **(d)** Here, A_2B_3 can also be written as A_4B_6.

Since, *hcp* has six atoms, so 'B' forms *hcp* lattice and 'A' is present in void.

Total tetrahedral voids = 12

$\therefore$ Fraction of tetrahedral voids occupied by

$A = 4/12 = \frac{1}{3}$

44. **(c)** $CH_3-\underset{\overset{|}{CH_3}}{CH}-\underset{\overset{|}{CH_3}}{CH}-CH_3$. Since it contains only two types of H-atoms hence it will give only two mono chlorinated compounds viz.

$$ClCH_2-\overset{\overset{CH_3}{|}}{CH}-\overset{\overset{CH_3}{|}}{CH}-CH_3$$

1–Chloro–2,3–dimethyl butane

and $CH_3-\overset{\overset{CH_3}{|}}{\underset{\underset{Cl}{|}}{C}}-\overset{\overset{CH_3}{|}}{CH}-CH_3$

2–Chloro–2,3–dimethyl butane

45. **(c)** Let solubility of $PbCl_2 = s$

$$PbCl_2 \rightleftharpoons Pb^{2+} + 2Cl^-$$

Moles $\quad s \quad\quad s \quad\quad 2s$

$$K_{sp} = [Pb^{2+}][Cl^-]^2$$

$\therefore \quad 1.7 \times 10^{-5} = (s)(2s)^2$

or $\quad 1.7 \times 10^{-5} = 4s^3$

$$\therefore \quad s = \sqrt[3]{\frac{1.7 \times 10^{-5}}{4}} = 1.62 \times 10^{-2}$$

46. (d) d^4 in high spin octahedral complex

e_g ↑ —

t_{2g} ↑ ↑ ↑

$CFSE = (-0.4x + 0.6y)\Delta_0$

Where, $x \rightarrow$ electrons in t_{2g} orbital

$y \rightarrow$ electrons in e_g orbital

$CFSE = [0.6 \times 1] + [-0.4 \times 3] = -0.6\ \Delta_0$

47. (d) Aniline ($C_6H_5NH_2$) $\xrightarrow[\text{0 °C}]{NaNO_2, HCl}$ (diazotisation) (A) Benzene diazonium chloride ($C_6H_5\overset{+}{N}{\equiv}NCl^-$) $\xrightarrow{CuCN}$

(B) Cyanobenzene (C_6H_5CN) $\xrightarrow{LiAlH_4}$ (C) Benzylamine ($C_6H_5CH_2NH_2$)

48. (b) Nylon is a polyamide polymer

49. (a) Reaction involved:

$$\overset{+3}{C_2}O_4^{2-} \longrightarrow 2\overset{+4}{C}O_2 + 2e^-$$

Oxidation number of C-atom increased.

$\therefore$ The number of electrons involved in producing one mole of CO_2 is 1.

50. (d) $\lambda = \dfrac{h}{mv}$

$\therefore \quad mv = \frac{h}{\lambda} = \frac{6.625 \times 10^{-34}}{0.33 \times 10^{-9}} = 2.01 \times 10^{-24}\ \text{kg m sec}^{-1}$

51. **(300)** ΔH = Heat of formation at constant pressure

ΔE = Heat of formation at constant volume

T = 27 °C = 27 + 273 = 300 K.

R = 2 cal/degree/mole.

$$C(s) + \frac{1}{2}O_2(g) \longrightarrow CO(g)$$

$$\Delta n = n_p - n_r = 1 - \frac{1}{2} = \frac{1}{2}$$

$$\Delta H = \Delta E + \Delta n_g RT \quad \text{or} \quad \Delta H - \Delta E = \Delta n_g RT$$

$$= \frac{1}{2} \times 2 \times 300 = 300 \text{ cal}$$

$\therefore$ Heat of formation of CO at constant pressure and at constant volume at 27 °C will differ from one another by 300 cal.

52. **(5)**

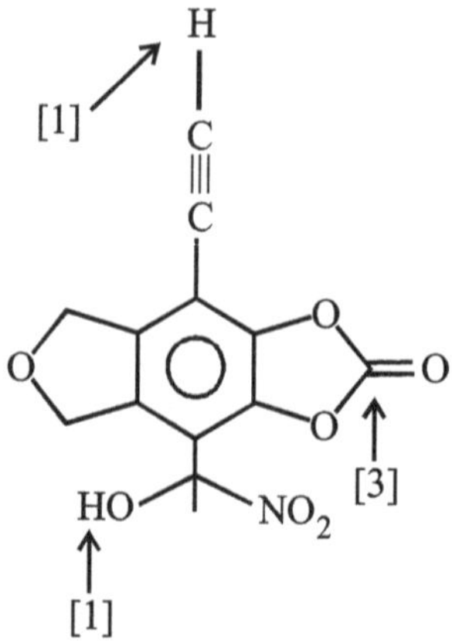

H
[1]
C
C
O
O
O
O Total = 5.
[3]
HO
NO_2
[1]

53. **(32)** $O_2\%$ = 20%

Metal% = 80%.

100g of metal oxide contains 80g metal and 20g oxygen

$\therefore$ Eq. wt. of metal = mass of metal × 8/ mass of oxygen

$$= \frac{80 \times 8}{20} = 32\text{ g}$$

54. **(4)** The total number of isomers for the complex compound

$[Cu^{II}(NH_3)_4][Pt^{II}Cl_4]$ is four.

These four isomers are

$[Cu(NH_3)_3Cl]\,[Pt(NH_3)Cl_3]$,

$[Cu(NH_3)Cl_3]\,[Pt(NH_3)_3Cl]$,

$[CuCl_4][Pt(NH_3)_4]$

and $\left[Cu(NH_3)_4\right]\left[PtCl_4\right]$.

The isomer $[Cu(NH_3)_2Cl_2][Pt(NH_3)_2Cl_2]$ does not exist due to both parts being neutral.

55. **(3)** 10 volume solution of H_2O_2 means that 1L of this H_2O_2 solution will give 10 L of oxygen at STP.

$2H_2O_2(l) \longrightarrow O_2(g) + H_2O(l)$

$2 \times 34g$ 22.7 L at STP

$= 68g$

Thus, 22.4L of O_2 is produced from 68 g H_2O_2 at STP. 10 L of O_2 at STP is produced from $\frac{68 \times 10}{22.4}$ g

$= 29.9 g H_2O_2 = 30$ g

Therefore, strength of H_2O_2 in 10 volume of H_2O_2 solution,

$= 30$ g/L $= 3\%$ H_2O_2 solution.

56. **(68)** $\% \text{ of Br} = \frac{\text{Atomic mass} \times \text{Br} \times m_1}{\text{Molecular mass of Ag Br} \times m} \times 100$

m_1 = mass of AgBr obtained

m = mass of organic compound taken

Now,

$\% \text{ of Br} = \frac{80 \times 0.2397}{188 \times 0.15} \times 100 = 68$

57. **(0)** $Zn^+ \rightarrow 1s^2\,2s^2\,2p^6\,3s^2\,3p^6\,3d^{10}\,4s^1$.

Outermost electron is in 4*s* subshell, so m = 0

58. **(12)** $16e^- + S_8^- \longrightarrow 8S^{2-}$

$12H_2O + S_8 \longrightarrow 4S_2O_3^{2-} + 24H^+ + 16e^-$

$2S_8 + 12H_2O \longrightarrow 8S^{2-} + 4S_2O_3^{2-} + 24H^+$

For balancing in basic medium add OH^- equal to H^+.

$2S_8 + 12H_2O + 24OH^- \longrightarrow 8S^{2-} + 4S_2O_8^{2-} + 24H_2O$

$$2S_8 + 24OH^- \longrightarrow 8S^{2-} + 4S_2O_8^{2-} + 12H_2O$$

$$S_8 + 12OH^- \longrightarrow 4S^{2-} + 2S_2O_8^{2-} + 6H_2O$$

$\therefore a = 12.$

59. **(19)** Using Raoult's law

$$P_s = \chi_A P_A^0 + \chi_B P_B^0 = \frac{1}{3}\times 21 + \frac{2}{3}\times 18 = 19 \text{ kPa}$$

60. **(5)** Mohr's salt $\Rightarrow (NH_4)_2 Fe(SO_4)_2 . 6H_2O$
Potash alum $\Rightarrow KAl(SO_4)_2 . 12H_2O$

$$= \frac{6}{12} = 0.5 = 5\times 10^{-1}$$

MATHEMATICS

61. **(a)** Since $\left(7+4\sqrt{3}\right)\left(7-4\sqrt{3}\right)=1,$

$\therefore$ The given equation becomes

$$y + \frac{1}{y} = 14 \text{ where } y = \left(7 - 4\sqrt{3}\right)^{x^2-4x+3}$$

$\Rightarrow y^2 - 14y + 1 = 0 \Rightarrow y = 7 \pm 4\sqrt{3}$

Now $y = 7 + 4\sqrt{3} \Rightarrow x^2 - 4x + 3 = -1 \Rightarrow x = 2, 2$

Also $y = 7 - 4\sqrt{3} \Rightarrow x^2 - 4x + 3 = 1 \Rightarrow x = 2 \pm \sqrt{2}$

62. **(a)** $f(x) = x^{3/2} + x^{-3/2} - 4\left(x + \frac{1}{x}\right)$

$$f(x) = \left(\sqrt{x} + \frac{1}{\sqrt{x}}\right)^3 - 3\left(\sqrt{x} + \frac{1}{\sqrt{x}}\right) - 4\left[\left(\sqrt{x} + \frac{1}{\sqrt{x}}\right)^2 - 2\right]$$

Let $\sqrt{x} + \frac{1}{\sqrt{x}} = t \ (x > 0)$

Let $g(t) = t^3 - 3t - 4t^2 + 8$

$g(t) = t^3 - 4t^2 - 3t + 8$

$g'(t) = 3t^2 - 8t - 3 = (t-3)(3t+1)$

$g'(t) = 0 \Rightarrow t = 3 \ (t \neq -1/3)$

$g''(t) = 6t - 8$

$g''(3) = 10 > 0 \Rightarrow g(3)$ is minimum

$g(3) = 27 - 9 - 36 + 8 = -10$

63. **(a)** term of $\left(\frac{x}{2}-\frac{3}{x^2}\right)^{10}$ is ${}^{10}C_t\left(\frac{x}{2}\right)^{10-t}\left(\frac{-3}{x^2}\right)^t$.

Here, $x^{-t+10-2t}=x^4 \Rightarrow -3t+10=4 \Rightarrow t=2$

Hence coefficient of x^4 is ${}^{10}C_2\left(\frac{1}{2}\right)^8(3)^2=\frac{405}{256}$

64. **(b)** Given plane $3x+y+2z+6=0$

and line $\frac{x-1/3}{2b/3}=\frac{y-3}{-1}=\frac{z-1}{a}$

Since plane is parallel to line, then

$3\left(\frac{2b}{3}\right)+(1)(-1)+2(a)=0$

$\Rightarrow 2b-1+2a=0 \Rightarrow a+b=1/2$

Now, $3a+3b=3/2$

65. **(b)** $f(x)=\sqrt{1+\log_e(1-x)}$ value of f(x) is real when

$1+\log_e(1-x)\geq 0$ and $1-x>0$

$\Rightarrow \log_e(1-x)\geq -1$ and $x<1$

$\Rightarrow \log_e(1-x)\geq \log_e e^{-1}$ and $x<1$

$\Rightarrow 1-x\geq \frac{1}{e}$ and $x<1 \Rightarrow x\leq \frac{e-1}{e}$ and $x<1$.

66. **(c)** $f(x)=[x]^2-[x^2]$

Check continuity at x = 0

$\lim_{x\to 0^+} f(x)=\lim_{x\to 0^+}[x]^2-[x^2]=0$

$\lim_{x\to 0^-} f(x)=\lim_{x\to 0^-}[x]^2-[x^2]$

$=(-1)^2-0=1$

Thus, discontinuous at x = 0

Check continuity at x = 1

$\lim_{x\to 1^+} f(x)=1-1=0$

$\lim_{x\to 1^-} f(x)=0-0=0$

Also f(1) = 0

Hence continuous at x = 1.

67. **(a)** $y=1+4x-x^2=5-(x-2)^2$

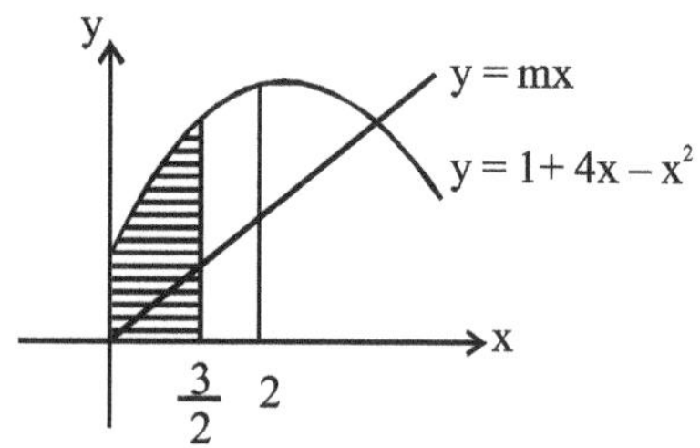

We have $\int_0^{3/2}(1+4x-x^2)dx = 2\int_0^{3/2} mx\,dx$

$$=\frac{3}{2}+2\left(\frac{9}{4}\right)-\frac{1}{3}\left(\frac{27}{8}\right)=m\cdot\frac{9}{4}$$

On solving we get $m=\frac{13}{6}$

68. **(b)** Series $3+33+333+.....+n$ terms
Given series can be written as,

$$=\frac{1}{3}[9+99+999+....+n \text{ terms}]$$

$$=\frac{1}{3}[(10-1)+(100-1)+(1000-1)+....+n \text{ terms}]$$

$$=\frac{1}{3}[10+10^2+....+10^n]-\frac{1}{3}[1+1+1+.....+n \text{ terms}]$$

$$=\frac{1}{3}\cdot\frac{10(10^n-1)}{10-1}-\frac{1}{3}n=\frac{1}{3}\left[\frac{10^{n+1}-10}{9}-n\right]$$

$$=\frac{1}{3}\cdot\left[\frac{10^{n+1}-9n-10}{9}\right]=\frac{1}{27}[10^{n+1}-9n-10]$$

69. **(a)** Let $I=\int\frac{1}{1+\sin x}dx=\int\frac{dx}{1+\frac{2\tan\frac{x}{2}}{1+\tan^2\frac{x}{2}}}$

$$\int\frac{\left(1+\tan^2\frac{x}{2}\right)dx}{1+\tan^2\frac{x}{2}+2\tan\frac{x}{2}}=\int\frac{\sec^2\frac{x}{2}\,dx}{1+\tan^2\frac{x}{2}+2\tan\frac{x}{2}}$$

Substitute

$\tan\frac{x}{2} = t \Rightarrow \frac{1}{2}\sec^2\frac{x}{2}dx = dt \Rightarrow \sec^2\frac{x}{2}dx = 2dt$.

Then

$$I = \int \frac{2dt}{1+t^2+2t} = 2\int \frac{dt}{(1+t)^2} = 2\frac{-1}{(1+t)} + C$$

$$= \frac{-2}{1+\tan\frac{x}{2}} + C = 1 - \frac{2}{1+\tan\frac{x}{2}} + (C-1) = \frac{\tan\frac{x}{2}-1}{\tan\frac{x}{2}+1} + b,$$

Where b = $C - 1$, a new constant

$$= -\frac{1-\tan\frac{x}{2}}{1+\tan\frac{x}{2}} + b = -\tan\left(\frac{\pi}{4}-\frac{x}{2}\right) + b = \tan\left(\frac{x}{2}-\frac{\pi}{4}\right) + b.$$

Clearly $a = -\frac{\pi}{4}$ and $b \in \mathbf{R}$

70. **(d)** Given expression can be written as

$$y = \tan^{-1}\left[\frac{2^x(2-1)}{1+2^x.2^{x+1}}\right] = \tan^{-1}\left[\frac{2^{x+1}-2^x}{1+2^x.2^{x+1}}\right]$$

$$= \tan^{-1}(2^{x+1}) - \tan^{-1}(2^x)$$

$$\Rightarrow \frac{dy}{dx} = \frac{2^{x+1}\log 2}{1+2^{2(x+1)}} - \frac{2^x \log 2}{1+2^{2x}}$$

$$\therefore \left(\frac{dy}{dx}\right)_{x=0} = (\log 2)\left(\frac{2}{5}-\frac{1}{2}\right) = \log 2\left(-\frac{1}{10}\right)$$

71. **(d)** We have, $\cos\frac{2\pi}{7} + \cos\frac{4\pi}{7} + \cos\frac{6\pi}{7}$

$$= \frac{1}{2\sin\frac{\pi}{7}}\left[2\sin\frac{\pi}{7}\cos\frac{2\pi}{7} + 2\sin\frac{\pi}{7}\cos\frac{4\pi}{7} + 2\sin\frac{\pi}{7}\cos\frac{6\pi}{7}\right]$$

$$= \frac{1}{2\sin\frac{\pi}{7}}\left[\left(\sin\frac{3\pi}{7}-\sin\frac{\pi}{7}\right)+\left(\sin\frac{5\pi}{7}-\sin\frac{3\pi}{7}\right)+\left(\sin\frac{7\pi}{7}-\sin\frac{5\pi}{7}\right)\right]$$

$$= -\frac{1}{2} \qquad \left[\because \sin\frac{7\pi}{7} = \sin\pi = 0\right]$$

72. (b) Consider the differential equation

$$\frac{dy}{dx} = y\tan x - y^2 \sec x$$

Divide by y^2 on both the sides, we get

$$\frac{1}{y^2}\left(\frac{dy}{dx}\right) = \frac{\tan x}{y} - \sec x \quad ...(1)$$

Let $\frac{1}{y} = z$

Differentiating both sides, we get:

$$\frac{-1}{y^2} \cdot \frac{dy}{dx} = \frac{dz}{dx}$$

Put value of $\frac{1}{y^2}\frac{dy}{dx}$ in the equation(1), we get

$$-\left(\frac{dz}{dx}\right) - (\tan x)z = -\sec x$$

$$\Rightarrow \left(\frac{dz}{dx}\right) + (\tan x)z = \sec x$$

This is the linear diff equation in 'z' i.e.

This is of the form $\frac{dz}{dx} + \text{P}.z = \text{Q}$

then integrating factor = $e^{\int \text{P}dx}$

∴ In the given question

$$\text{I.F.} = e^{\int \tan x\, dx} = e^{\log(\sec x)} = \sec x$$

73. (c) Here equation of the circle
$(x^2 + y^2 - 10x) + \lambda(y - 2x) = 0$
Now centre $C\,(5 + \lambda, -\lambda/2)$ lies on the chord again.

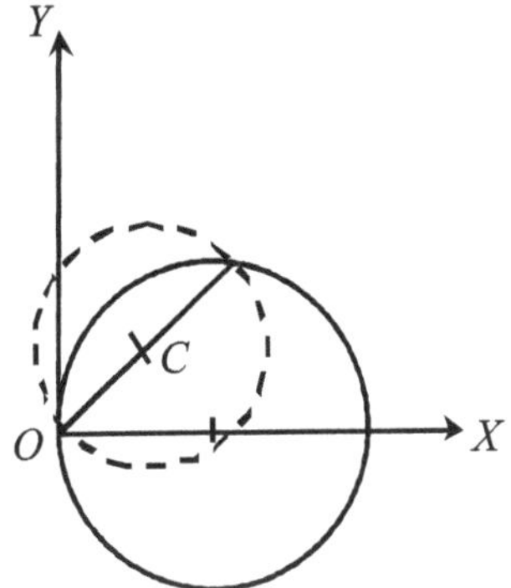

$\therefore \frac{-\lambda}{2} = 2(5+\lambda)$

$\therefore \lambda = -4$

Hence $x^2 + y^2 = 10x + 4y - 8x$

or $x^2 + y^2 - 2x - 4y = 0$

74. (c) Since, $\vec{a}$ and $\vec{b}+\vec{c}$ are mutually perpendicular.

$\therefore \quad \vec{a}.(\vec{b}+\vec{c}) = 0 \Rightarrow \vec{a}.\vec{b}+\vec{c}.\vec{a} = 0$ ...(i)

Similarly, $\vec{b}.\vec{c}+\vec{a}.\vec{b} = 0$ ...(ii)

and $\vec{c}.\vec{a}+\vec{b}.\vec{c} = 0$ ...(iii)

On adding eqs. (i), (ii) and (iii), we get

$2(\vec{a}.\vec{b}+\vec{b}.\vec{c}+\vec{c}.\vec{a}) = 0$

Now, $|\vec{a}+\vec{b}+\vec{c}|^2 = |\vec{a}|^2 + |\vec{b}|^2 + |\vec{c}|^2 + 2(\vec{a}.\vec{b}+\vec{b}.\vec{c}+\vec{c}.\vec{a})$

$= |\vec{a}|^2| + |\vec{b}|^2 + |\vec{c}|^2$

$= 9 + 16 + 25 \quad (\because |\vec{a}| = 3, |\vec{b}| = 4, |\vec{c}| = 5)$

$= 50$

$\Rightarrow \quad |\vec{a}+\vec{b}+\vec{c}| = 5\sqrt{2}$.

75. (c) $\begin{vmatrix} a-x & c & b \\ c & b-x & a \\ b & a & c-x \end{vmatrix} = 0$

$$\Rightarrow \begin{vmatrix} a+b+c-x & c & b \\ a+b+c-x & b-x & a \\ a+b+c-x & a & c-x \end{vmatrix} = 0$$

$$\Rightarrow (\Sigma a - x)\begin{vmatrix} 1 & c & b \\ 1 & b-x & a \\ 1 & a & c-x \end{vmatrix} = 0$$

$\Rightarrow x = \Sigma a = 0$

or $1\{(b-x)(c-x)-a^2\} - c\{c-x-a\} + b\{a-b+x\} = 0$

(by expanding the determinant.)

or $x^2 - (a^2+b^2+c^2) + (ab+bc+ca) = 0$

or $x^2 - \Sigma a^2 + \Sigma ab = 0$

or $x^2 - (\Sigma a^2) - \frac{1}{2}(\Sigma a^2) = 0$

$[\because a+b+c = 0 \Rightarrow (a+b+c)^2 = 0$

$\Rightarrow \Sigma a^2 + 2\Sigma ab = 0 \Rightarrow \Sigma ab = -\frac{1}{2}\Sigma a^2]$

or $\quad x = \pm\sqrt{\frac{3}{2}\Sigma a^2}$

$\therefore$ the solution is $x = 0$ or $\pm\sqrt{\frac{3}{2}\Sigma a^2}$.

76. **(b)** $I_1 = \int_0^1 2^{x^2}dx,\ I_2 = \int_0^1 2^{x^3}dx,\ I_3 = \int_1^2 2^{x^2}dx,\ I_4 = \int_1^2 2^{x^3}dx$

$\forall\ 0 < x < 1,\ x^2 > x^3$

$\Rightarrow \int_0^1 2^{x^2}dx > \int_0^1 2^{x^3}dx \Rightarrow I_1 > I_2$.

Also $\forall\ 1 < x < 2\ \ x^2 < x^3 \Rightarrow \int_1^2 2^{x^2}dx < \int_1^2 2^{x^3}dx \Rightarrow I_3 < I_4$

77. **(c)** Given, $f(x) = |x|$ and $g(x) = [x-3]$

For $-\frac{8}{5} < x < \frac{8}{5};\ 0 \le f(x) < \frac{8}{5}$

Now, for $0 \le f(x) < 1$,

$g(f(x)) = [f(x) - 3] = -3 \quad [\because -3 \le f(x) - 3 < -2]$

for $1 \le f(x) < 1.6$

$g(f(x)) = -2 \quad [\because -2 \le f(x) - 3 < -1.4]$

$\therefore$ required set is $\{-3, -2\}$.

78. **(d)** We know that $P(A \cup B) \ge \max\{P(A), P(B)\} = \frac{2}{3}$

$P(A \cap B) \le \min\{P(A), P(B)\} = \frac{1}{2}$

and $P(A \cap B) = P(A) + P(B) - P(A \cup B) \ge P(A) + P(B) - 1 = \frac{1}{6}$

$\Rightarrow \frac{1}{6} \le P(A \cap B) \le \frac{1}{2}$

$P(A' \cap B) = P(B) - P(A \cap B)$

$\therefore \frac{2}{3} - \frac{1}{2} \le P(A' \cap B) \le \frac{2}{3} - \frac{1}{6}$

$\Rightarrow \frac{1}{6} \le P(A' \cap B) \le \frac{1}{2}$

79. **(d)** Let $P(a \sec\theta, b \tan\theta)$ and $Q(a \sec\theta, -b \tan\theta)$ be end points of double ordinates and $C(0, 0)$, is the centre of the hyperbola.
Now $PQ = 2b \tan\theta$

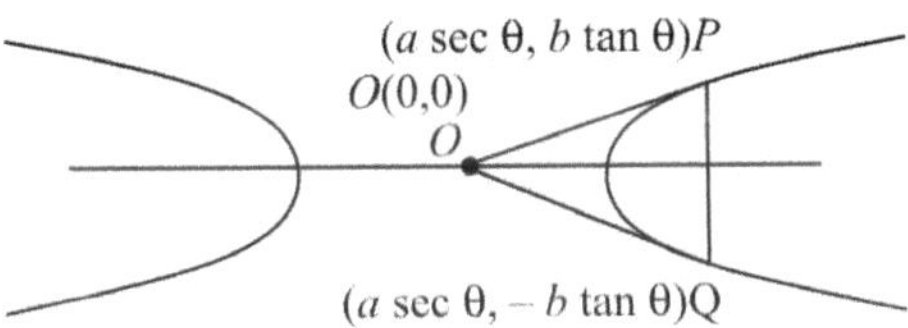

$OQ = OP = \sqrt{a^2 \sec^2\theta + b^2 \tan^2\theta}$

Since, OPQ is an equilateral triangle (given)

$\therefore OQ = OP = PQ,$

$\therefore 4b^2 \tan^2\theta = a^2 \sec^2\theta + b^2 \tan^2\theta$

$\Rightarrow 3b^2 \tan^2\theta = a^2 \sec^2\theta \Rightarrow 3b^2 \sin^2\theta = a^2$

$\Rightarrow 3a^2(e^2-1)\sin^2\theta = a^2,$ $\left[\because e=\sqrt{1-\frac{b^2}{a^2}}\right]$

$\Rightarrow 3(e^2-1)\sin^2\theta = 1$

$\Rightarrow \frac{1}{3(e^2-1)} = \sin^2\theta < 1, \quad (\because \sin^2\theta < 1)$

$\Rightarrow \frac{1}{e^2-1} < 3 \Rightarrow e^2-1 > \frac{1}{3} \Rightarrow e^2 > \frac{4}{3} \Rightarrow e > \frac{2}{\sqrt{3}}.$

80. **(b)** Let p be the length of the perpendicular from the origin on the given line. Then its equation in normal form is

$x\cos 30° + y\sin 30° = p \Rightarrow \sqrt{3}x + y = 2p$

This meets the coordinate axes at $A\left(\frac{2p}{\sqrt{3}}, 0\right)$ and $B(0, 2p)$.

$\therefore$ Hence, area of $\Delta OAB = \frac{1}{2}\left(\frac{2p}{\sqrt{3}}\right)2p$

$= \frac{2p^2}{\sqrt{3}}$

$\because$ are a of triangle is $\frac{50}{\sqrt{3}}$.

$\therefore \frac{2p^2}{\sqrt{3}} = \frac{50}{\sqrt{3}} \Rightarrow p = \pm 5.$

Hence the lines are $\sqrt{3}x + y \pm 10 = 0$.

81. **(6)** The first equation can be written as

$2\sin\frac{1}{2}(x+y)\cos\frac{1}{2}(x-y)$

$= 2\sin\frac{1}{2}(x+y)\cos\frac{1}{2}(x+y)$

$\therefore$ Either $\sin\frac{1}{2}(x+y) = 0$ or $\sin\frac{1}{2}x = 0$ or $\sin\frac{1}{2}y = 0$

$\because x+y=1, x+y=-1, x-y=-1, x-y=1$

When $x+y=0$, we have to reject $x+y=1$

$x+y=-1$ and solve it with $x-y=1$

or $x-y=-1$ which gives $\left(\frac{1}{2}, -\frac{1}{2}\right)$ or $\left(-\frac{1}{2}, \frac{1}{2}\right)$ as the possible solution.

Again solving with $x=0$, we get $(0, \pm 1)$ and solving with $y=0$, we get $(\pm 1, 0)$ as the other solution. Thus we have six pairs of solutions for x and y.

82. (120) Using L-Hospital's rule,

$$\lim_{x\to 0}\left\{\frac{\sin x - x + \frac{x^3}{6}}{x^5}\right\} = \lim_{x\to 0}\frac{\cos x - 1 + \frac{3x^2}{6}}{5x^4}$$

$$= \lim_{x\to 0}\frac{-\sin x + \frac{6x}{6}}{20x^3} = \lim_{x\to 0}\frac{-\cos x + 1}{60x^2}$$

$$= \lim_{x\to 0}\frac{\sin x}{120x} = \lim_{x\to 0}\frac{\cos x}{120} = \frac{1}{120}$$

83. (750) Let edge of the cube be x cm.

Volume of the cube be $x^3 cm^3$.

Given, $\frac{dx}{dt} = 10$ cm/sec

Now, $v = x^3 \Rightarrow \frac{dv}{dt} = 3x^2\frac{dx}{dt}$

$$\Rightarrow \frac{dv}{dt} = 3(5)^2(10)\,cm^3/\text{sec} = 750\,cm^3/\text{sec}.$$

84. (0) Given $2x = -1 + \sqrt{3}i \Rightarrow x = \frac{-1+\sqrt{3}i}{2} = \omega$

Now $(1-\omega^2+\omega)^6 - (1-\omega+\omega^2)$

$= (-\omega^2-\omega^2)^6 - (-\omega-\omega)^6 \quad (\because \ 1+\omega+\omega^2 = 0)$

$= (-2\omega^2)^6 - (-2\omega)^6 = (-2)^6(\omega^3)^4 - (-2)^6(\omega^3)^2$

$= (-2)^6 - (-2)^6 = 0 \quad (\because \ \omega^3 = 1)$

85. (13986)

The non-zero perfect square digits are 1, 4 and 9.
1 can occur at units place in $3 \times 3 = 9$ ways.
$\therefore$ Sum due to 1 at units place is 1×9. Similarly,
sum due to 1 at tens place is $1 \times 10 \times 9$ and
sum due to 1 at hundreds place $1 \times 100 \times 9$. We can deal with the digits 4 and 9 in a similar way.
Thus, sum of the desired number is
$(1+4+9)(1+10+100)(9) = 13986$.

86. (48) $z(1+i) + \bar{z}(1+i) \geq -10$

$\Rightarrow \quad (z+\bar{z})+i(z-\bar{z}) \geq -10$

$\Rightarrow \quad x-y+5>0$

And $|z+5| \leq 4$ is interior of a circle with centre -5 and radius 4.

$\therefore \quad |z+1|$ represents the distance of z from -1.

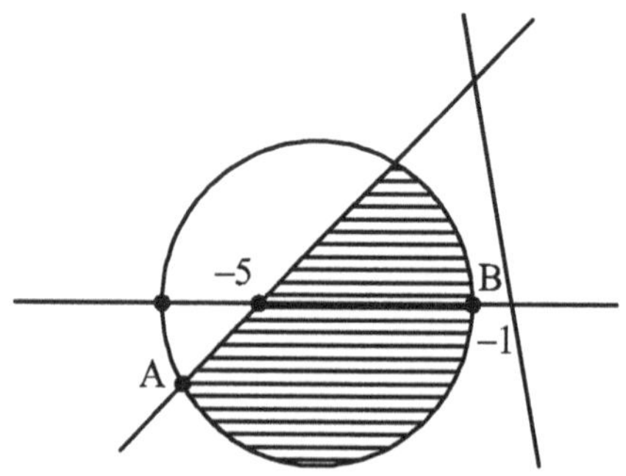

$|z+1|$ is maximum at A.

On solving equation of circle and line we get

$A(-2\sqrt{2}-5, -2\sqrt{2})$

$|z+1|^2 = AB^2 = (2\sqrt{2}+4)^2 + (2\sqrt{2})^2$

$\alpha + \beta\sqrt{2} = 32 + 16\sqrt{2}$

So, $\alpha + \beta = 32 + 16 = 48$.

87. **(777)** It is given that there are 15 players, 6 bowlers, 7 batsman, 2 wicketkeepers

So, total number of ways for at least 4 bowlers, 5 batsman and 1 wicketkeeper

$= {}^6C_4({}^7C_6 \times {}^2C_1 + {}^7C_5 \times {}^2C_2) + {}^6C_5 \times {}^7C_5 \times {}^2C_1 = 777$

88. **(1)** For domain $\log_5(\log_3(18x - x^2 - 77)) > 0$

$\Rightarrow \quad \log_3(18x - x^2 - 77) > 1$

$\Rightarrow \quad 18x - x^2 - 77 > 3$

$\Rightarrow \quad x^2 - 18x + 80 < 0$

$\Rightarrow (x-8)\quad(x-10)\quad < 0$

$+$		$-$	$+$
$-\infty$	8	10	∞

$\therefore x \in (8, 10)$

$\Rightarrow \quad a = 8$ and $b = 10$

$$\therefore\ I=\int_8^{10}\frac{\sin^3 x}{\sin^3 x+\sin^3(18-x)}dx \quad ...(i)$$

$$I=\int_8^{10}\frac{\sin^3(18-x)}{\sin^3(18-x)+\sin^3 x}dx \quad ...(ii)$$

Adding (i) and (ii) we get

$$2I=\int_8^{10}1.\,du=10-8=2$$

$\therefore I=1.$

89. (8) Since plane is perpendicular to the line joining points $(-2,-21,29)$ and $(-1,-16,23)$

$\therefore$ Normal vecter of plane is

$$\overline{n}=\hat{i}+5\hat{j}-6\hat{k}$$

Let A $(\lambda, 2, 1)$ and $(4,-2,2)$

$\because\ \overline{AB}\perp\overline{n}$

$\Rightarrow (\lambda-4)+5\times4-6(-1)=0$

$\Rightarrow \lambda-4+20+6=0$

$\Rightarrow \lambda=-22$

Hence, $\left(\frac{\lambda}{11}\right)^2-4\left(\frac{\lambda}{11}\right)-4=8$

90. (2) Equation of tangent to the given ellipse is,

$$\frac{x\cos\theta}{b}+\frac{y\sin\theta}{2a}=1$$

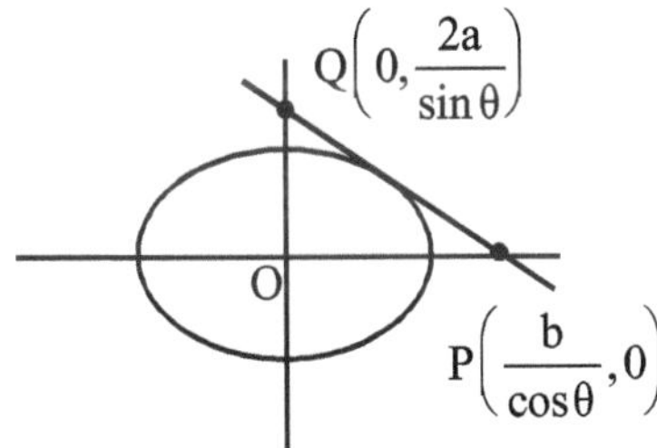

So, area $(\Delta OPQ)=\frac{1}{2}\times\frac{b}{\cos\theta}\times\frac{2a}{\sin\theta}$

$$=\frac{2ab}{\sin 2\theta}\geq 2ab \Rightarrow k=2$$

MOCK TEST-5

PHYSICS

1. **(a)**

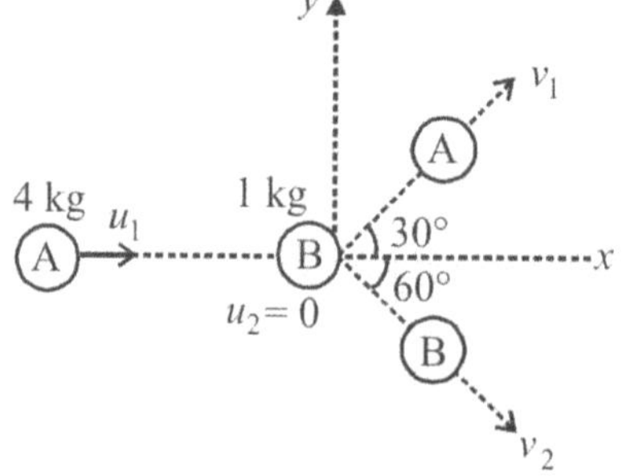

Apply the law of conservation of linear momentum along a direction perpendicular to the direction of motion (i.e. along y-axis), we get

$0 + 0 = 4v_1 \sin 30° - v_2 \sin 60°$

$4v_1 \sin 30° = v_2 \sin 60°$

$$\frac{v_1}{v_2} = \frac{\sin 60°}{4 \sin 30°} = \frac{\sqrt{3}}{4}$$

2. **(d)** Mass per unit length of the wire = ρ

Mass of L length, $M = \rho L$

and since the wire of length L is bent in a form of circular loop therefore

$$2\pi R = L \Rightarrow R = \frac{L}{2\pi}$$

Moment of inertia of loop about given axis $= \frac{3}{2} MR^2$

$$= \frac{3}{2} \rho L \left(\frac{L}{2\pi}\right)^2 = \frac{3\rho L^3}{8\pi^2}$$

3. **(c)** $V_{in} = \frac{-GM}{2R}\left[3 - \left(\frac{r}{R}\right)^2\right],$

$$V_{surface} = \frac{-GM}{R}, V_{out} = \frac{-GM}{r}$$

4. **(c)** Electric field, $E \propto \frac{1}{K}$

As $K_1 < K_2$ so $E_1 > E_2$

Hence graph (c) correctly dipicts the variation of electric field E with distance d.

5. (a) Let each plate moves a distance x from its initial position.
Let q charge flows in the loop. Using Kirchoff's voltage law

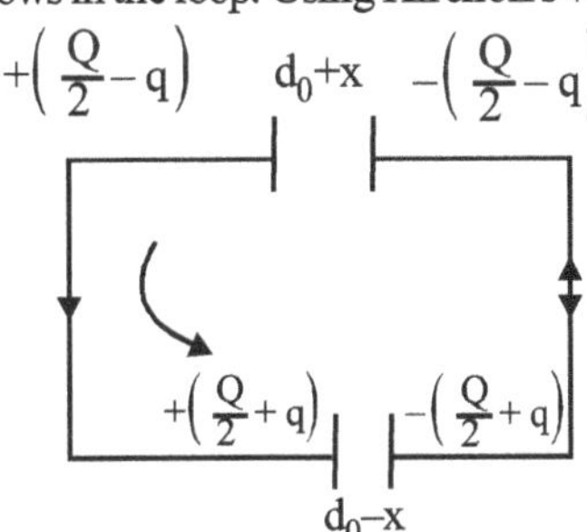

$$\frac{\left(\frac{Q}{2}-q\right)(d_0+x)}{\epsilon_0 A}-\frac{\left(\frac{Q}{2}+q\right)(d_0-x)}{\epsilon_0 A}=0$$

$$\therefore \; q=\frac{Qx}{2d_0} \; ; \; I=\frac{dq}{dt}=\frac{Q}{2d_0}\left(\frac{dx}{dt}\right)=\frac{Q}{2d_0}u_0$$

6. (a) The magnetic field varies inversely with the distance for a long conductor.
That is, $B \propto \frac{1}{d}$
so, graph (a) is the correct one.

7. (d) Applying dimensional method :
$v_c = \eta^x \rho^y r^z$
$[M^0LT^{-1}] = [ML^{-1}T^{-1}]^x [ML^{-3}T^0]^y [M^0LT^0]^z$
Equating powers both sides
$x+y=0; -x=-1 \therefore x=1$
$1+y=0 \therefore y=-1$
$-x-3y+z=1$
$-1-3(-1)+z=1$
$-1+3+z=1$
$\therefore z=-1$

8. (d)

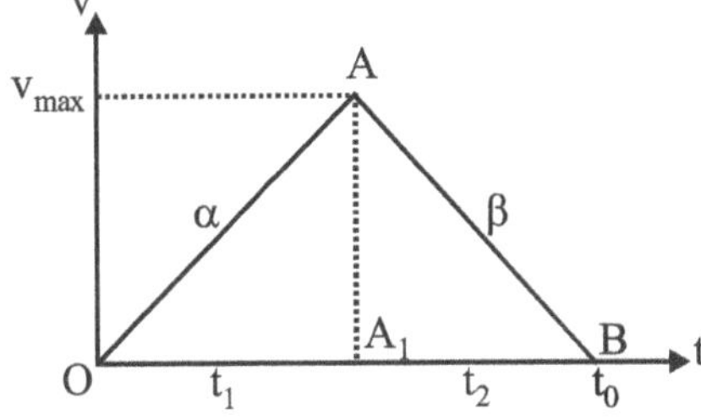

In fig., $AA_1 = v_{max.} = \alpha t_1 = \beta t_2$

But $t = t_1 + t_2 = \frac{v_{max}}{\alpha} + \frac{v_{max}}{\beta}$

$$= v_{max}\left(\frac{1}{\alpha} + \frac{1}{\beta}\right) = v_{max}\left(\frac{\alpha+\beta}{\alpha\beta}\right)$$

or, $v_{max} = t\left(\frac{\alpha\beta}{\alpha+\beta}\right)$

9. **(c)** Given, $u\cos\theta = \frac{\sqrt{3}u}{2}$

$$\Rightarrow \cos\theta = \frac{\sqrt{3}}{2} \Rightarrow \theta = 30°$$

Range (R) $= \frac{u^2 \sin 2\theta}{g} = \frac{u^2 \sin 60°}{g} = \frac{\sqrt{3}u^2}{2g}$

Maximum height $= \frac{u^2 \sin^2\theta}{2g} = \frac{u^2 \sin^2 30°}{2g} = \frac{u^2}{8g}$

Now, Range $= P \times H$

$$\Rightarrow \frac{\sqrt{3}u^2}{2g} = P \times \frac{u^2}{8g} \Rightarrow P = 4\sqrt{3}$$

10. **(d)** The electron ejected with maximum speed v_{max} are stopped by electric field $E = 4N/C$ after travelling a distance $d = 1m$

$$\frac{1}{2}mv_{max}^2 = eEd = 4eV$$

The energy of incident photon $= \frac{1240}{200} = 6.2$ eV

From equation of photo electric effect

$$\frac{1}{2}mv_{max}^2 = h\nu - \phi_0$$

$$\therefore \phi_0 = 6.2 - 4 = 2.2 \text{ eV}$$

11. **(d)** Shortest wavelength comes from $n_1 = \infty$ to $n_2 = 1$ and longest wavelength comes from $n_1 = 6$ to $n_2 = 5$ in the given case.

Hence $\frac{1}{\lambda_{min}} = R\left(\frac{1}{1^2} - \frac{1}{\infty^2}\right) = R$

$$\frac{1}{\lambda_{max}} = R\left(\frac{1}{5^2} - \frac{1}{6^2}\right) = R\left(\frac{36-25}{25\times 36}\right) = \frac{11}{900}R$$

$$\therefore \frac{\lambda_{max}}{\lambda_{min}} = \frac{900}{11}$$

12. (c) The range of energy of β-particles is from zero to some maximum value.
13. (c) According to Newton's law of cooling, the temperature goes on decreasing with time non-linearly.

14. (c) The equation for the line is

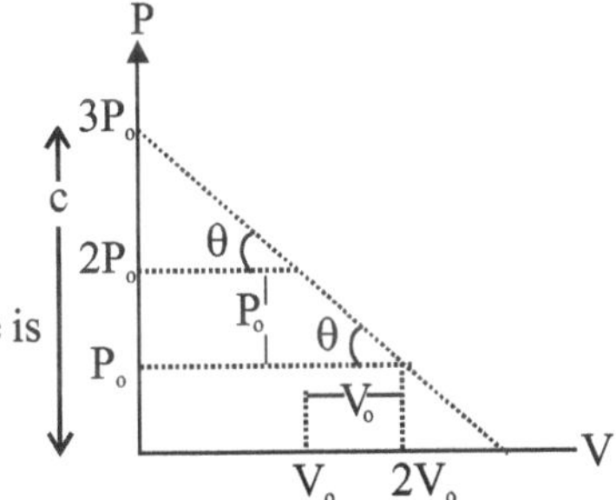

$$P = \frac{-P_0}{V_0}V + 3P \text{ [slope} = \frac{-P_0}{V_0}, c = 3P_0]$$

$$PV_0 + P_0V = 3P_0V_0 \qquad ...(i)$$

But $PV = nRT$

$$\therefore P = \frac{nRT}{V} \qquad ...(ii)$$

From (i) and (ii)

$$\frac{nRT}{V}V_0 + P_0V = 3P_0V_0$$

$$\therefore nRT\,V_0 + P_0V^2 = 3P_0V_0 \qquad ...(iii)$$

For temperature to be maximum $\frac{dT}{dV} = 0$

Differentiating e.q. (iii) by 'V' we get

$$nRV_0\frac{dT}{dV} + P_0(2V) = 3P_0V_0$$

$$\therefore nRV_0\frac{dT}{dV} = 3P_0V_0 - 2P_0V$$

$$\frac{dT}{dV}=\frac{3P_0V_0-2P_0V}{nRV_0}=0$$

$$V=\frac{3V_0}{2} \qquad \therefore\ P=\frac{3P_0}{2} \qquad \text{[From (i)]}$$

$$\therefore\ T_{max}=\frac{9P_0V_0}{4nR} \quad \text{[From (iii)]}$$

15. (b) $P_1 > P_2$

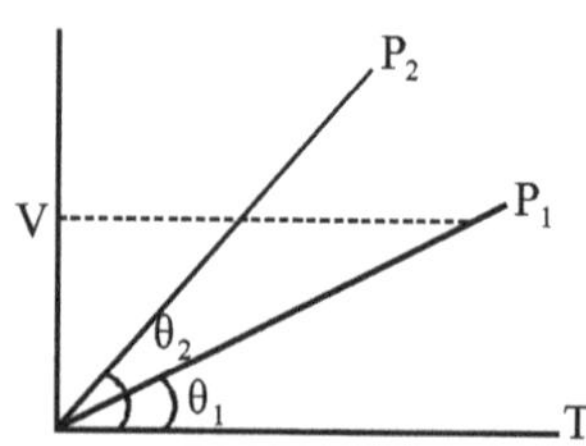

As V = constant $\Rightarrow P \propto T$

Hence from V–T graph $P_1 > P_2$

16. (d) At t = 2 sec, the particle crosses mean position.

At t = 4 sec, its velocity is 4 ms^{-1}

For simple harmonic motion, y = a sin ωt

$$\therefore\ y = a\sin\left(\frac{2\pi}{T}\right)t$$

$$y_1 = a\sin\left[\left(\frac{2\pi}{16}\right)\times 2\right] = a\sin\left(\frac{\pi}{4}\right)=\frac{a}{\sqrt{2}} \qquad \text{...(i)}$$

After 4 sec or after 2 sec from mean position, $y_1=\frac{a}{\sqrt{2}}$,

velocity = 4 ms^{-1}

$$\therefore\ \text{Velocity} = \omega\sqrt{a^2-y_1^2}$$

$$\Rightarrow\ 4=\left(\frac{2\pi}{16}\right)\sqrt{a^2-\frac{a^2}{2}} \qquad \text{[from (i)]}$$

$$\Rightarrow\ 4=\frac{\pi}{8}\times\frac{a}{\sqrt{2}} \ \text{ or } a=\frac{32\sqrt{2}}{\pi} \text{ metre.}$$

17. **(d)** Here, induced e.m.f.

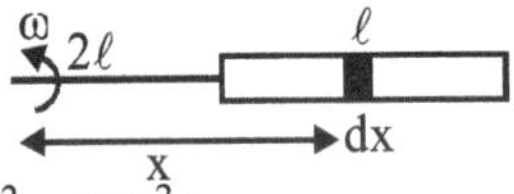

$$e = \int_{2\ell}^{3\ell} (\omega x)B dx = B\omega \frac{[(3\ell)^2 - (2\ell)^2]}{2}$$

$$= \frac{5B\ell^2\omega}{2}$$

18. **(c)** Charge on the capacitor at any time t is given by

$q = CV(1 - e^{t/\tau})$

at $t = 2\tau$

$q = CV(1 - e^{-2})$

19. **(b)** $\because$ The E.M. wave are transverse in nature i.e.,

$$= \frac{\vec{k} \times \vec{E}}{\mu\omega} = \vec{H} \qquad \text{...(i)}$$

where $\vec{H} = \frac{\vec{B}}{\mu}$

and $\frac{\vec{k} \times \vec{H}}{\omega\varepsilon} = -\vec{E}$ ...(ii)

$\vec{k}$ is $\perp$ $\vec{H}$ and $\vec{k}$ is also $\perp$ to $\vec{E}$

or In other words $\vec{X} \parallel \vec{E}$ and $\vec{k} \parallel \vec{E} \times \vec{B}$

20. **(b)** Acceleration of block AB $= \frac{3mg}{3m + m} = \frac{3}{4}g$

Acceleration of block CD $= \frac{2mg}{2m + m} = \frac{2g}{3}$

Acceleration of image in mirror AB = 2 × acceleration of mirror =

$2\left(\frac{-3g}{4}\right) = \frac{-3}{2}g$

Acceleration of image in mirror CD $= 2\left(\frac{2g}{3}\right) = \frac{4g}{3}$

$\therefore$ Acceleration of the two images w.r.t. each other

$$= \frac{4g}{3} - \left(\frac{-3g}{2}\right) = \frac{17g}{6}$$

21. **(2.5)** If C_e be the effective capacitance, then

$$V_C = \frac{1}{2}V_0$$

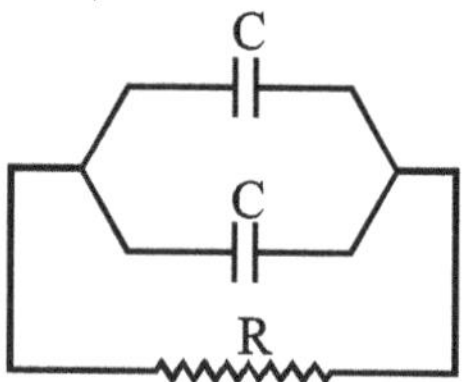

$$\frac{q}{C_e} = \frac{q_0}{2C_e}$$

$$\Rightarrow \quad q_0(1-e^{-t/RC_e}) = \frac{q_0}{2} \Rightarrow t = RC_e \ln 2$$

For parallel grouping

$$C_e = \frac{2C}{2}$$

$$\therefore \quad t_2 = 2RC\ln 2$$

For series grouping,

$$C_e = \frac{C}{2}$$

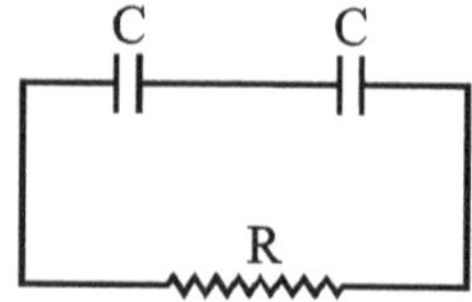

$$\therefore \quad t_1 = \frac{RC}{2}\ln 2$$

$$\therefore \quad \frac{t_2}{t_1} = \frac{1}{4} \Rightarrow t_2 = 2.5s$$

22. **(22)** $v_e = 11$ Km/s.

$R_p = 2R$ $\qquad\qquad \rho' = \rho$

$$\because g = \frac{GM}{R^2} = \frac{G.\frac{4}{3}\pi R^3\rho}{R^2} = 4\pi GR\rho$$

$$g_p = \frac{G\frac{4}{3}\pi {R_p}^3\rho}{{R_p}^2} = 4\pi GR_p\rho$$

$$= 2\times(4\pi GR\rho) = 2\times g$$

$$v_e' = \sqrt{2g_pR_p} = \sqrt{2\times 2g\times 2R} = 2\sqrt{2gR}$$

$$= 2\times 11 = 22 \text{ km/s.}$$

23. **(70)**

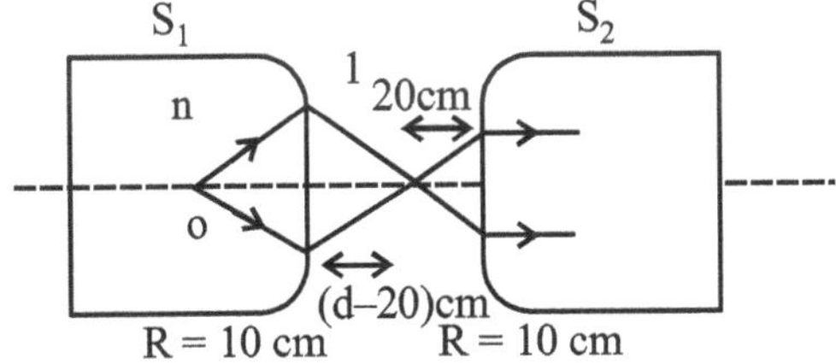

At glass rod S_2
$1 \to n$ refraction

$$\frac{n}{\infty} - \frac{1}{u_2} = \frac{n-1}{+10}$$

$\Rightarrow u_2 = -20\text{cm}$
At glass rod S_1
For $n \to 1$ refraction
$v_1 = d - 20$

$$\frac{1}{d-20} - \frac{n}{(-50)} = \frac{1-n}{-10}$$

$$\frac{1}{d-20} - \frac{n}{(-50)} = \frac{1-n}{-10}$$

$$\frac{1}{d-20} + \frac{n}{50} = +\frac{1}{20}$$

d = 70 cm

24. **(0.3)** The displacement of particle, executing SHM

$$y = 5\sin\left(4t + \frac{\pi}{3}\right) \quad \text{...(i)}$$

Velocity of particle, $\frac{dy}{dt} = \frac{5d}{dt}\sin\left(4t + \frac{\pi}{3}\right)$

$$= 5\cos\left(4t + \frac{\pi}{3}\right)4 = 20\cos\left(4t + \frac{\pi}{3}\right)$$

Velocity at $t = \left(\frac{T}{4}\right)$

$$\left(\frac{dy}{dt}\right)_{t=\frac{T}{4}} = 20\cos\left(4 \times \frac{T}{4} + \frac{\pi}{3}\right)$$

$\Rightarrow u = 20\cos\left(T + \frac{\pi}{3}\right)$ ...(ii)

Comparing the given equation with standard equation of SHM y = a sin (ωt + ϕ), we get ω = 4.

As $\omega = \frac{2\pi}{T} \Rightarrow T = \frac{2\pi}{\omega} \Rightarrow T = \frac{2\pi}{4} \Rightarrow T = \left(\frac{\pi}{2}\right)$

Now, putting value of T in Eq. (ii), we get

$$u = 20\cos\left(\frac{\pi}{2} + \frac{\pi}{3}\right) = -20\sin\frac{\pi}{3}$$

$$= -20 \times \frac{\sqrt{3}}{2} = -10 \times \sqrt{3}$$

The kinetic energy of particle,

$$KE = \frac{1}{2}mu^2$$

$$\because\ m = 2g = 2 \times 10^{-3}\,kg$$

$$= \frac{1}{2} \times 2 \times 10^{-3} \times \left(-10\sqrt{3}\right)^2$$

$$= 10^{-3} \times 100 \times 3 = 3 \times 10^{-1} \Rightarrow K.E. = 0.3J$$

25. **(0.144)** Here, $E = 9V$; $V_z = 6$; $R_L = 1000\Omega$ and $R_s = 100\Omega$,

Potential drop across series resistor

$V = E - V_Z = 9 - 6 = 3V$

Current through series resistance R_S is

$$I = \frac{V}{R} = \frac{3}{100} = 0.03\,A$$

Current through load resistance R_L is

$$I_L = \frac{V_Z}{R_L} = \frac{6}{1000} = 0.006\,A$$

Current through Zener diode is

$I_Z = I - I_L = 0.03 - 0.006 = 0.024$ amp.

Power dissipated in Zener diode is

$P_Z = V_Z I_Z = 6 \times 0.024 = 0.144$ watt

26. **(20)** Energy stored in stretched catapult is converted into kinetic energy of stone

$$\frac{1}{2}.\frac{YA}{L}.x^2=\frac{1}{2}mv^2$$

$$\frac{0.5\times10^9\times10^{-6}\times(0.04)^2}{0.1}=\frac{20}{1000}v^2$$

$\Rightarrow$ $v^2 = 400 \therefore v = 20$ m/s

27. **(5)** Minimum force required to pull the block

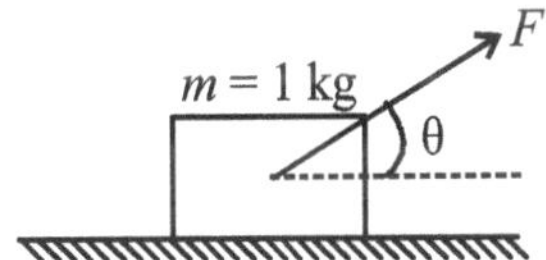

$$F_{\min}=\frac{\mu Mg}{\sqrt{1+\mu^2}}=\frac{\frac{1}{\sqrt{3}}\times1\times10}{\sqrt{1+\left(\frac{1}{\sqrt{3}}\right)^2}}=\frac{\frac{1}{\sqrt{3}}\times10}{\sqrt{1+\frac{1}{3}}}=5\text{ N}$$

28. **(80)** Flux, $\phi=\vec{B}.\vec{A}$

$$\phi=\frac{4}{\pi}\times10^{-3}\left(1-\frac{t}{100}\right).\pi R^2$$

$$\phi=4\times10^{-3}\times(1)^2\left(1-\frac{t}{100}\right)$$

From Faraday's law of electromagnetic induction,
Induced emf,

$$\varepsilon=\frac{-d\phi}{dt}$$

or, $$\varepsilon=\frac{-d}{dt}\left(4\times10^{-3}\left(1-\frac{t}{100}\right)\right)$$

or, $$\varepsilon=4\times10^{-3}\left(\frac{1}{100}\right)=4\times10^{-5}\text{V}$$

$\text{If } B = 0;\ 1 - \frac{t}{100} = 0$

$\therefore t = 100\text{ s}$

Energy dissipated by the coil $= \frac{\varepsilon^2}{R} t$

$$= \frac{(4 \times 10^{-5})^2}{2 \times 10^{-6}} \times 100$$

$$= \frac{16 \times 10^{-10} \times 100}{2 \times 10^{-6}} = 0.08\text{ J} = 80\text{ mJ}$$

29. **(3)** Centre of mass of solid hemisphere of radius R lies at a distance $\frac{3R}{8}$ above the centre of flat side of hemisphere.

$$\therefore h_{cm} = \frac{3R}{8} = \frac{3 \times 8}{8} = 3\text{ cm}$$

30. **(1)** Power factor for RL circuit

$$\cos\phi = \frac{R}{\sqrt{R^2 + X_L^2}} = \frac{R}{\sqrt{R^2 + 3R^2}} = \frac{1}{\sqrt{10}}$$

Power factor for LCR circuit

$$\cos\phi' = \frac{R}{\sqrt{R^2 + \left(X_L^2 - X_C^2\right)}} = \frac{R}{\sqrt{R^2 + R^2}} = \frac{1}{\sqrt{2}}$$

$$\frac{\cos\phi'}{\cos\phi} = \frac{\sqrt{10}}{\sqrt{2}} = \frac{\sqrt{5}}{1}$$

$\therefore x = 1$

CHEMISTRY

31. **(d)** (a) $Ba(N_3)_2 \xrightarrow{\Delta} Ba + 3N_2$

(b) $(NH_4)_2Cr_2O_7 \xrightarrow{\Delta} Cr_2O_3 + N_2 + 4H_2O$

(c) $NH_4NO_2 \xrightarrow{\Delta} N_2 + 2H_2O$

(d) $(NH_4)_2SO_4 \xrightarrow{\Delta} 2NH_3 + H_2SO_4$

NH_3 is evolved in case of (d) .

32. (b) Aspirin is analgesic and antipyretic.

33. (b) $\Delta H = E_{a(f)} - E_{a(b)}$

Thus energy of activation for reverse reaction depend upon whether reaction is exothermic or endothermic.

If reaction is exothermic, $\Delta H = -\text{ve}$, $E_{a(b)} > E_{a(f)}$

If reaction is endothermic, $\Delta H = +\text{ve}$ $E_{a(b)} < E_{a(f)}$

34. (c) Liquation process, Mond's process and, van Arkel process are the refining processes that are applied depending upon the nature of the metal under treatment and nature of the impurities whereas amalgamation process is used for the extraction of noble metals like gold, silver, etc, from native ores. The metal is recovered from the amalgam by subjecting it to distillation, where the mercury distils over leaving behind the metal.

Ore + Hg → Amalgam —Distilled→ Hg-vapours / Metal

35. (c)

Name of oxo acids	Oxidation state
Hypophosphorous acid (H_3PO_2)	+1
Orthophosphorous acid (H_3PO_3)	+3
Hypophosphoric acid ($H_4P_2O_6$)	+4
Orthophosphoric acid (H_3PO_4)	+5

36. (d) Soap helps to lower the surface tension of solution, thus soap get stick to the dust particles and grease, and these are removed by action of water.

37. (d) H_3BO_3 acts as a Lewis acid and accepts OH^- ions to form $[B(OH)_4]^-$

38. (a) $\underset{P_0 - 2x}{2NH_3(g)} \rightleftharpoons \underset{x}{N_2(g)} + \underset{3x}{3H_2(g)}, \quad K = \frac{1}{K_p}$

$$\therefore K = \frac{1}{K_p} = \frac{x(3x)^3}{P_{NH_3^2}}$$

$$\Rightarrow P^2_{NH_3} = 3^3 x^4 K_p$$

$$\Rightarrow P_{NH_3} = 3^{\frac{3}{2}} x^2 K_p^{\frac{1}{2}}$$

$$= \frac{3^{\frac{3}{2}} . P^2 K_p^{\frac{1}{2}}}{16}$$

39. **(d)** We can distinguish between formic acid and acetic acid by their action on Fehling's solution. Formic acid gives a red ppt of cuprous oxide but acetic acid does not give red ppt.

40. **(c)** $E^\circ_{cell} = \frac{0.0591}{n} \log K_{eq}$

$$\therefore 0.591 = \frac{0.0591}{1} \log K_{eq}$$

$$\text{or } \log K_{eq} = \frac{0.591}{0.0591} = 10$$

$$\text{or } K_{eq} = 1 \times 10^{10}$$

41. **(d)** $Hg_2Cl_2 + 2NH_4OH \longrightarrow Hg_2NH_2Cl + NH_4Cl + 2H_2O$

42. **(b)** $Ce^{4+} \xrightarrow{e^-} Ce^{3+}$ $\quad E^\circ = +1.74$ V

Positive SRP means greater oxidising power. So, Ce^{4+} can be easily reduced to Ce^{3+}. Hence, Ce^{4+} is less stable than Ce^{3+}.

43. **(c)** $-CH_3$ group is *o, p*–directing.

44. **(b)** Sodium cyanide ($Na + C + N \rightarrow NaCN$).
(Lassaigne's test)

45. **(b)** Magnesium reacts with air to form oxide and nitride. On reaction with water the oxide gives hydroxide and nitride gives hydroxide and ammonia.

$$2Mg + O_2 \rightarrow \underset{(X)}{2MgO}$$

$$3Mg + N_2 \rightarrow \underset{(Y)}{Mg_3N_2}$$

$$MgO + H_2O \rightarrow \underset{(P)}{Mg(OH)_2}$$

$$Mg_3N_2 + H_2O \rightarrow \underset{(P)}{3Mg(OH)_2} + \underset{(Q)}{2NH_3}$$

46. **(c)** Peptization involves conversion of freshly prepared precipitate into colloidal particles using a suitable electrolyte.

47. (b) $\Delta T_b = K_b \times m \times i = 0.52 \times 1 \times 2 = 1.04$
$\therefore \ \Delta T_b = 100 + 1.04 = 101.04\,°C$

48. (d) Oxidation state of Cr in $[Cr(NH_3)_4Cl_2]^+$.
Let it be x, $1 \times x + 4 \times 0 + 2 \times (-1) = 1$ Therefore $x = 3$.

49. (a) Higher the value of reduction potential higher will be the oxidising power whereas lower the value of reduction potential higher will be the reducing power.

50. (b) $k = \frac{2.303}{t} \log \frac{a}{(a-x)}$
$(a-x)$ is the concentration left after 100 sec.

$$2.7 \times 10^{-3} = \frac{2.303}{100} \log \frac{0.29}{(a-x)}$$

$$\Rightarrow \frac{0.27}{2.303} = \log \frac{0.29}{(a-x)} \Rightarrow 0.117 = \log \frac{0.29}{(a-x)}$$

$\Rightarrow (a-x) = 0.22$ M.

51. (0) It is zero order reaction

52. (38) $M(NO_3)_n \rightarrow M_2(SO_4)_n$ (n = Valency of metal)
g eq. $M(NO_3)_n$ = g eq. of $M_2(SO_4)_n$

$$\frac{1.0}{E(M) + E(NO_3^-)} = \frac{0.86}{E(M) + E(SO_4^{2-})}$$

$$\Rightarrow \quad \frac{1}{E + \frac{62}{1}} = \frac{0.86}{E + \frac{96}{2}} \Rightarrow E = 38g$$

53. (2)

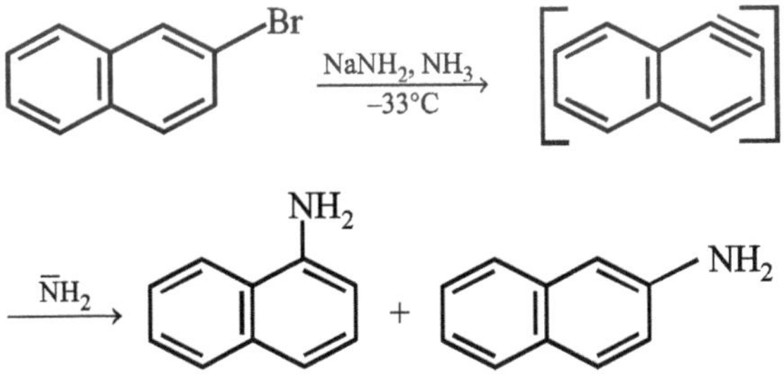

Br — $\xrightarrow[-33°C]{NaNH_2,\ NH_3}$

$\xrightarrow{\bar{N}H_2}$ NH_2 + NH_2

54. (279) $\wedge^{\infty}_{BaCl_2} = \frac{1}{2}\lambda^{\infty}_{Ba^{2+}} + 2\lambda^{\infty}_{Cl^-}$

$= 127 + 2 \times 76 = 279 \text{ S cm}^2 \text{ mol}^{-1}$

55. **(–208.1)** Cyclohexene $+ H_2 \longrightarrow$ Cyclohexane ; $\Delta H = -119.5$ kJ

Benzene $+ 3H_2 \longrightarrow$ Cyclohexane ; $\Delta H = 3(-119.5)$

$= -358.5$ kJ

The resonance energy provides extra stability to the benzene molecule so it has to be overcome, for hydrogenation to take place.

So $\Delta H = -358.5 - (-150.4) = -208.1$ kJ

56. **(2)** T-shaped molecule means central atom has 3 sigma bond and 2 lone pairs of electron.

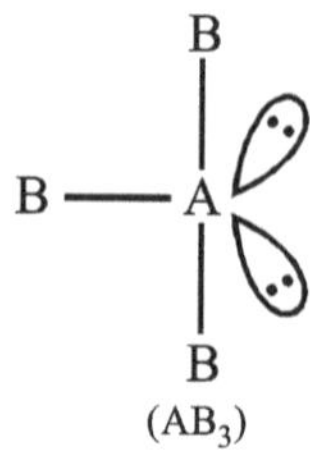

57. **(10)** $H \overset{\sigma}{-} C(H)(H) \overset{\sigma}{=} C(H) \overset{\sigma}{-} C(H) \overset{\sigma}{-} C \overset{\sigma}{\equiv} C \overset{\sigma}{-} H$

Numbers of σ bonds = 10

58. **(1)** $W = \frac{E}{F} \times I \times t$

$$10 = \frac{122.6}{96500 \times 6} \times x \times 10 \times 3600$$

$x = 1.311 \approx 1$

59. **(4)** $P_4(s) + 3OH^-(aq) + 3H_2O(l) \longrightarrow PH_3(g) + 3H_2PO_2^-(s)$
(A)

$$\underset{1\text{ mole}}{H_2\overset{1}{P}O_2^-} + \underset{(\text{Excess})}{Ag^+} + 2H_2O \longrightarrow \overset{0}{Ag} + H_3\overset{+5}{P}O_4 + 3H^+$$

$$\left[e^- + Ag^+ \longrightarrow Ag\right] \times 4$$

$$P^{+1} \longrightarrow P^{+5} + 4e^-$$

$$4Ag^+ + P^{+1} \longrightarrow 4Ag + P^{+5}$$

60. **(1)** $P(V_m - b) = RT$

$\Rightarrow \quad PV_m - Pb = RT$

$$\Rightarrow \quad \frac{PV_m}{RT} = 1 + \frac{Pb}{RT}$$

$$\Rightarrow \quad Z = 1 + \frac{Pb}{RT}$$

$$\Rightarrow \quad \left(\frac{\partial Z}{\partial P}\right)_T = \frac{b \times 1}{RT}$$

$\therefore \quad x = 1$

MATHEMATICS

61. **(a)** The equation is $x^2 + px + q = 0$

Let α be one of the root, then as per problem, second root is α^2.

From the principle of quadratic equation.

$\alpha^2 + \alpha = -p$ ....(1)

and $\alpha^3 = q$ ...(2)

From eq (1) + eq (2):

$\alpha^3 + \alpha^2 + \alpha = q - p$

$\Rightarrow \quad \alpha(\alpha^2 + \alpha + 1) = q - p$

$\Rightarrow \quad \alpha(-p + 1) = q - p$ [since $\alpha^2 + \alpha = -p$ from eq^n (1)]

$$\Rightarrow \quad \alpha = \frac{q-p}{1-p} = \frac{p-q}{p-1}$$

Putting this value of α in equation (1)

$$\left(\frac{p-q}{p-1}\right)^2 + \left(\frac{p-q}{p-1}\right) = -p$$

$$\Rightarrow \quad \frac{p^2 - 2pq + q^2}{(p-1)^2} + \frac{p-q}{(p-1)} = -p$$

$$\Rightarrow \quad \frac{p^2 - 2pq + q^2 + (p-1)(p-q)}{(p-1)^2} = -p$$

$\Rightarrow\ p^2 - 2pq + q^2 + p^2 - pq - p + q = -p(p^2 - 2p + 1)$

$\Rightarrow\ 2p^2 - 3pq + q^2 - p + q = -p^3 + 2p^2 - p.$

$\Rightarrow\ p^3 - 3pq + q + q^2 = 0$

$\Rightarrow\ p^3 - q(3p - 1) + q^2 = 0$

62. (b) Let $M(h, k)$

Given, $AM = 2AB$

$\Rightarrow AB + BM = 2AB$

$\Rightarrow AB = BM$

So B is mid point of AM

$$B = \left(\frac{h}{2}, \frac{k+3}{2}\right)$$

$\because$ Point B lies on the circle.

$\therefore$ B satisfies the equation of circle. i.e.,

$$\left(\frac{h}{2}\right)^2 + 4\left(\frac{h}{2}\right) + \left(\frac{k+3}{2} - 3\right)^2 = 0$$

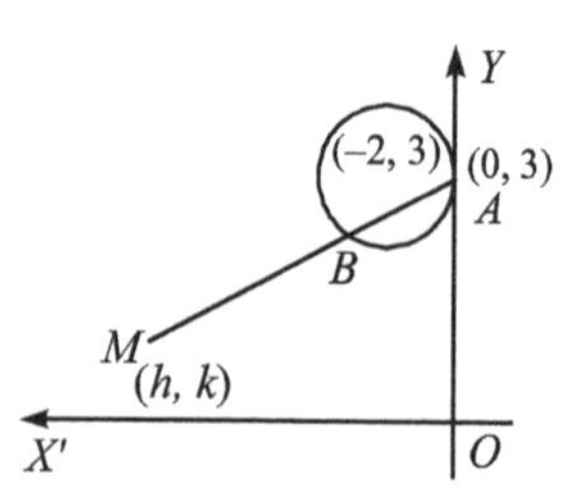

$$\Rightarrow \frac{h^2}{4} + \frac{8h}{4} + \frac{(k-3)^2}{4} = 0$$

or $x^2 + y^2 + 8x - 6y + 9 = 0$, which is a circle.

63. (b) We have $f(x) = \begin{cases} (x-1)\sin\left(\dfrac{1}{x-1}\right) & \text{if } x \neq 1 \\ 0 & \text{if } x = 1 \end{cases}$

$$Rf'(1) = \lim_{h\to 0} \frac{f(1+h) - f(1)}{h}$$

$$= \lim_{h\to 0} \frac{h\sin\frac{1}{h} - 0}{h} = \lim_{h\to 0} \sin\frac{1}{h}$$

which does not exist.

$\therefore f$ is not differentiable at $x = 1$

$$\text{Also } f'(0) = \left[\sin\frac{1}{(x-1)} - \frac{x-1}{(x-1)^2}\cos\left(\frac{1}{x-1}\right)\right]_{x=0}$$

$$= -\sin 1 + \cos 1$$

$\therefore f$ is differentiable at $x = 0$

64. (b) $n(A) = 40\%$ of $10,000 = 4,000$

$n(B) = 20\%$ of $10,000 = 2,000$

$n(C) = 10\% \text{ of } 10{,}000 = 1{,}000$

$n(A \cap B) = 5\% \text{ of } 10{,}000 = 500$

$n(B \cap C) = 3\% \text{ of } 10{,}000 = 300$

$n(C \cap A) = 4\% \text{ of } 10{,}000 = 400$

$n(A \cap B \cap C) = 2\% \text{ of } 10{,}000 = 200$

We want to find $n(A \cap B^c \cap C^c) = n[A \cap (B \cup C)^c]$

$= n(A) - n[A \cap (B \cup C)]$

$= n(A) - n[(A \cap B) \cup (A \cap C)]$

$= n(A) - [n(A \cap B) + n(A \cap C) - n(A \cap B \cap C)]$

$= 4000 - [500 + 400 - 200] = 4000 - 700 = 3300.$

65. **(d)** Given function $f(x) = Pe^{2x} + Qe^{x} + Rx$ ...(i)

Given conditions $f(0) = -1,\ f'(\log 2) = 31$

and $\int_0^{\log 4} [f(x) - Rx]dx = \frac{39}{2}$

differentiate equation (i)

$f'(x) = 2Pe^{2x} + Qe^{x} + R$ ...(ii)

Put $x = \log 2$ in equation (ii)

$f'(\log 2) = 2Pe^{2\log 2} + Qe^{\log 2} + R$

$31 = 8P + 2Q + R$ ...(iii)

and, put $x = 0$ in equation (i)

$f(0) = Pe^{2\times 0} + Qe^{0} + R.0$

$= P + Q - 1 = P + Q$

$\Rightarrow P = -1 - Q$ ...(iv)

Thus $\int_0^{\log 4} [f(x) - Rx]dx = \frac{39}{2}$

$\Rightarrow \int_0^{\log 4} [Pe^{2x} + Qe^{x} + Rx - Rx]dx = \frac{39}{2}$

$\Rightarrow \int_0^{\log 4} [Pe^{2x} + Qe^{x}]dx = \frac{39}{2}$

$$\Rightarrow \left[\frac{Pe^{2x}}{2} + Qe^{x}\right]_0^{\log 4} = \frac{39}{2}$$

$$\Rightarrow \frac{P}{2}\times 16 + 4Q - \frac{P}{2} - Q = \frac{39}{2}$$

$$\Rightarrow \frac{15P}{2} + 3Q = \frac{39}{2} \qquad \text{... (v)}$$

From (iv) and (v), we get

$$\frac{15P}{2} + 3(-1-P) = \frac{39}{2}$$

$$\Rightarrow \frac{9P}{2} = \frac{45}{2} \Rightarrow P = 5$$

and $Q = -1 - P = -1 - 5 = -6$

and from equation (iii)

$31 = 8\times 5 + 2\times -6 + R$

$31 = 40 - 12 + R$

$\therefore\ P = 5; Q = -6, R = 3$

66. (a) $\lim\limits_{x\to 0^+} x^m(\log x)^n = \lim\limits_{x\to 0^+} \frac{(\log x)^n}{x^{-m}}, \left(\frac{\infty}{\infty}\text{ Form}\right)$

$$= \lim_{x\to 0^+} \frac{n(\log x)^{(n-1)}\frac{1}{x}}{-mx^{-m-1}} \qquad \text{[Using L-Hospital's rule]}$$

$$= \lim_{x\to 0^+} \frac{n(\log x)^{(n-1)}}{-mx^{-m}}, \left(\frac{\infty}{\infty}\text{ Form}\right)$$

$$= \lim_{x\to 0^+} \frac{n(n-1)(\log x)^{(n-2)}\frac{1}{x}}{(-m)^2 x^{-m-1}}$$

[Again using L-Hospital's rule]

$$= \lim_{x\to 0^+} \frac{n(n-1)(\log x)^{n-2}}{m^2 x^{-m}}, \left(\frac{\infty}{\infty}\text{ Form}\right)$$

....

....

$$= \lim_{x \to 0^+} \frac{n!}{(-m)^n x^{-m}} = 0$$

67. **(a)** We have ; $f(x) = \sin x - \cos x - ax + b$

$\Rightarrow f'(x) = \cos x + \sin x - a$

$\Rightarrow f'(x) < 0 \ \forall\ x \in R$

$\Rightarrow (\cos x + \sin x) < a \ \forall\ x \in R$

As the max. value of $(\cos x + \sin x)$ is $\sqrt{2}$

The above is possible when $a \geq \sqrt{2}$

68. **(d)** $$\frac{\sin 3B}{\sin B} = \frac{3 \sin B - 4 \sin^3 B}{\sin B} = 3 - 4 \sin^2 B$$

$$= 3 - 4 + 4\cos^2 B = -1 + \frac{4(a^2 + c^2 - b^2)^2}{4(ac)^2}$$

$$= -1 + \frac{\left(\frac{a^2 + c^2}{2}\right)^2}{(ac)^2} = -1 + \frac{(a^2 + c^2)^2}{4(ac)^2}$$

$$= \frac{(a^2 + c^2)^2 - 4a^2c^2}{4(ac)^2} = \left(\frac{c^2 - a^2}{2ac}\right)^2.$$

69. **(a)** We have, $y = (1 + x)^y + \sin^{-1}\left(\sin^2 x\right)$ ...(i)

when $x = 0$, we have $y = 1$

Differentiating (i) w.r.t. x we get

$$\frac{dy}{dx} = (1 + x)^y \left\{\frac{dy}{dx} \log(1 + x) + \frac{y}{1 + x}\right\} + \frac{\sin 2x}{\sqrt{1 - \sin^4 x}}$$

$$\Rightarrow \left(\frac{dy}{dx}\right)_{(0,1)} = 1 \Rightarrow -\left(\frac{dx}{dy}\right)_{(0,1)} = -1.$$

So the equation of the normal at (0, 1) is

$y - 1 = -1(x - 0) \Rightarrow x + y = 1$

70. **(b)** Parametric equation of the hyperbola $xy = c^2$ is $(ct, c/t)$

and equation of circle is $x^2 + y^2 = a^2$ ...(i)

Put $x = ct$ and $y = c/t$ in (i)

$$(ct)^2 + \left(\frac{c}{t}\right)^2 = a^2$$

$$c^2 t^4 + c^2 - a^2 t^2 = 0 \quad ...(ii)$$

From (ii), $t_1 t_2 t_3 t_4 = \frac{c^2}{c^2} = 1$

71. **(b)** Integration by parts is given as

$$\int \underset{\text{I}}{\text{u}}\,\underset{\text{II}}{\text{v}}\,dx = u\int v\,dx - \int\left[\frac{d}{dx}(u)\int v\,dx\right]dx$$

Let $I = \int 32x^3 (\log x)^2 dx$

Integrate it by parts, using ILATE so, we choose $(\log x)^2$ as I[st] function and x^3 as IInd function

$$= 32\left\{(\log x)^2 \frac{x^4}{4} - \int 2\log x \frac{1}{x}.\frac{x^4}{4}\,dx\right\}$$

$$= \frac{32}{4}x^4(\log x)^2 - 16\int x^3 \log x\; dx$$

$$= 8x^4(\log x)^2 - 16\left\{\log x.\frac{x^4}{4} - \int \frac{1}{x}.\frac{x^4}{4}\,dx\right\}$$

$$= 8x^4(\log x)^2 - 4x^4 \log x + 4\int x^3 dx$$

$$= 8x^4(\log x)^2 - 4x^4 \log x + x^4 + C$$

$$= x^4\left\{8(\log x)^2 - 4\log x + 1\right\} + C$$

72. **(a)** Let $u = \tan^{-1}\frac{2x}{1-x^2}$ ...... (i)

and $v = \sin^{-1}\frac{2x}{1+x^2}$ ...... (ii)

In equation (i) put, $x = \tan\theta$

$$\therefore \quad u = \tan^{-1}\left[\frac{2\tan\theta}{1-\tan^2\theta}\right] = \tan^{-1}(\tan 2\theta)$$

$\Rightarrow u = 2\theta \Rightarrow \dfrac{du}{d\theta} = 2$ ...... (iii)

In equation (ii), put $x = \tan\theta$

$\therefore v = \sin^{-1}\left[\dfrac{2\tan\theta}{1+\tan^2\theta}\right] = \sin^{-1}(\sin 2\theta)$

$\Rightarrow v = 2\theta \Rightarrow \dfrac{dv}{d\theta} = 2$ .... (iv)

From equations (iii) and (iv),

$\dfrac{du}{dv} = \dfrac{du}{d\theta} \times \dfrac{d\theta}{dv} = 2 \times \dfrac{1}{2} = 1$

$\therefore$ required differential coefficient will be 1.

73. (c)

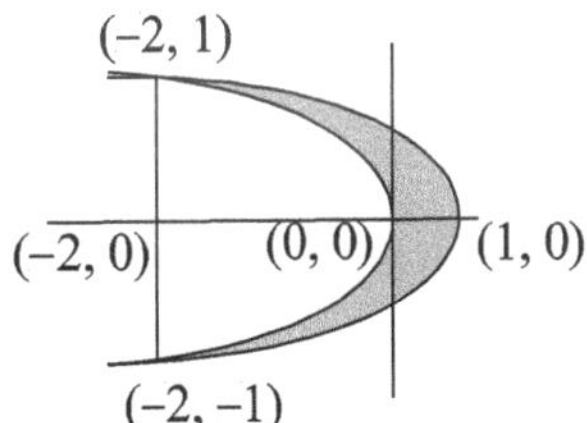

Parabola : $y^2 = \dfrac{-x}{2}$ and $y^2 = \dfrac{1}{3}(1-x)$

On solving, we get $x = -2, y = \pm 1$

$\therefore$ required Area $= 2\left[\dfrac{1}{\sqrt{3}}\int_{-2}^{1}\sqrt{(1-x)}\,dx - \dfrac{1}{\sqrt{2}}\int_{-2}^{0}\sqrt{-x}dx\right]$

$= 2\left\{\left[\dfrac{1}{\sqrt{3}} \times \dfrac{-2}{3}(1-x)^{3/2}\right]_{-2}^{1} - \left[\dfrac{1}{\sqrt{2}} \times \dfrac{-2}{3}(-x)^{3/2}\right]_{-2}^{0}\right\}$

$= 2\left\{\left(\dfrac{2}{3\sqrt{3}}.3\sqrt{3}\right) - \left(\dfrac{2}{3\sqrt{2}}.2\sqrt{2}\right)\right\} = \dfrac{4}{3}.$

74. (c) The inverse of the proposition $(p \wedge \sim q) \to r$ is

$\sim (p \wedge \sim q) \to \sim r$

$\equiv \sim p \vee \sim(\sim q) \to \sim r$

$\equiv \sim p \vee q \to \sim r$

75. **(c)** The rth term in the expansion of $\left(\frac{3}{2}x^2-\frac{1}{3x}\right)^9$ is

$$T_{r+1}={}^9C_r\left(\frac{3}{2}x^2\right)^{9-r}\left(-\frac{1}{3x}\right)^r$$

$$={}^9C_r\left(\frac{3}{2}\right)^{9-r}\left(-\frac{1}{3}\right)^r x^{18-3r} \qquad \text{...(i)}$$

The coefficient of the term independent of x in the expansion of $(1+x+2x^3)$

$$\left(\frac{3}{2}x^2-\frac{1}{3x}\right)^9 \qquad \text{...(ii)}$$

= Sum of the coefficient of the terms x^0, x^{-1} and x^{-3} in

$$\left(\frac{3}{2}x^2-\frac{1}{3x}\right)^9.$$

For x^0 in (i) above, $18-3r=0\Rightarrow r=6$.
for x^{-1} in (i) above, there exists no value of r and hence no such term exists.
For x^{-3} in (i), $18-3r=-3\Rightarrow r=7$
$\therefore$ for term independent of x, in (ii) the coefficient

$$=1\times{}^9C_6(-1)^6\left(\frac{3}{2}\right)^{9-6}\left(\frac{1}{3}\right)^6+2\times{}^9C_7(-1)^7\left(\frac{3}{2}\right)^{9-7}\left(\frac{1}{3}\right)^7$$

$$=\frac{9.8.7}{1.2.3}\cdot\frac{3^3}{2^3}\cdot\frac{1}{3^6}+2\frac{9.8}{1.2}(-1)\frac{3^2}{2^2}\cdot\frac{1}{3^7}=\frac{7}{18}-\frac{2}{27}=\frac{17}{54}.$$

76. **(a)** We have $\frac{dy}{dx}=\frac{f'(x)}{f(x)}y-\frac{y^2}{f(x)}\Rightarrow\frac{dy}{dx}-\frac{f'(x)}{f(x)}y=-\frac{y^2}{f(x)}$

Divide by y^2

$$y^{-2}\frac{dy}{dx}-y^{-1}\frac{f'(x)}{f(x)}=-\frac{1}{f(x)}$$

Put $y^{-1} = z \Rightarrow -y^{-2}\frac{dy}{dx} = \frac{dz}{dx}$

$$-\frac{dz}{dx} - \frac{f'(x)}{f(x)}(z) = -\frac{1}{f(x)} \Rightarrow \frac{dz}{dx} + \frac{f'(x)}{f(x)}z = \frac{1}{f(x)}$$

$$\text{I.F.} = e^{\int \frac{f'(x)}{f(x)}dx} = e^{\log f(x)} = f(x)$$

$\therefore$ The solution is $z(f(x)) = \int \frac{1}{f(x)}(f(x))dx + c$

$$\Rightarrow y^{-1}(f(x)) = x + c \Rightarrow f(x) = y(x+c)$$

77. (d) Given $\angle A - \angle B = \theta \Rightarrow \tan(A - B) = \tan\theta$

$$\Rightarrow \frac{\tan A - \tan B}{1 + \tan A - \tan B} = \tan\theta \quad ...(i)$$

In right angled triangle CDA,

$$\tan A = \frac{k}{a-h}$$

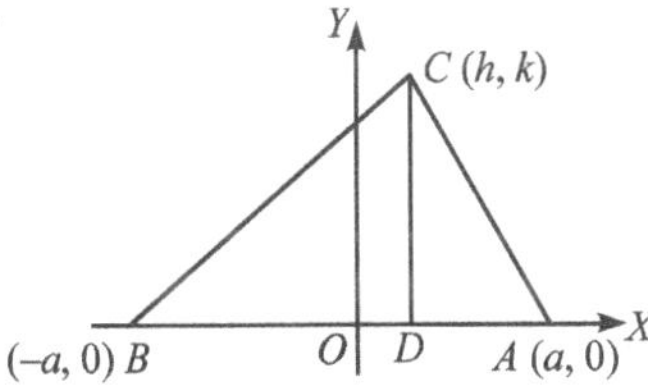

Similarly in triangle CDB,

$$\tan B = \frac{k}{a+h}$$

Substitute the values of $\tan A$ and $\tan B$ in (i), we get

$h^2 - k^2 + 2hk \cot\theta = a^2$

Hence the locus is $x^2 - y^2 + 2xy \cot\theta = a^2$.

78. (a) Equation of planes passing through intersecting the planes $3x - y - 4z = 0$ and $x + 3y + 6 = 0$ is,

$$(3x - y - 4z) + \lambda(x + 3y + 6) = 0$$

$(3+\lambda)x+(3\lambda-1)-4z+6\lambda=0$ ......(i)

Given, distances of plane (i) from origin is 1.

$$\therefore \frac{6\lambda}{\sqrt{(3+\lambda)^2+(3\lambda-1)^2+(-4)^2}}=1$$

or $36\lambda^2=10\lambda^2+26$ or $\lambda=\pm1$

Put the value of λ in (i),

$\therefore (3x-y-4z)\pm(x+3y+6)=0$

or $4x+2y-4z+6=0$ or $2x+y-2z+3=0$

and $2x-4y-4z-6=0$ or $x-2y-2z-3=0$

Thus the required planes are $x-2y-2z-3=0$ and $2x+y-2z+3=0$.

79. (a) Since, angles of Δ are in AP.
Let, third side is x.
$\Rightarrow(\alpha-\delta)+\alpha+(\alpha+\delta)=180°\Rightarrow\alpha=60°$
Use cosine law in ΔABC

$$\cos 60° = \frac{(10)^2+(9)^2-x^2}{2.(10).(9)} \Rightarrow \frac{1}{2}=\frac{181-x^2}{2.(90)}$$

$\Rightarrow x^2=91\Rightarrow x=\sqrt{91}.$

80. (a) $\vec{a}=(1,-1,2)$, $\vec{b}=(-2,3,5)$, $\vec{c}=(2,-2,4)$

So, $\vec{a}=(1,-1,2)\equiv\hat{i}-\hat{j}+2\hat{k};\hat{b}$

$=(-2,3,5)\equiv -2\hat{i}+3\hat{j}+5\hat{k}$

and $\vec{c}=(2,-2,4)\equiv 2\hat{i}-2\hat{j}+4\hat{k}$

$\Rightarrow \vec{a}-2\vec{b}+3\vec{c}=(\hat{i}-\hat{j}+2\hat{k})-2(-2\hat{k}+3\hat{j}+5\hat{k})$

$+3(2\hat{i}-2\hat{j}+4\hat{k})$

$=11\hat{i}-13\hat{j}+4\hat{k}$ and $(\vec{a}-2\vec{b}+3c).\hat{i}=11.$

81. (120) As the greater side of a triangle has greater angle opposite to it.

$\therefore$ The angle (say C) opposite to $\sqrt{a^2+b^2+ab}$ = c (say) is the greatest in this case.

Now, $\cos C = \dfrac{a^2+b^2-c^2}{2ab}$

$= \dfrac{a^2+b^2-(a^2+b^2+ab)}{2ab}$ $[\because c^2 = a^2+b^2+ab]$

$= \dfrac{-ab}{2ab} = \dfrac{-1}{2}$; $C = 120°$

82. (198) $\begin{bmatrix} a & b & c \\ d & e & f \\ g & h & i \end{bmatrix}\begin{bmatrix} a & d & g \\ b & e & h \\ c & f & i \end{bmatrix}$

Sum of diagonal elements,

$a^2+b^2+c^2+d^2+e^2+f^2+g^2+h^2+i^2 = 5$

Case – I: Five (1's) and four (0's)

${}^9C_5 = 126$

Case – II: One (2) and one (1)

${}^9C_2 = 2! = 72$

$\therefore$ Total = 198

83. (2) We know that, $|z_1 - z_2| \geq ||z_1| - |z_2||$ ...(i)

Here $|z_1| = 12$ and $|z_2 - 3 - 4i| = 5$

but $|z_2 - (3+4i)| \geq ||z_2| - |3+4i||$

$\Rightarrow 5 \geq |z_2| - 5$

$\Rightarrow |z_2| \leq 10$

Also from (i) $|z_1 - z_2|$ will have least value when $|z_2|$ has greatest value i.e. 10

$\therefore |z_1 - z_2| \geq 12 - 10 = 2$

Thus min. value of $|z_1 - z_2|$ is 2.

84. (1875) $x_1 x_2 x_3 x_4 x_5 = 2 \times 3 \times 5^2 \times 7$ we can assign 2, 3 or 7 to any of variable.
We can assign entire 5^2 to just one variable in 5 ways or can assign.
$5^2 = 5 \times 5$ to two variables in ${}^5C_2$ ways
${}^5C_1 + {}^5C_2 = 5 + 10 = 15$ ways
Required number of solutions $= 5 \times 5 \times 5 \times 15 = 1875$

85. (0.55) Total number of cases obtained by taking multiplication of only two numbers out of $100 = {}^{100}C_2$.
Out of hundred (1, 2, ..., 100) given numbers, there are the numbers 3, 6, 9, 12, ..., 99, which are 33 in number such that when any one of these is multiplied with any one of remaining 67 numbers or any two of these 33 are multiplied, then the resulting products is divisible by 3. Then the number of numbers which are the products of two of the given number are divisible by $3 = {}^{33}C_1 \times {}^{67}C_1 + {}^{33}C_2$.
Hence the required probability

$$= \frac{{}^{33}C_1 \times {}^{67}C_1 + {}^{33}C_2}{{}^{100}C_2} = \frac{2739}{4950} = 0.55$$

86. (10) Let $z = x + iy$

$$x + iy + \alpha|x + iy - 1| + 2i = 0$$

$$\Rightarrow x + \alpha\sqrt{(x-1)^2 + y^2} + i(y+2) = 0 + 0i$$

$$\Rightarrow y + 2 = 0 \text{ and } x + \alpha\sqrt{(x-1)^2 + y^2} = 0$$

$$\Rightarrow y = -2 \text{ and } \alpha^2 = \frac{x^2}{x^2 - 2x + 5}$$

Now, $\frac{x^2}{x^2 - 2x + 5} \in \left[0, \frac{5}{4}\right]$

$$\therefore \alpha^2 \in \left[0, \frac{5}{4}\right] \Rightarrow \alpha \in \left[-\frac{\sqrt{5}}{2}, \frac{\sqrt{5}}{2}\right]$$

$$\therefore p = -\frac{\sqrt{5}}{2}; q = \frac{\sqrt{5}}{2}$$

$$\Rightarrow 4(p^2+q^2) = 4\left(\frac{5}{4}+\frac{5}{4}\right) = 10$$

87. **(31650)** If group C has one student then number of groups

$${}^{10}C_1[2^9-2] = 5100$$

If group C has two students then number of groups

$${}^{10}C_2[2^8-2] = 11430$$

If group C has three students then number of groups

$$= {}^{10}C_3 \times [2^7-2] = 15120$$

So, total groups = 31650.

88. **(5)** $\int_0^{\pi}\left(\sin^3 x\right).e^{-\sin^2 x}dx = \frac{1}{e}\int_0^{\pi}\sin^2 x.e^{\cos^2 x}.\sin xdx$

Let cosx = t, then sin x dx = –dt

$$\therefore \int_0^{\pi}\left(\sin^3 x\right)e^{-\sin^2 x}dx$$

$$= \frac{1}{e}\int_1^{-1}\left(t^2-1\right)e^{t^2}dt = \frac{2}{e}\int_0^1\left(1-t^2\right)e^{t^2}dt$$

Let, $t^2 = z, dt = \frac{dz}{2\sqrt{z}}$

$$= \frac{1}{e}\int_0^1\left(\frac{1}{\sqrt{z}}-\sqrt{z}\right)e^z dz$$

$$= \frac{1}{e}\left[e^z.2\sqrt{z}\Big|_0^1 - \int_0^1 2e^z.\sqrt{z}dz - \int_0^1\sqrt{z}e^z dz\right]$$

$$= \frac{1}{e}\left[2e-3\int_0^1 e^t.\sqrt{t}dt\right] = 2-\frac{3}{e}\int_0^1\sqrt{t}e^t dt$$

$\Rightarrow \quad \alpha = 2$ and $\beta = 3$

So, $\alpha+\beta = 5$

89. **(6)** If $\vec{r} = \vec{a} + \lambda\vec{b}$ and $\vec{r} = \vec{c} + \lambda\vec{d}$

$\therefore\ \vec{a} - \vec{c} = (\alpha + 4)\hat{i} + 2\hat{j} + 3\hat{k}$

$$\frac{\vec{b} \times \vec{d}}{|\vec{b} \times \vec{d}|} = \frac{(2\hat{i} + 2\hat{j} + \hat{k})}{3}$$

Then shortest distance between two lines is,

$$\frac{(\vec{a} - \vec{c}) . (\vec{b} \times \vec{d})}{|\vec{b} \times \vec{d}|} = 9$$

$$\Rightarrow \quad ((\alpha + 4)\hat{i} + 2\hat{j} + 3\hat{k}) . \frac{(2\hat{i} + 2\hat{j} + \hat{k})}{3} = 9$$

$$\Rightarrow \quad 2\alpha + 15 = 27 \Rightarrow \alpha = 6$$

90. **(9)** Let $f(x) = \dfrac{4}{\sin x} + \dfrac{1}{1 - \sin x}$

$\Rightarrow f'(x) = 0 \Rightarrow \sin x = 2/3$

$$\therefore f(x)_{\min} = \frac{4}{2/3} + \frac{1}{1 - 2/3} = 9$$

$f(x)_{\max.} \to \infty$

(x) is continuous function

$\therefore\ \alpha_{\min} = 9$

www.ingramcontent.com/pod-product-compliance
Ingram Content Group UK Ltd.
Pitfield, Milton Keynes, MK11 3LW, UK
UKHW021701190726
13853UKWH00001B/385